Louis

Armstrong

A CULTURAL LEGACY

edited by **Marc H. Miller**

essays by **Donald Bogle**

Richard A. Long

Marc H. Miller

Dan Morgenstern

Queens Museum of Art, New York

in association with

University of Washington Press,

Seattle and London

This publication has been prepared to accompany the exhibition Louis Armstrong: A Cultural Legacy, organized by the Queens Museum of Art, in cooperation with the Louis Armstrong Archives at Queens College, City University of New York. The traveling version was organized and developed for circulation by the Smithsonian Institution Traveling Exhibition Service (SITES).

EXHIBITION TOUR:
The Queens Museum of Art, Queens, New York
Museum of African American Life and Culture, Dallas, Texas
Terra Museum of Art, Chicago, Illinois
New Orleans Museum of Art, New Orleans, Louisiana
Strong Museum, Rochester, New York
Telfair Academy of Arts and Sciences, Savannah, Georgia
National Portrait Gallery, Washington, D.C.

This project has been funded in part by the National Endowment for the Humanities, a federal agency, and the New York State Council on the Arts. The exhibition is part of America's Jazz Heritage, A Partnership of the Lila Wallace-Reader's Digest Fund and the Smithsonian Institution.

The exhibition has been made possible by major corporate support from Mobil Foundation, Inc. Additional support for this project has been provided by GRP Records, Inc. The catalogue has been funded, in part, by the Marshall and Marilyn R. Wolf Foundation.

The Queens Museum of Art
The New York City Building
Flushing Meadows Corona Park
Queens, New York 11368

The Queens Museum of Art is housed in the New York City Building which is owned and operated by the City of New York, and its operation is supported in part with public funds provided by the New York City Department of Cultural Affairs and the Office of Queens Borough President Claire Shulman. Additional support is provided with public funds from the New York State Legislature and the New York State Council on the Arts.

ISBN: 0-295-97382-x (cloth)
ISBN: 0-295-97383-8 (ppb)

Library of Congress Cataloging-in-Publication Data

Louis Armstrong: a cultural legacy / edited by Marc H. Miller; essays by Donald Bogle...(et al...)
    p. cm.
    Catalog of an exhibition held at the Queens Museum of Art and other locations throughout the United States.
    Includes bibliographical references and index.
    ISBN 0-295-97382-X--ISBN 0-295-97383-8 (paper)
    1. Armstrong, Louis. 1900-1971--Exhibitions. 2. Jazz--Exhibitions. I, Miller, Marc H. II. Bogle, Donald. III. Queens Museum of Art.
ML 141,N4A76   94-21134
781.65' 092--dc20   CIP
                    MN

Cover: Calvin Bailey, Portrait of Louis Armstrong, 1948. Louis Armstrong Archives, Queens College, City University of New York.

Back cover: Lisette Model, Louis Armstrong at the Newport Jazz Festival (1954–56). National Portrait Gallery, Smithsonian Institution,Courtesy Lisette Model Foundation.

Page 1: The exertion of playing the trumpet is evident in this extreme close-up of Armstrong taken by Philippe Halsman in 1966. © Yvonne Halsman.

Page 2: The "Columbia" B Flat trumpet used by Armstrong in Chicago in the late 1920s. Kislak National Bank.

Page 4 : Ben Shahn's ink portrait of Armstrong was commissioned for the film documentary Satchmo the Great (1957). Dr. John I. Dintenfass.

Contents

William Woodward, *Second Ursulines Convent and Priest's House* (1912). The New Orleans of Armstrong's youth was a city of contrasts. Traditions of joy and celebration coexisted with harsh economic disparities often rooted in race. New Orleans Museum of Art, Gift of the Stern Family, New Orleans.

Armstrong with his mother Mayann and his sister Beatrice, 1922. This picture taken by Villard Paddio, a local New Orleans photographer, just before Armstrong moved to Chicago is the only surviving portrait of Armstrong's family. Louis Armstrong Archives, Queens College, City University of New York.

My father left home when I was real little. I had a great mother. She didn't have much power, but she did all she could for me.
Louis Armstrong, *Life*, April 15, 1966

Acknowledgments

The Queens Museum of Art is very proud to present this exhibition chronicling the accomplishments of Louis Armstrong, whose home was in Corona, Queens, for the last thirty years of his life. During this period, Armstrong served as a cultural ambassador to many countries of the world through the international language of jazz. In his music and travels, he embodied the Museum's mission to offer audiences the opportunity to understand and appreciate cultures other than one's own. The visual and performing arts provide abundant clues to the social and economic identities of people of another time and place. Funded through generous planning and implementation grants from the National Endowment for the Humanities, a federal agency, this exhibition and publication explore Armstrong's life in the context of 20th-century American history, his role in the development of jazz, and the relationship of jazz to the visual arts. Additional support was provided through America's Jazz Heritage, A Partnership of the Lila Wallace-Reader's Digest Fund and the Smithsonian Institution.

Many individuals and institutions helped make the exhibition "Louis Armstrong: A Cultural Legacy" and the accompanying catalogue a reality. The Museum is grateful to Marc H. Miller, who initiated this project, curated the exhibition, and edited the catalogue. We are also indebted to Donald Bogle, Richard Long, and Dan Morgenstern who not only served as exhibition advisors, but also contributed essays for this publication.

Crucial to the success of this project has been the support and cooperation of Queens College, City University of New York, and its Louis Armstrong Archives. This rich collection was both the inspiration and backbone of the exhibition and catalogue. It was a pleasure working with Dr. Shirley Strum Kenny, President of Queens College, to honor a distinguished Queens resident and whose vision resulted in the preservation and documentation of the Archives. Julian T. Euell, Director of the Louis Armstrong House, also under the care of the College, was an early supporter and important advisor on this project. Michael Cogswell, Curator of the Armstrong Archives, was not only an important advisor but also diligently supervised the task of preparing objects for loan and reproduction. We would also like to thank Ceil Cleveland, Vice President for Institutional Relations, and her predecessor Susan Zimmerman for their assistance.

We are particularly grateful to the Smithsonian Institution Traveling Exhibition Service (SITES) which is developing and organizing the touring version of this exhibition with us. Special thanks are due to Betty Teller for incorporating this exhibition into the America's Jazz Heritage series and to Marquette Folley, who as the SITES project director helped sharpen the focus of the exhibition and supervised many crucial aspects. Others at SITES assisted in a variety of capacities including Crisley McCarson, Andrea Stevens, Viki Possoff, and Jane Markowitz. Most appreciated was the assistance of Kenneth Young and Rosemary Regan at the Smithsonian's Office of Exhibits Central, which designed, edited, and fabricated the traveling exhibit. Audiovisual material for the exhibition was prepared under the supervision of Jacquie Gales Webb of the Smithsonian's Office of Telecommunications.

The exhibition and catalogue would not have been possible without the generosity of many lenders. While acknowledged elsewhere in this publication, the exceptional generosity of the Historic New Orleans Collection; Hogan Jazz Archive, Tulane University; Howard University Gallery of Art; Frank Driggs Collection; Institute of Jazz Studies, Rutgers University; and John Kisch Separate Cinema Collection deserves special mention. This volume is also a tribute to the professional assistance of Donald R. Ellegood, University of Washington Press, and Tish O'Conner and Dana Levy, Perpetua Press. Photographers Lisa Kahane in New York and Jan White Brantley in New Orleans displayed special diligence. The Estate of Romare Bearden graciously permitted reproduction of the artist's collages.

The Louis Armstrong Educational Foundation, its President David Gold, and Vice President Phoebe Jacobs have provided invaluable encouragement and advice for this project.

While space does not permit a detailed description of their contributions, we would also like to thank the following individuals for their assistance in the realization of this project: Richard Allen, J. Lee Anderson, George Arevalo, Kostanze Bachmann, Eleanor Barefoot, Maricia Battle, Kathy Benson, Kathleen Bickford, Jack Bradley, Terry Brown, Barbara Buckley, John Bullard, Donna Cassidy, Michael Chertok, Beverly Cox, Stanley Dance, Terry Dintenfass, Laurel Duplessis, Eddie Edwards, Wayne Everard, Sam Gill, Howard Gotlieb, Amy Henderson, Tad Jones, Robert Kashey, Marilyn Kushner, Peggy LaBorde, Alfred Lemmon, David Leopold, David Levering Lewis, Phyllis Magidson, Howard Mandelbaum, Don Marquis, Terry Martin, Dr. Wilbur E. Meneray, Alan Moore, Girard Mouton III, Albert Murray, Estill Curtis Pennington, Bruce Raeburn, Sally Reeves, Van Romans, Al Rose, Jocelyn Rotily, Jack Stewart, David Streiff, Frederick Voss, Veronique Wiesinger, Wilma Wilcox, Tom Wolf.

I wish to thank the Board of Trustees of The Queens Museum of Art for their support of this important exhibition. I am also grateful to the Museum staff who were instrumental in bringing the exhibition to fruition. Among them, Jane Farver, Director of Exhibitions, and Cheryl Epstein Wolf, Research Assistant, coordinated the project from the earliest planning stages through its installation in our newly renovated galleries with the assistance of exhibition designer Christopher Warnick. Curator of Education Sharon Vatsky and Administrative/Editorial Assistant Maura Hutchens have been instrumental in the interpretive components of the exhibition. We appreciate the efforts, energy and expertise on the part of staff members: Christina Yang, Dawn Giegerich, Arnold Kanarvogel, and Steven Jo in the Curatorial Department; Paula Sharp and Jeff Oppenheim and in the Development Department; Facility Manager Louis Acquavita; and members of the Museum's Education, Development, Security and Business Departments. Former staff members whose contributions are recognized include Steven Klindt, Ileen Sheppard, and David Freilach.

CARMA C. FAUNTLEROY
Executive Director
The Queens Museum of Art

Holding his trademark handkerchief, Armstrong is a central figure in Jacob Lawrence's painting *Harlem Nightclub Scene*, from the 1950s. Dr. John I. Dintenfass.

Shot with a wide-angle lens from above, this full-length portrait by Philippe Halsman appeared in 1966 on the cover of *Life* magazine, which designed a special pull-out cover to accommodate it. © Yvonne Halsman.

Foreword

Queens College is delighted to contribute materials The Louis Armstrong Archives to the exhibition "Louis Armstrong: A Cultural Legacy." The Archives, a collection of Armstrong's personal memorabilia—was discovered in Louis Armstrong's home in Corona, Queens, after the death in 1983 of Armstrong's wife, Lucille. It provides an exceedingly personal view of Armstrong's life offstage.

Lucille Armstrong left their home to New York City. Queens College was given license to operate the Armstrong House in 1986. The collection was installed in the new Archival Center in the Benjamin S. Rosenthal Library at Queens College. Small groups now tour the House itself, which contains Louis and Lucille's furnishings. Louis Armstrong loved children, and we currently sponsor jazz concerts for school children and young people in the garden of the only home he ever owned.

With funding from the National Endowment for the Humanities, the Louis Armstrong Education Foundation, and the Ford Foundation, the Queens College archivists have catalogued the collection, which in the spring of 1994 was opened to scholars and researchers.

Throughout his life, Louis Armstrong created reel-to-reel tapes that documented his life and career. Of the 650 tapes in the collection, more than 200 of them contain candid conversations and other spoken-word material. Armstrong had a wonderful habit of turning on the tape recorder while he was visiting with friends and colleagues. Dozens of these tapes capture back-stage "rap sessions," during which Armstrong and his friends swap jokes and gossip about band trips and other musicians. He decorated each of his tape boxes with collages created from photographs, news clippings, and other materials. Several of his hand-decorated boxes are reproduced in this catalog.

Jazz historians have long known that Armstrong was a prolific diarist. The Archives house hundreds of pages of autobiographical manuscripts, many pages in Armstrong's own hand, which include both reminiscences of his remarkable life and career and observations about people and events.

Another highlight of the collection is the wealth of previously unknown photographs of Armstrong and his contemporaries. The Archives contain more than 5,000 photos, dating from the 1920s to 1983. This catalog presents for the first time a number of previously undiscovered photographs.

The collection reveals the spirit of the man. Here "Pop's Things"—conceived, created, decorated, cherished, meticulously collected, and even to some degree catalogued by Pops himself—

illuminate the artist vividly. Pops pasted clippings of his first British tour in his scrapbook. He decorated the tape boxes, carefully clipping reviews, photos, favorite images, even Valentines, Scotch taping them in artistic collages. He wrote in longhand wonderful stories of his childhood, his first acquaintance with jazz, his years in a waifs' home, and his loving relationship with a Jewish family in New Orleans. He wrote of Lucille, their home in Queens, his barber shop, even the hospital where he recuperated from a heart attack. Louis's rough-edged voice filled with wit, comedy, insight and affection, comes through as clearly in his writings as in his music.

The collection is extraordinary not only for its physical treasures, but also for its brilliant insights into an historical period in which people were caught by surprise, even shocked, to find such musical genius and artistry in a young Black man from a background of extreme poverty. The Archives detail the battles that a Black artist had to fight in order to triumph as Louis Armstrong did. His rise came in an era, not so long ago, that has faded in our collective memory as we face the prejudices of our own day. The Archives help us remember.

Armstrong wrote in his diary of his mentor: "It is really too bad that the world did not have a chance to dig the real Joe King Oliver and his greatness. His conceptions of things—life, music, people in general were really wonderful." The same can be said of Louis Armstrong. We are pleased to share some of these with you, the viewers of this exhibition. And we invite you to visit the collection.

SHIRLEY STRUM KENNY
President
Queens College of the City University of New York

TIME

THE WEEKLY NEWSMAGAZINE

Artzybasheff

LOUIS ARMSTRONG
When you got to ask what it is, you never get to know.
(Music)

Armstrong's rise to the top ranks of American culture was reflected in his selection as the cover subject of *Time* magazine on February 21, 1949. The illustration is by Boris Artzybasheff. Copyright 1949, Time, Inc. Reprinted by permission.

In 1974 Romare Bearden commemorated the story of jazz with a series of collages entitled *Of the Blues*. *Showtime* features Armstrong on the left. Collection of Dolores and Stanley Feldman, Courtesy Estate of Romare Bearden.

1 Louis Armstrong: A Cultural Legacy

Marc H. Miller

If historians were to select an individual to personify twentieth-century American culture, one leading candidate would certainly be the jazz musician Louis "Satchmo" Armstrong (1901–1971). Although not the inventor of jazz, Armstrong was its premier performer and principal molder of the mature vocabulary of this original American art form. As jazz rose to popularity in the 1920s, a period often called the "Jazz Age," and then exerted its influence on a wide range of musical forms, Armstrong emerged as one of the most famous and important musicians of his era. During a century when the United States had political and cultural impact throughout the world, Armstrong and jazz were among the nation's best known and most influential exports.

A central figure in the culture of his times, Armstrong's impact extended well beyond the field of music. His talent as a musician opened opportunities for him as an actor, comedian, spokesperson and writer; his success on stage allowed him to become a major player in a changing entertainment world dominated by phonograph recordings, sound film, radio, television, glossy magazines, and other new media. These new communications devices allowed Armstrong to reach audiences throughout America and much of the world during his fifty-year career. The force of his creativity and personality left its mark on dance, theater, the visual arts, fashion, poetry, and literature. Armstrong's story also touched the social and political currents of his time. Armstrong's life intersected with social changes through which

Armstrong is shown soon after he achieved national fame in this 1931 portrait by the commercial photographer Theatrical of Chicago. Courtesy Institute of Jazz Studies, Rutgers University.

Ralston Crawford's photograph shows the intersection of Jane Alley and Perdido Street near where Armstrong was born. Soon after this photograph was taken in 1956, the neighborhood was completely transformed by urban renewal. Hogan Jazz Archives, Howard-Tilton Memorial Library, Tulane University, New Orleans, Louisiana.

African-American creativity triumphed over prejudice to emerge in the forefront of American culture.

Armstrong himself would celebrate his role as an American child of this century by appropriating July 4, 1900, as his birthdate. In his writings and interviews, his rise from poverty to worldwide fame emerges as an example of the American myth of the self-made man. Always open to people and ideas, Armstrong reached out and absorbed all that was around him. Both his life and music reflect the synthesis of cultures long recognized as the heart of American originality. When on July 4, 1976, five years after his death, the city of New Orleans celebrated the U.S. Bicentennial by dedicating a statue (p. 227) to the hometown musician, Armstrong's ascension into the pantheon of American culture was complete.

Few would have predicted success for Louis Armstrong, born in the poorest section of New Orleans, not on July 4, 1900 as he claimed, but on the more prosaic August 4, 1901.[1] The grand-child of slaves, Armstrong was at the bottom of the ladder in a city where strict racial divisions prevented easy advancement. His mother, Mary Albert (Mayann), was not yet sixteen years old when she moved from rural Boutte, Louisiana, to New Orleans to live with her cousin Isaac Miles and his family. Their home was in Jane Alley, a dirt street adjacent to the city's House of Detention. Years later Armstrong would describe the neighborhood in his autobiography *Satchmo: My Life in New Orleans* (1955):

At age seven, young Louis went to work for the Karnofsky family, who owned a business buying and selling junk. Armstrong later recalled his closeness to the Karnofskys (shown here around 1917) and how the family helped him buy his first horn. Courtesy The Karnofsky Family.

It was called the Battlefield because the toughest characters in town used to live there, and would shoot and fight so much. In that one block between Gravier and Perdido Streets more people were crowded than you ever saw in your life.[2]

Mayann soon met neighbor William Armstrong, a laborer (and later a supervisor) at a turpentine factory. The couple never married but Mayann bore two children by Will: Louis and two years later Beatrice (Mama Lucy). Living in cramped quarters with Will's mother, Josephine Armstrong, the couple soon went their separate ways, leaving the children to be raised by their grandmother.

Louis was five and Beatrice three when they were reunited with their mother a few miles away at Liberty and Perdido. This was the heart of New Orleans' black vice district, and it would be Armstrong's home until he left New Orleans at the age of twenty-one. At a time when women had few options, Mayann may have had professional reasons for living there, as hinted in Armstrong's own carefully chosen words: "Whether my mother did any hustling, I cannot say. If she did, she certainly kept it out of my sight."[3]

In later years, Armstrong and other writers romanticized the circumstances of his youth. The poverty and deprivation were neutralized as part of a rags-to-riches story in which talent and determination triumph over disadvantage. Armstrong emphasized the positive elements of his childhood: closeness with his mother, sister, and cousins, his many neighborhood friends, and the importance of church for both his mother and grandmother. But growing

The bugle and cornet that Armstrong used at the Waifs Home. New Orleans Jazz Club Collections, Louisiana State Museum. © Jan White Brantley.

The director of the Home for Colored Waifs was Captain Joseph Jones. This postcard was probably produced in 1931 when Armstrong's triumphal return to New Orleans focused attention on his early years. Louis Armstrong Archives, Queens College, City University of New York.

COLORED
1913

WAIFS' (JONES')
NEW ORLEANS, LOUISIANA

HOME
1913

When Armstrong was eleven, the juvenile court sent him to the Home for Colored Waifs for firing a pistol on New Year's eve. There he had his first formal music lessons and eventually became the leader of the home's brass band. Frank Driggs Collection.

up in poverty amidst whorehouses, saloons, and gambling joints, with a succession of stepfathers (some abusive), was undoubtedly tough. This kind of childhood determined Armstrong's mature personality, instilling the sensitivity, hardness, and drive integral to success.[4]

Necessity made Armstrong a hard worker. From the age of seven he earned his keep with a succession of menial jobs: scavenging discarded produce, working on a junk wagon, unloading banana boats, washing dishes, and selling newspapers. The best of these jobs, delivering coal, brought him to the Karnofsky family, recent Jewish immigrants whose kindness he long remembered. The Karnofskys taught him Russian lullabies and helped him acquire his first cornet.[5] Even at a young age Louis's talent for music earned him money: he formed a quartet with a group of young friends, sang on street corners at night, and passed the hat.

In the rough environment of Liberty and Perdido, skirmishes with the law were inevitable. Armstrong was probably involved in more then one altercation before the twelve year old was arrested for firing off a gun as he celebrated New Year's Eve, 1913. It was good fortune that a judge placed him in the Colored Waif's Home, a reform school administered by an African-American, Captain Joseph Jones. This well-run home instilled discipline and provided some vocational training. Under the tutelage of Peter Davis, Armstrong also received his first formal training in music.

Armstrong's natural talents for music assured his future.

During Armstrong's youth, music was everywhere in New Orleans: dances, picnics, bars, parades, funerals, brothels, riverboats. This 1911 charity picnic featured music by the Magnolia Orchestra. Hogan Jazz Archive, Howard-Tilton Memorial Library, Tulane University, New Orleans, Louisiana.

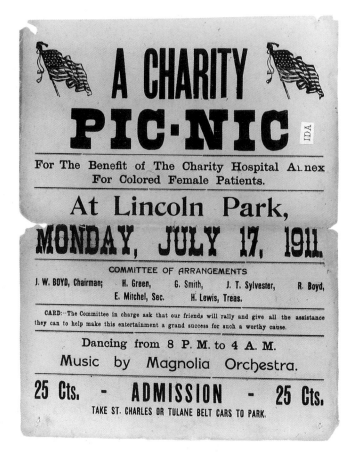

The disadvantages he encountered in New Orleans were compensated by the city's rich musical traditions. Leaving the Waif's Home at the age of thirteen, Armstrong entered a dynamic milieu. Music was everywhere in New Orleans: picnics, parades, bars, dance halls, and on the street. The city was home to a host of talented musicians, Buddy Bolden (1868?–1931), Jelly Roll Morton (1885–1941), Sidney Bechet (1897–1959), John Robichaux (1886–1939), and Armstrong's mentor Joseph "King" Oliver (1885–1938). In this musical melting pot the African-American songs of the plantation mixed with turn-of-the-century ragtime and classical traditions, forming the dynamic new music called jazz.

In later years Armstrong wrote, "Jazz and I grew up side by side,"[6] a good summation of his early career. In New Orleans, Armstrong played at all the venues linked with the birth of jazz. He performed in the city's marching bands, in holiday parades, and in the traditional funeral marches in which hymns are played on the way to the cemetery and raucous celebratory tunes on the way back. Although the brothels in the city's notorious pleasure district of Storyville employed only piano players, Armstrong worked the district's rowdy bars. He also played nighttime dance cruises on the riverboats that brought jazz to cities and towns along the Mississippi River.

From our vantage point, the birth of jazz stands out as a major event, but the rarity of contemporary artifacts and pictorial illustrations reflect the fragile place the music first occupied. The painter Jules Pascin (1885–1930), photographer Arnold Genthe (1869–1942), and numerous local artists portrayed New Orleans at

Many of the original New Orleans groups were photographed by the African-American photographer Arthur P. Bedou. The John Robichaux Orchestra was the most accomplished Creole group in the early 1900s when Armstrong began playing. Hogan Jazz Archives, Howard-Tilton Memorial Library, Tulane University, New Orleans, Louisiana.

Bedou shows the Armand Piron-Clarence Williams Band dressed for a vaudeville appearance, c. 1914. As both a musician and an entrepreneur, Williams (left) helped popularize jazz. Hogan Jazz Archives, Howard-Tilton Memorial Library, Tulane University, New Orleans, Louisiana.

the beginning of the century, but the new African-American music scene was not included. Simple broadsides advertising dances and a few commercial photographs of musicians reflect the circumstances in the black community (p. 22). Even before the turn of the century, the dynamic music and dance of New Orleans' African-American community had attracted the attention of their white neighbors. Between 1887 and 1891 some issues of the New Orleans newspaper *The Mascot* featured covers lampooning black musicians and dancers, convincing testimony both to the music's emerging profile and to the condescending amusement initially shown it by whites in the city.[7]

By 1920 many of the jazz musicians had left New Orleans, an exodus sometimes attributed to the wartime shutdown of Storyville in 1917, but actually part of the broader movement of southern blacks north in search of better opportunities. The cautious and pragmatic Armstrong lingered longer than most. Not until 1922,

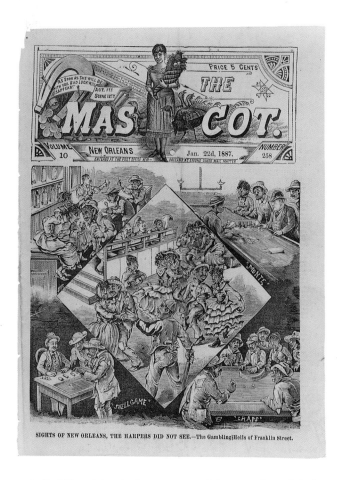

SIGHTS OF NEW ORLEANS, THE HARPERS DID NOT SEE.—The Gambling Hells of Franklin Street.

Left: Although jazz had many venues, it is often associated with New Orleans' red-light districts. Armstrong grew up on Perdido Street, the heart of the black vice district. Many of his early appearances were in dance halls like the one illustrated on the cover of the January 22, 1887, edition of *The Mascot*, a local newspaper. Louisiana State Museum.

Right: The racial prejudice of the time is reflected in police photographs of black prostitutes who were arrested for vagrancy if they worked the streets of Storyville, a district that catered only to white patrons and featured only white or light Creole prostitutes. New Orleans City Archives, Louisiana Division, New Orleans Public Library.

When I got my first job in New Orleans playing in a honky-tonk—Matranga's at Franklin and Perdido—I was 17, and it was the same as Carnegie Hall to me. Yeah. Night I made my debut, I thought I was somebody.

Louis Armstrong, *Life*, April 15, 1966

when his hometown mentor Joe Oliver invited him to join his new band in Chicago, did Armstrong go north. The gifted musician made an easy transition. Chicago's nightclubs were booming during the Prohibition years, and the young jazzman had a job with one of the city's most popular bands. Chicago—America's "Second City," national rail hub, and publications and entertainment center—was a good place for a talented musician playing an exciting new music to launch a national career.

Armstrong settled on the city's South Side, a rapidly growing district sometimes called "Bronzeville" or the "Black Belt." Only Harlem rivaled Chicago's South Side as a center for African-American creativity and entrepreneurship. Robert Abbott (1870–1940) published *The Chicago Defender*, a newspaper circulated in black communities around the country. From 1928 Oscar DePriest (1871–1951) represented the South Side in Congress, the first black elected to the House of Representatives since Reconstruction. Along State Street and 35th, in a thriving nightclub and theater scene, the exciting new music and dance that migrated to Chicago from New Orleans was refined and promoted. Archibald Motley, Jr. (1891–1981), a painter who moved to Chicago from New Orleans as a boy, made expressive renderings of the district's streets and nightclubs (p. 39), capturing the dynamic new world that Armstrong encountered.[8]

In the rough and tumble atmosphere of New Orleans, Armstrong was close to musicians like Joe Oliver, but also palled around with gamblers and pimps. A sense of the hardness of

Although the brothels of Storyville employed only piano players, musical jobs were plentiful in the district's bars. E. J. Bellocq's photographs romanticize the prostitutes who worked there, c. 1905. Courtesy Fraenkel Gallery, San Francisco.

Armstrong's early life is evident in his candid description of his short and tumultuous marriage to Daisy Parker in 1918:

> When I married Daisy (my first wife) she was a prostitute....And the way those tough men such as gamblers, pimps, etc., got along with their wives and whores, that was the same way that I had to get along with Daisy....Many times she and I went to jail from fighting in the streets.[9]

Although he never lost his infatuation with the demimonde, many of whom were early fans of jazz, in Chicago Armstrong hobnobbed with the elite entertainer celebrities of the Black Belt. In 1924 he married Lil Hardin (1898–1971), the pianist in Oliver's group. With her college degree, urbane style, and business acumen, the sophisticated Lil had a strong influence on Armstrong. He later recalled the large gap in social class that had separated them at first:

> I was wrapped up in music and did not pay any attention at first to the fact that Lil was stuck (had a crush) on me....*Who was I?* to think that a big high powered chick like Lillian Hardin who came to Chicago from Memphis Tenn – the year of 1917 – right out of Fisk University – valedictorian of her class – who me? – I thought to myself. I just couldn't conceive the idea.[10]

Working with King Oliver's Creole Jazz Band and later with other groups in Chicago, Armstrong perfected his skills and learned a range of music to accompany dancers, nightclub floor shows, and

A newspaper advertisement for music and dance cruises on the S.S. *Capitol*. Joseph Merrick Jones Steamboat Collection, Manuscripts Department, Howard-Tilton Memorial Library, Tulane University, New Orleans, Louisiana.

Right: Armstrong worked on steamboats owned by the Streckfus Brothers. Photograph by Charles Franck, 1920s. Historic New Orleans Collection.

silent films. His virtuoso trumpet work soon captured attention. Composer Hoagy Carmichael recalled the impact Armstrong had on him and the young trumpet player Bix Beiderbecke in summer 1923:

> We took two quarts of bathtub gin, a package of muggles [marijuana], and headed for the black-and-tan joint where King Oliver's band was playing….[Armstrong] slashed into Bugle Call Rag. I dropped my cigarette and gulped my drink. Bix was on his feet, his eyes popping…"Why, I moaned, why isn't everybody in the world here to hear that?" I meant it. Something as unutterably stirring as that deserved to be heard by the world.[11]

Armstrong's career would swiftly unfold. In late 1924 he worked for a year with the Fletcher Henderson Band in New York, America's entertainment capital. His arrival coincided with the publication of the "Harlem: Mecca of a New Negro" issue of the popular journal *Survey Graphics* in March of 1925, spotlighting the broad flourishing of African-American creative enterprise that came to be called the Harlem Renaissance.[12] The movement helped launch many black artists, but during a decade christened the "Jazz Age" by F. Scott Fitzgerald, the practitioners of the new syncopated music and dance held center stage. Illustrators like John Held, Jr. (1889–1958) (p. 33), and Miguel Covarrubias (1904–1957) (p. 40) captured an era when jazz was embraced by the youth culture and Harlem was chic for both black and white.[13] Armstrong

Arthur P. Bedou's photograph of the Fate Marable Band on S.S. *Capitol*, c. 1920. Left to right: Henry Kimball, Boyd Atkins, Fate Marable (at piano), Johnny St. Cyr, David Jones, Norman Mason, Armstrong, George Brashear, Baby Dodds. Frank Driggs Collection.

There was a saying in New Orleans. When some musician would get a job on the riverboats with Fate Marable, they'd say, 'Well, you're going to the conservatory.' That's because Fate was such a fine musician and the men who worked with him had to be really good.

Zutty Singleton, drummer, Fate Marable Band, Hear Me Talkin' To Ya, 1955

was at the heart of it, playing second trumpet in the Henderson Band at the Roseland Dance Hall on Broadway as a mostly white audience did the Charleston, Black Bottom, and other new dances.

Just as Armstrong's career was taking off, technological change was transforming the entertainment business. Between 1910 and 1920 sales of the phonograph record began to overtake sales of sheet music, the traditional mode of distribution. After 1920 this technology, which enabled stars of the era to reach unprecedently large and geographically dispersed audiences, became available to black performers. Armstrong made his first recordings with King Oliver's Creole Jazz Band in Chicago in 1923, and in New York his recording career gained momentum. As the jazz age unfolded, New York's record industry, the nation's largest, stoked the craze for blues and dance music with a slew of new recordings. During his one year in New York, Armstrong appeared as a sideman on more than fifty records with Bessie Smith, Ma Rainey, and Sidney Bechet. Called "race records" because they were intended for black customers, these blues and jazz recordings quickly demonstrated cross-racial appeal. In a nation where whites and blacks were segregated, the passive medium of the phonograph was an important bridge that built the cross-racial culture of the jazz age.

In late 1925 Armstrong returned to Chicago, and with his wife Lil serving as his advisor, he enjoyed increasing success. Soon the Armstrongs purchased a large home on the South Side where they lived with Lil's mother and young Clarence Hatfield,[14] a mildly retarded

Chicago

Louis Armstrong in Chicago, c. 1927.
Courtesy Chris Albertson.

In Chicago's nightclub district, music and dance from New Orleans flourished. The Pekin Cafe (top right) and the Plantation Cafe (bottom left) were two of its most popular clubs. Chicago Historical Society, IChi-20428, IChi-14428.

Armstrong went to Chicago in 1922 at the invitation of his mentor Joe "King" Oliver who had moved north five years before. This photograph was taken soon after Armstrong's arrival. Frank Driggs Collection.

A scrapbook page charts Armstrong's professional success in Chicago, c. 1928. Louis Armstrong Archives, Queens College, City University of New York.

King Oliver's Creole Jazz Band was photographed by Daguerre of Chicago, c. 1922–24. Left to right: Honore Dutrey, Baby Dodds, Oliver (in back), Armstrong, Lil Hardin, Bill Johnson, Johnny Dodds. Floyd Levin's Jazz Archive.

Louis Armstrong's Hot Five,
Exclusive Okeh Record Artists

Top: Louis and Lil Armstrong, Earl Hines, and others boating at Idlewild, Michigan, 1928. Courtesy Chris Albertson.

Bottom: A snapshot of Armstrong and friends at one of Chicago's beaches, c. 1928. Louis Armstrong Archives, Queens College, City University of New York.

Opposite
Top: This photograph by Woodard Studios taken in the fall of 1928 shows Armstrong with his new Hot Five. Left to right: Zutty Singleton, Mancy Cara, Jimmy Strong, Fred Robinson, Armstrong, and Gene Anderson. Frank Driggs Collection.

Bottom: Louis Armstrong's Hot Five was formed in 1925 specifically for recording. Left to right: Johnny Dodds, Armstrong, Johnny St. Cyr, Kid Ory, Lil Hardin Armstrong. Photograph by Daguerre of Chicago. Historic New Orleans Collection, William Russell Collection.

Armstrong's fourteen-month stint beginning in late 1924 with the Fletcher Henderson Band brought him to New York, America's entertainment capital. Left to right: Kaiser Marshall, Charlie Green, Coleman Hawkins, Howard Scott, Buster Bailey, Armstrong, Don Redman, Elmer Chambers, Charlie Dixon, Bob Escudero, Henderson. Photograph by White Studios, 1924. Frank Driggs Collection.

cousin of Armstrong for whom he cared after the death of his mother. Armstrong appreciated Lil's sophistication, but the differences in their backgrounds were already straining the relationship. In the late 1920s, while still married to Lil, Armstrong began seeing Alpha Smith, an adoring young fan who would become his third wife in 1938.[15]

In Chicago, Armstrong was a headline attraction with a sign placed outside clubs proclaiming him "The World's Greatest Trumpet Player." Inside Armstrong wowed audiences with extended solos full of musical invention, virtuosity, and stamina. While only a few had the chance to see Armstrong perform live in the 1920s, his radio broadcasts from Chicago's Savoy were heard throughout the midwest and northeast. Records he made as leader of Armstrong's Hot Five and Hot Seven in Chicago between 1925 and 1928 capture his maturing genius and established his reputation around the country. Stephen Longstreet's (b. 1907) 1927 drawing of a flapper next to a phonograph (p. 102)[16] and Jan Matulka's (1890–1972) 1929 painting *Still Life Arrangement with Phonograph and African Sculpture* (p. 35)[17] document both directly and symbolically the emergence of the medium that brought Armstrong and jazz into homes throughout America.

In 1929, as Armstrong returned to New York by car, he discovered how widespread his reputation had become through radio and records. Jazz was still going strong, and through record company executive Tommy Rockwell, Armstrong found work at Connie's Inn and other leading nightclubs in Harlem. "The night life of Harlem now surpasses Broadway itself," announced the show

The Henderson band worked the Roseland Dance Hall on Broadway where a mostly white audience did the Charleston, Black Bottom, and other new jazz-based dances. John Held, Jr.'s illustration *Teaching Old Dogs New Tricks* (1926) captures the spirit of the times. Collection of Robert C. Graham, Sr.

business magazine *Variety*. The district's clubs, eating spots, and other attractions were charted in a map by E. Simms Campbell (p. 75), whose illustrated "Harlem Sketches" appeared in African-American papers around the country.[18] The bacchanal mood of Harlem on the eve of the Depression is evoked in numerous paintings, including Reginald Marsh's (1898–1954) *Tuesday Night At the Savoy Ballroom* (p. 35) done the year after (1930) Armstrong was a star attraction at the popular club.[19]

Once in New York Armstrong soon moved from Harlem to Broadway when a version of *Hot Chocolates*, the popular floor show at Connie's Inn, moved to the Hudson Theater as the latest in a string of black musicals on Broadway spotlighting the new music and dance. This raucous mix of music, dance, comedy, and attractive chorus girls was depicted in a drawing by Winold Reiss (1886–1953) (p. 45), an Austrian artist who four years before had illustrated the Harlem issue of *Survey Graphics* (pp. 38, 73). On Broadway, Armstrong's nightly rendition of "Ain't Misbehavin'" was a highlight of the all-black revue. An editorial in the *New York Herald Tribune* noted the significance of success on the Great White Way, the center of the nation's entertainment.

> When Broadway sets its sign and seal upon a movement it is made...it means that the Negro, not merely as a vaudeville joke and not merely as a highbrow cult, has arrived.[20]

Armstrong enjoyed high favor among the white intellectuals of the day. Eugene O'Neill, who had addressed African themes in his 1920 play *Emperor Jones* (starring the black actor/singer Paul

Reginald Marsh's painting *Tuesday Night at the Savoy Ballroom* (1930) captures the revelry at a famous Harlem nightclub where Armstrong frequently performed. Rose Art Museum, Brandeis University, Waltham, Massachussetts, Gift of the Honorable William Benton, New York.

Still Life Arrangement with Phonograph and African Sculpture (1929) by Jan Matulka commemorates the invention that brought Armstrong and jazz into homes throughout America. Whitney Museum of American Art, Gift of Gertrude Vanderbilt Whitney, 31.298.

Opposite: The jazz age inspired many visual artists. A 1916 watercolor by Charles Demuth shows a jazz band at Marshall's, an early New York club. Collection of Irwin Goldstein, M.D.

Robeson), wrote to writer, photographer, and longtime advocate of Harlem Renaissance artists Carl Van Vechten in September of 1929:

> "The St. James Infirmary" is right up my alley! I am now memorizing the words. Do you know Mr. Armstrong? If so give him my fraternal benediction. He is a darl.[21]

O'Neill was surely responding to Armstrong's expressive treatment of the song's darkly tragic story. Armstrong's link to the literary community also played out in another of his key musical innovations, scat singing. His improvisational approach to written lyrics—mixing, jumbling, and reinventing the words along expressive musical lines—echoed new directions in literature. Tristan Tzara, poet and *chef d'ecole* of the *Dada* movement in Paris in the early 1920s, related Armstrong's scat to the sound poetry of the avant-garde movement:

> Louis Armstrong is a poet whose efforts of expressing himself in words are frustrated with each successive trial, because in the final analysis, poetry cannot be put into words. In his personal language, however, this poetry touches the sensitivity of individuals from all four corners of the world.[22]

While Armstrong surely appreciated the respect accorded him by intellectuals, he was a popular artist and strived for the widest mass audience. Working on Broadway and in the floor shows of Harlem made Armstrong an all-around entertainer. "I got to be around great actors like Bill Robinson," he later explained, "so I found out, the main thing is live for that audience."[23] As he moved into the 1930s, he emphasized his singing and his onstage gift for gab and comedy. Increasingly in his repertoire he abandoned the hot jazz classics of New Orleans and Chicago in favor of popular show tunes and Tin Pan Alley favorites. Armstrong's unique fusion of modes would change the world of popular music and the shape of jazz.

In 1929 Armstrong returned to New York by automobile. Snapshots show Armstrong at Niagara Falls and with Zutty Singleton soon after their arrival in Manhattan. Frank Driggs Collection.

In 1930 Armstrong relocated to California for an extended engagement at Frank Sebastian's New Cotton Club in Culver City. In Hollywood he made his first appearance in film, another new medium that played a role in his rise to national fame. In November of 1930 the musician was arrested for marijuana possession outside the Cotton Club, receiving a six-month suspended sentence. More troubling were gun-point confrontations with the gangsters who controlled nightclubs during the years of Prohibition. When Armstrong returned to Chicago in 1931, rival gangs vied over the popular star, making life increasingly uncomfortable for him and his manager Johnny Collins.[24]

Convinced it was unsafe to work in the gangster-dominated clubs of Chicago and New York, Armstrong and Collins assembled a band, hired a bus, and began a grueling ten-month tour of Pitts-

Armstrong first played with the Dickerson Orchestra in Chicago in 1926, and the band followed him to New York. This photograph by Apeda, a leading New York portrait studio, commemorates their appearance at Connie's Inn in Harlem in 1929. New Orleans Jazz Club Collections, Louisiana State Museum.

burgh, Baltimore, Memphis, Houston, and other smaller cities. Such tours were particularly difficult for black performers, as Armstrong recalled:

> We used to tour the South.... We couldn't get into hotels. Our money wasn't even good. We'd play night clubs and spots which didn't have a little boy's room for Negroes. We'd have to go outside, often in the freezing cold, and in the dark.[25]

Armstrong's appeal crossed racial lines but he still had to appear in many segregated venues. During a three-month return visit to his hometown of New Orleans in 1931, Armstrong enjoyed a hero's welcome in the black community with a parade, honorary banquet, and special "Armstrong" souvenir cigar. Still the city's Jim Crow laws prevented blacks from attending his performance. On opening night, as 5,000 whites crowded into the Suburban Garden, 10,000 blacks sat on the levee hoping to catch the music through the open windows.

In 1932 Armstrong and Collins headed for Europe, first for a short four-month stay and then, after a return to America, for a longer eighteen-month tour. Jazz in Europe, said one critic, ranked with "the movie and the dollar as the foremost exponent of modern Americanism."[26] French artist Paul Colin's portfolio of lithographs (pp. 42, 60), *Le Tumulte Noir* (1927), captures the excitement of Jazz-Age Paris where the African-American singer/dancer

Opposite: Winold Reiss's *Interpretation of Harlem Jazz (Harlem at Night)* originally appeared in the "Harlem: Mecca of the New Negro" issue of *Survey Graphics* magazine in March 1925. Collection of Mr. and Mrs. W. Tjark Reiss.

Top: Archibald Motley Jr.'s *Saturday Night* (1935) captures the ambiance of the clubs where Armstrong and jazz came to maturity. Howard University Gallery of Art, Permanent Collection, Washington, D.C.

Bottom: Motley's painting *Black Belt* (1934) shows the South Side of Chicago, the neighborhood where Armstrong lived and worked in the 1920s. Hampton University Museum, Hampton, Virginia.

Harlem Nightclubs

The night life of Harlem now surpasses that of Broadway itself. From midnight until after dawn it is a seething cauldron of Nubian mirth and hilarity.

Variety, October 16, 1929

The popular young caricaturist Miguel Covarrubias frequently visited the nightclubs of Harlem. His drawing of a blues singer and a dancer with a cap were reproduced in W. C. Handy, *Blues: An Anthology* (1926). Prints and Photographs Division, Library of Congress.

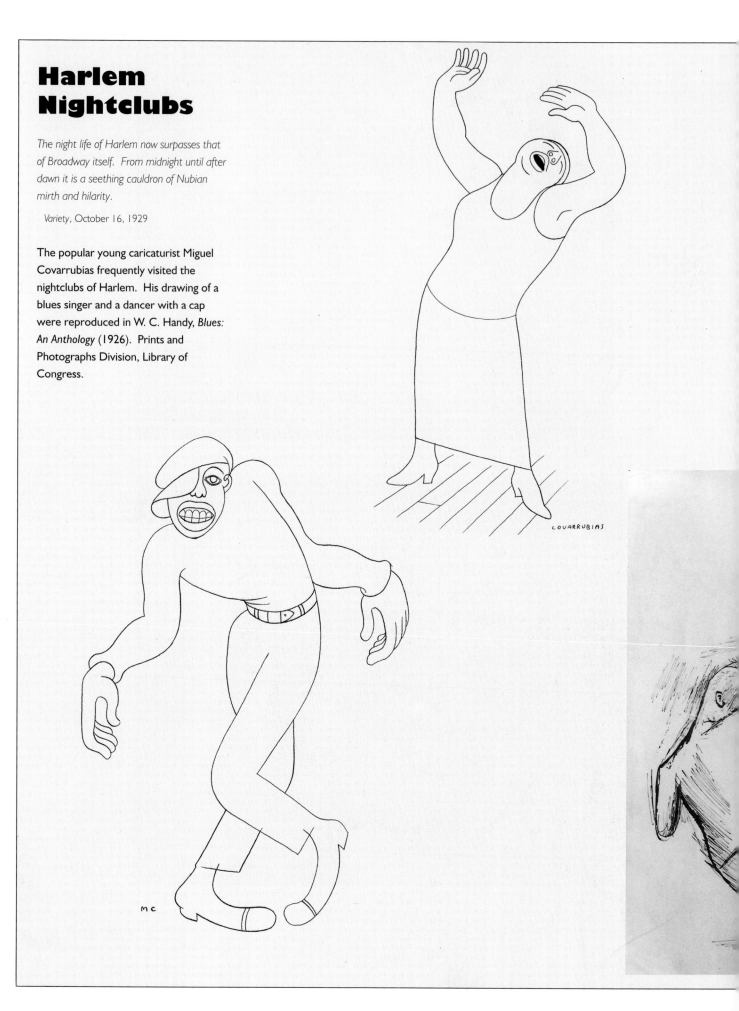

The exuberant dancing at the Savoy, a cavernous Harlem club that held thousands of patrons, is captured in drawings by Adolf Dehn, 1929. Estate of Adolf Dehn, Courtesy Harmon-Meek Gallery, Naples, Florida.

By the 1920s, the Jazz Age was
international. French artist Paul Colin's
depiction of a jazz band is from *Le Tumulte
Noir* (1927), a portfolio of lithographs
celebrating the vogue for African-American
music and dance in Paris. Art & Artifacts
Division, Schomburg Center for Research in
Black Culture, The New York Public
Library, Astor, Lenox and Tilden
Foundations.

Theaters used for jazz concerts often had wall paintings that enhanced their ambiance. These murals showing jazz musicians were done for a roller-skating rink in Lehighton, Pennsylvania, in 1933. The artist was 23-year-old Franz Kline, a local who later won fame as an abstract expressionist. Jazz Mural Collection of Larry and Charlene Graver.

Opposite: Armstrong made it to Broadway in 1929 in the cast of *Hot Chocolates*. A drawing by Winold Reiss captures the raucous mix of music, dance, comedy, and attractive chorus girls that characterized *Hot Chocolates* in its original incarnation at Connie's Inn in Harlem. Collection of Mr. and Mrs. W. Tjark Reiss, Courtesy Shepherd Gallery, New York.

Blanding Sloan's woodcut, *Jazz—The New Possession* (c. 1925), makes overt the sexuality that many associated with the new music. National Museum of American Art, Smithsonian Institution, Museum purchase made possible by Emily Tuckerman and Charles Albert.

Jules Pascin, well known for his depictions of Paris nightlife, often visited the jazz clubs of Harlem during an extended visit to New York in the mid-1920s. Collection of E. William Judson.

Armstrong's rendition of "Ain't Misbehavin'," composed by Fats Waller and Andy Razaf, was singled out as "a highlight of the premiere" of *Hot Chocolates*. Private Collection, New York.

Campbell Studios, New York, *Fats Waller*, 1924. Courtesy Institute of Jazz Studies, Rutgers University.

Rex Studio, Columbus, Ohio, *Andy Razaf*, early 1920s. Photographs & Prints Division, Schomburg Center for Research in Black Culture, The New York Public Library, Astor, Lenox and Tilden Foundations.

Opposite

Top: The sound of jazz inspired many abstract paintings. The starting point for *Swing Music (Louis Armstrong)* (1938) by the American artist Arthur Dove was Armstrong's hit record "Public Melody Number One." Emulsion, oil, and wax on canvas, 44.7 x 55.8 cm. Alfred Stieglitz Collection, 1949.540, photograph © 1992, The Art Institute of Chicago. All Rights Reserved.

Bottom: Artist and jazz fan Misha Reznikoff did numerous paintings based on jazz. Armstrong's Hot Five classic inspired the oil painting *Cornet Chop Suey* (1938). Courtesy The Reznikoff Artistic Partnership.

Stuart Davis, *Hot Still Scape for Six Colors— 7th Avenue Style*, 1940. Gift of the William H. Lane Foundation and the M. and M. Karolik Collection by exchange, Courtesy Museum of Fine Arts, Boston.

Josephine Baker was the star of the moment, and Bricktop's, the Montmartre nightclub run by African-American Ada "Bricktop" Smith, was the place to be seen.[27]

With his records already known, Armstrong was enthusiastically received from his first concert at the London Palladium. In Europe, Armstrong fired the erratic Collins and let Europeans secure him bookings. Backed by either local white orchestras or with a pickup band of Paris-based African-American musicians that included Bricktop's husband Peter DuConge, Armstrong toured England, Belgium, Sweden, Denmark, France, Switzerland, and Italy. In England he was called "Satchmo," a variant of his nickname "Satchelmouth" that would stick for the rest of his career and even appears on his tombstone.[28] In Europe he met young jazz fans like Robert Goffin from Belgium, Leonard Feather of England, and the Frenchmen Hugues Panassie and Charles Delaunay, who later became key supporters.

Back in America in 1935, Armstrong took on a new manager: Joe Glaser, the owner of the Sunset Club in Chicago. Armstrong and Glaser were a well-matched pair, and the association between them was lifelong. Backed by Glaser's aggressive business skills, Armstrong's career soared. As the changing musical taste of the Depression era sank the careers of other jazz musicians of the 1920s, a revamped Armstrong not only flourished but also helped set the style of the new Swing era. Sporting an elegant upscale look, a new repertoire of songs, and up-to-date band arrangements, Armstrong and his Orchestra were constantly on tour doing both concerts and dances around the country.

By the late 1930s and 1940s, Armstrong's central role in mainstream American culture was reflected in the visual arts. Arthur Dove (1880–1946), inspired by Armstrong's hit record "Public Melody Number One," painted *Swing Music (Louis Armstrong)* (1938), an abstraction in which lines and colors express the spirit of music (p. 46). Much of the modernist painter Mischa Reznikoff's (1905–1971) oeuvre of the late 1930s and 1940s is devoted to abstract interpretations of jazz, and *Swing That Music* (1942), *Cornet Chop Suey* (1938), and others are specifically based on Armstrong records (p. 46). Jazz-inspired paintings connected to Armstrong were done by Stuart Davis (1892–1964) (p. 47) and Davis' sometime-student, George Wettling (1907–1968), a white jazz drummer who frequently worked with the trumpeter (p. 127).[29] Davis explained the great appeal that Armstrong had for him and other visual artists:

> Every artist has models of greatness in the Arts which guide his development. Louis Armstrong has always been one of the most important for me. Not to illustrate his musical ideas, but as an example of direct expression which transforms its Subject Matter into Art.[30]

Music was the source of Armstrong's extraordinary success, but it was amplified by his engaging public personality and buttressed by skillful communication of his life story and his views on

Opposite: As Armstrong toured the country in the early 1930s, he often gave fans and friends autographed copies of this portrait by Theatrical of Chicago. This picture is inscribed to Isaac Miles, Armstrong's closest relative on his mother's side. Hogan Jazz Archives, Howard-Tilton Memorial Library, Tulane University, New Orleans, Louisiana.

Following his success in *Hot Chocolates*, Armstrong headed for Los Angeles where he fronted the Les Hite Band during an extended booking at Frank Sebastian's Cotton Club in Culver City. Frank Driggs Collection.

A snapshot shows Armstrong with his wife Lil outside the Hotel Somerville in Los Angeles, 1930. Frank Driggs Collection.

jazz. Always available for interviews and photo sessions, his version of events influenced many written histories of jazz. Armstrong was himself a prolific writer. Traveling with his typewriter, he worked backstage and in hotel rooms on letters, magazine articles, and manuscripts. His book *Swing That Music* (1936) was the first life story of a jazz musician, and it masterfully positioned its author in the changing jazz scene. Armstrong tells the story of his rise in jazz, and coauthor Horace Gerlach defines the current world of Swing, illustrating with scores how other jazz players would play Armstrong's tune "Swing that Music." His second autobiography, *Satchmo: My Life in New Orleans* (1954) was the most successful of many postwar books on jazz. Its colorful tales of youth in turn-of-the-century New Orleans established Armstrong as a mythic figure in the popular imagination.[31]

As a popular black performer whose appeal crossed racial lines, Armstrong greatly expanded opportunities for black performers. From the late 1930s on, he was one of a handful of African-Americans regularly appearing in Hollywood films. In 1937 he was the first black performer to host a national radio program, substituting for Rudy Vallee on the Fleischmann's Yeast Hour. Usually without fanfare, Armstrong broke long-standing barriers against black performers in theaters and clubs around the country.

In 1942 he married Lucille Wilson, a dancer he had met three years before at New York's Cotton Club. Although both whites and blacks of Armstrong's generation often equated beauty with light skin pigmentation, it was a prejudice he did not share as he later

An advertisement for a 1932 appearance by Armstrong at the Trianon in Indianapolis. Frank Driggs Collection.

In 1931 Armstrong assembled a band, hired a bus, and took to the road. Snapshots show the bus, and Armstrong looking at a poster advertising his old Chicago friends Buck and Bubbles. Louis Armstrong Archives, Queens College, City University of New York.

related in an *Ebony* magazine article entitled "Why I Like Dark Women":

When I first saw her, the glow of her deep-brown skin got me deep down...Lucille was the first girl to crack the high-yellow color standard used to pick girls for the famous Cotton Club chorus line. I think she was a distinguished pioneer.[32]

The couple bought a modest house in Corona, Queens, a predominantly white suburban neighborhood where other successful black musicians like Clarence Williams (1893–1965) also lived. It was Armstrong's first permanent residence since his breakup with Lil a decade before, and it remained his home until his death nearly thirty years later.[33] The relationship with Lucille, his fourth wife, would also last.

After a brief lull in work during the war, Armstrong quickly reestablished himself in a postwar period that saw many changes in jazz. Small clubs, like those on 52nd Street in New York, replaced large theaters and dance halls, and the big orchestras of the 1930s gave way to smaller combos. Armstrong followed the trend, breaking up his orchestra and forming a septet, Louis Armstrong's All Stars. As the Swing era ended, the jazz world divided between the new direction of bebop and the traditional sound of New Orleans/ Chicago jazz. With his band of veteran performers like Jack Teagarden and Earl Hines, Armstrong was the leader of the school known as Dixieland.

Return to New Orleans, 1931

A three-month engagement at New Orleans's Suburban Gardens in 1931 offered Armstrong a chance to visit his hometown. Photographer Villard Paddio captured all the high points of his triumphal return. Historic New Orleans Collection, William Russell Collection.

New Orleans musicians honored Armstrong with a banquet at the Astoria Hotel as recorded in photographs by Villard Paddio. Frank Driggs Collection.

Louis Armstrong and Lil Armstrong greet the director of the Waifs Home, Captain Joseph Jones, and Armstrong's first music teacher, Peter Davis. Photograph by Villard Paddio. Hogan Jazz Archives, Howard-Tilton Memorial Library, Tulane University, New Orleans, Louisiana.

Returning to the Colored Waifs Home (now called the Municipal Boys' Home), Armstrong and his orchestra posed with the home's brass band in this photograph by Villard Paddio. Hogan Jazz Archives, Howard-Tilton Memorial Library, Tulane University, New Orleans, Louisiana.

During his stay in New Orleans, Armstrong sponsored a local baseball team, providing them with new caps, uniforms, and gear. They called themselves "Armstrong's Secret Nine." Photograph by Villard Paddio. Historic New Orleans Collection, William Russell Collection.

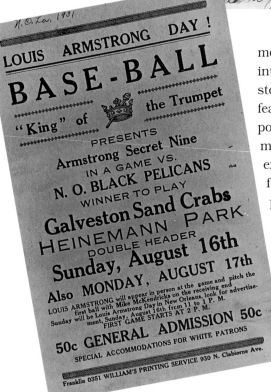

A broadside announces a baseball game between Armstrong's Secret Nine and the New Orleans Black Pelicans. Louis Armstrong Archives, Queens College, City University of New York.

In his middle years, Armstrong was no longer the young modern but a historical figure lionized as an originator of the internationally popular American art form. A *Time* magazine cover story in February 1949 and Edward R. Murrow and Fred Friendly's feature film documentary, *Satchmo the Great* (1957), cemented the popular perception of Armstrong as the fountainhead of jazz. In *Life* magazine, Richard Meryman summed up Armstrong's exalted if exaggerated status: "It is a simple fact of jazz music, the only art form America ever wholly originated, that virtually all that is played today comes in some way from Louis Armstrong." [34]

During the 1940s and 1950s broadly based scholarly interest in jazz fed the Dixieland revival and Armstrong's status as founding father. The careers of long-forgotten jazz veterans were revived, many new books on jazz history were published, and visual artists rushed to document jazz's fast-disappearing past. Ralston Crawford's ambitious series of close to ten thousand photographs (pp. 18, 134) and an extended series by Lee Friedlander (p. 135) exemplify the high quality of the documentation of New Orleans jazz. [35] These images show the original world of New Orleans jazz: reverential portraits of now-elderly originators, threatened historical sites, and living traditions like the jazz funeral. As they recall the world of Armstrong's youth, they also show us its aging face and reveal the new historicizing respect that recharged the career of Armstrong and other veteran musicians.

Although traditional jazz lacked the avant-garde excitement

Photographs by Gibson of Chicago capture Armstrong's charisma and energy in 1933. Louis Armstrong Archives, Queens College, City University of New York.

of bebop, it enjoyed a much larger audience, and in the hands of Armstrong it still had kick. Armstrong's All Stars worked nightclubs, concert halls, jazz festivals, and college campuses playing to a mix of jazz aficionados, younger fans, and older folks nostalgic for the good old prewar days. At Disneyland, Armstrong's traditional jazz mixed easily with the faux turn-of-the-century ambiance of the California theme park. Armstrong's 1962 reunion with fellow New Orleans musicians and "Hot Five" veterans Johnny St. Cyr and Kid Ory on the *Mark Twain*, a recreated Mississippi riverboat at Disneyland, aptly symbolized the passage of jazz from cutting edge to mainstream aesthetic. In 1964 Armstrong demonstrated the mass appeal of his original brand of contemporary Dixieland nostalgia when his recording of "Hello Dolly," replaced the Beatles, "She Loves You" as number one on the *Billboard* chart.

Although Armstrong enjoyed fame and fortune, his later life was not free of controversy. America's racial climate changed swiftly after World War II, and as one of the nation's most successful blacks, Armstrong was inevitably drawn into the civil rights struggle. Born in the South at the turn of the century, Armstrong had emerged in a world hard on blacks. Racial prejudice was enforced by frequent incidents of mob violence, and blacks learned to avoid trouble with a ready smile and a quick, "Yes, sir." In show business the role of black entertainers was strictly circumscribed by

In Europe, 1932–1935

In 1932 Armstrong made his first trip to Europe, staying four months. After a brief return to the United States, he went back for an eighteen-month tour that ended in January 1935.

Elegant photographs of Armstrong by Ava Studio of London capture the mixture of new music and high fashion found in jazz-age Europe, c. 1933. Frank Driggs Collection.

Armstrong's Stockholm performance included a set with a local orchestra. Photograph by Peddy-Foto (B.A. "Peddy" Moberg). Louis Armstrong Archives, Queens College, City University of New York.

At a Stockholm reception, Armstrong is joined by another American, Marian Anderson, whose spiritual singing was popular in Europe. Frank Driggs Collection.

The arrival of Armstrong and his entourage at the railroad station of Stockholm, Sweden, was captured by a photojournalist for the daily newspaper *Stockholms-Tidningen*. Frank Driggs Collection.

Cartoon caricatures from the English magazine *Melody Maker* show Armstrong's first European concert at the Palladium in London in August 1932. At a time when the capabilities of photography were still limited, drawings captured Armstrong's lively, extroverted stage act. Courtesy Institute of Jazz Studies, Rutgers University.

the traditions of nineteenth-century minstrel shows where white men in blackface did comic portrayals of blacks that reinforced negative stereotypes. Like others of his generation, Armstrong worked within these harsh realities to forge a broadly popular image in the United States. Armstrong was proud of his success against the odds and was surprised when some criticized his compromises:

> Some folks, even some of my own people, have felt that I've been "soft" on the race issue. Some have even accused me of being an Uncle Tom of not being "aggressive." How can they say that? I've pioneered in breaking the color line in many Southern states... I've taken a lot of abuse, put up with a lot of jazz, even been in some pretty dangerous spots through no fault of my own for almost forty years.[36]

Armstrong expressed his view on race in *Ebony*, the most widely read magazine of black life. Most notable is his article "Daddy, How the Country Has Changed!" (May 1961), in which he discusses his role as a groundbreaker in the civil rights struggle. Privately Armstrong expressed his views in collages he made in the 1950s and 1960s. Cut-out newspaper photos of the baseball player Jackie Robinson pay tribute to another pioneer of American integration (p. 82). Another collage has images from "Pinky," a 1949 film about a light-complexioned black woman passing for white. Although he avoided speaking out on political issues, Armstrong was so outraged by the televised resistance to school integration in Little Rock,

Left: Charles Delaunay used his skills as a sketch artist to meet his idol Armstrong at a Paris recording session. The son of the esteemed artists Robert and Sonia Delaunay, Charles soon abandoned the visual arts to become a leading jazz promoter. From the publication *Noirs au Blanc.* Courtesy Institute of Jazz Studies, Rutgers University.

Right: Drawings of a smiling Armstrong by a Belgium artist with the initials M.G. were used to promote Armstrong's concert in Belgium. The Louis Armstrong Archives Queens College, City University of New York.

Arkansas, in 1957 that he denounced Governor Orville Faubus and President Dwight Eisenhower. Because of his reputation for being nonpolitical, his remarks had maximum effect.

As a world attraction, Armstrong and his music could not avoid the politicization that attends cultural change. Touring Europe in 1934, Armstrong avoided Nazi Germany, which was increasingly hostile to non-Aryan people and culture. In 1938 the Nazis labeled jazz "degenerate music," and as Hitler's power spread, jazz was banned in much of Europe. After 1945, the long-suppressed sound quickly reemerged, now as a symbol of freedom and liberation. Armstrong's 1948 return to Europe as the star of the Festival International du Jazz at Nice, France, was met with wild jubilation, a scene repeated during subsequent tours. Against the background of the emerging Cold War, the political implications of Armstrong's popularity were first articulated in the *New York Times* by Felix Belair:

> America's secret weapon is a blue note in a minor key. Right now its most effective ambassador is Louis (Satchmo) Armstrong. American jazz has now become a universal language. It knows no national boundaries, but everyone knows where it comes from and where to look for more.[37]

Through U. S. State Department–sponsored tours and Voice of America broadcasts, Armstrong's music was heard behind the Iron Curtain.

Ambassador Satch had a special impact in Africa in the

Nude Dancer on a Piano, modeled after Josephine Baker, and a stylized image of a jazz dancer were included in Paul Colin's portfolio of lithographs *Le Tumulte Noir* (1927). National Portrait Gallery, Smithsonian Institution.

1950s and 1960s, a time when many parts of the continent were making the transition from colonial rule to independence. Because Armstrong and jazz traced their roots to Africa, both the performer and music had wide appeal there. More than one hundred thousand people attended his 1956 concert at Accra, Gold Coast (soon to be the independent nation of Ghana). Armstrong's appeal in Africa was recognized by American commercial interests. In an innovative advertising ploy that has since become common, Pepsi-Cola sponsored Armstrong's 1960 tour of West Africa to promote new bottling plants in Nigeria and Ghana.[38] As more American blacks began to see themselves as part of a pan-African diaspora, Armstrong's success in Africa enhanced his reputation with African-Americans back home.

During his last years Armstrong continued to ride the wave of revolution. Just as he had on phonograph records, on radio, and in sound movies, Armstrong played well in the postwar media of television. In hundreds of shows broadcasts to millions, Armstrong won new fans with lively musical segments, often featuring improvised duets with such popular singers as Bing Crosby and Frank Sinatra, who had long been influenced by Armstrong's style and technique.

The late 1960s, marked by the assassinations of Robert Kennedy and the Reverend Martin Luther King, Jr., and the war in Vietnam, were difficult times for America. Times were also hard for Armstrong who in 1969 mourned the death of his manager and

A pencil sketch by the African-American painter Palmer Hayden shows the Paris nightclub Bal Noir, c. 1926. Palmer Cole Hayden Papers, Archives of American Art, Smithsonian Institution.

The American Ada "Bricktop" Smith, hostess of the popular Paris jazz club Bricktops, and Peter DuConge, a New Orleans-born clarinetist in Armstrong's European band, are shown in this 1929 wedding portrait. Photographs & Prints Division, Schomburg Center for Research in Black Culture, The New York Public Library, Astor, Lenox and Tilden Foundations.

Top left: Armstrong and his companion Alpha Smith (who later became his third wife) rest at a train station in England. Photograph by Fletcher Allen. Frank Driggs Collection.

Top right: Armstrong carries a snapshot camera and Alpha, a home movie camera, as they tour England. Frank Driggs Collection.

Left: Louis Armstrong poses with Justo Barreto, the leader of the quickly assembled Paris jazz band that accompanied Armstrong on his first tours of Europe. The snapshot is by band member Fletcher Allen. Frank Driggs Collection.

friend Joe Glaser and saw his own health begin to falter. Yet to the end, Armstrong retained his ability to produce inspiring music. His powerful recording of "What a Wonderful World" and "When You Wish Upon a Star" found a worldwide, cross-generational audience. Armstrong's spoken introduction to a remake of "What a Wonderful World," recorded less then twelve months before his death, captures the optimistic philosophy that audiences now associated with him:

> Seems to me it ain't the world that's so bad, but what we are doing to it. And all I'm saying is, see what a wonderful world it would be if only we would give it a chance. Love, baby, love. That's the secret. Yeah.

When the sixty-nine year-old Louis Armstrong died on July 6, 1971, his passing was front-page news throughout America. More than twenty-five thousand mourners filed by as his coffin lay in state at a New York City National Guard Armory. His widow, Lucille, received the condolences of political leaders, entertainers, and fans from around the world. As he moved permanently offstage, his musical contributions were universally hailed. His bebop-playing trumpet rival Dizzy Gillespie noted, "If it weren't for him, there wouldn't be any of us." But Armstrong's legacy was not only his music but also his infectious upbeat outlook on life. Coretta Scott King, the widow of Martin Luther King, Jr., remembered how the "eloquence of his horn" helped "bridge generation, racial, political, and national gaps.[39] The power of his music and personality has proved to be enduring. Permanently preserved by new twentieth-century technologies, Armstrong continues to perform with a freshness and vitality that reaffirms his stature as one of the most inspiring and influential musicians of his time.

NOTES

1. Armstrong first used the July 4, 1900, birthdate when he registered for the draft in 1918. The August 4, 1901, date comes from baptismal records and census reports discovered by New Orleans writer and researcher Tad Jones. See Gary Giddins, *Satchmo* (New York: Doubleday, 1988), 47–53.

2. Louis Armstrong, *Satchmo: My Life in New Orleans* (New York: Signet Book, 1955), 7.

3. Ibid., 8

4. Will Armstrong would eventually marry and have two children. As a provision for being released from the Waif's Home, Louis lived for a short time with his father's new family. His mother's life was more unsettled. Armstrong recalled at least six stepfathers. He was fond of Gabe and Tom but Albert and Slim were drinkers who often fought with him and his mother. See Armstrong, *Satchmo*, op. cit., 23–5.

5. Armstrong's strong attachment to the Karnofsky family is evident in a seventy-six page manuscript entitled "Louis Armstrong & the Jewish Family in New Orleans," begun March 31, 1969. Louis Armstrong Archives, Queens College, City University of New York.

6. Undated quote in Mike Pinfold, *Louis Armstrong* (New York: Universe Books, 1987), 20.

7. Arnold Genthe, *Impressions of Old New Orleans* (New York: Geroge H. Doran Co., 1926); For visual material from the early years of jazz, see Al Rose and Edmond Souchon, *New Orleans Jazz: A Family Album* (Baton Rouge: Louisiana State University Press,1967); Al Rose, *Storyville, New Orleans Being An Authentic Illustrated Account of the Notorious Red-Light District* (University of Alabama Press, 1974), which reproduces the illustrated covers of many issues of *The Mascot.*

8. For more about the South Side of Chicago, see Dempsey J. Travis, *An Autobiography of Black Jazz* (Chicago: Urban Research Institute, 1983). Chicago's Black Belt is also thoroughly discussed in Jontyle Theresa Robinson and Wendy Greenhouse, *The Art of Archibald J. Motley, Jr.* (Chicago Historical Society, 1991).

9. Letter from Armstrong to Max Jones, c. 1969, in Max Jones and John Chilton, *Louis: The Louis Armstrong Story* (Boston and Toronto: Little, Brown, and Company, 1971), 56.

10. Louis Armstrong, manuscript (written for Robert Goffin), c. 1944, writing tablet 1, 17. Collection of the Institute for Jazz Studies, Rutgers University.

11. Hoagy Carmichael, *The Stardust Road* (Bloomington, IN: Indiana University Press, 1946), 53.

12. For Harlem Renaissance, see David Levering Lewis, *When Harlem Was In Vogue* (New York: Oxford University Press, 1979); John S. Wright and Tracy E. Smith, *A Stronger Soul With A Finer Frame: Portraying African-Americans in the Black Renaissance*, exhibition catalogue (Minneapolis: University Art Museum, University of Minnesota, 1990).

13. The term "Jazz Age" was popularized by F. Scott Fizgerald's book of short stories, *Tales of the Jazz Age* (1924). For more on illustration of the Jazz Age, see Shelley Armitage, *John Held, Jr.: Illustrator of the Jazz Age* (Syracuse, NY: Syracuse University Press, 1987); Miguel Covarrubias (introduction by Frank Crowninshield), *Negro Drawings*, (New York: Knopf 1927).

14. Clarence was the illegitimate offspring of Armstrong's cousin Flora Miles and an elderly white man named Hatfield. His retardation was the result of a fall that took place when he was under Armstrong's care (see Armstrong, *Satchmo*, op. cit., 129–130). After the death of his mother, Clarence moved to Chicago to live with Armstrong who still (through his will) continues to provide his support. Numerous pictures from all phases of their lives show the close relationship between Armstrong and his "adopted son."

15. For more about the marital difficulties between Armstrong and Lil, and a detailed account of his relationship with Alpha Smith see: Armstrong, Goffin manuscript, op. cit., writing tablet 3, 12-30.

16. Stephen Longstreet is a successful writer whose credits include the screenplay for Th*e Al Jolson Story*. From the 1920s to the present day he has done tens of thousands of drawings about jazz. See Richard Wang (introduction), *Jazz-the Chicago Scene: The Art of Stephen Longstreet* (Chicago: The Joseph Regenstein Library, The University of Chicago, 1989); Stephen Longstreet, *Storyville to Harlem: Fifty Years in the Jazz Scene*, (New Brunswick, NJ: Rutgers University Press, 1986).

17. *Jan Matulka (1890-1972)*, published for the National Collection of Fine Arts and the Whitney Museum of American Art by the Smithsonian Institution Press, Washington D.C., 1980.

18. E. Simms Campbell would have a very successful career as an illustrator for *Esquire* magazine.

19. During the years 1910–1929, the jazz clubs of Harlem inspired many artists including Charles Demuth (1883–1935), Stuart Davis, Jules Pascin, Winold Reiss, Miguel Covarrubias, Stephen Longstreet, William Gropper (1897–1971), and Adolf Dehn (1896–1968). Although expressive line and color captures the animation and spirit of jazz, portrayals of blacks often reiterate the racial stereotypes of the day. See Guy C. McElroy, *Facing History: the Black Image in American Art 1710-1940* (San Francisco: Bedford Arts, and Washington, D.C: The Corcoran Gallery of Art, 1990).

20. *New York Herald Tribune*, 18 October 1929.

21. O'Neill letter quoted in Arthur and Barbara Gelb, *O'Neill* (New York: Dell, 1965), 403.

22. Undated statement by Tristan Tzara from liner notes by Alain Gerber, "Louis Armstrong 7 Satchmo's Discoveries 1936: 1938" (Jazz Heritage Series, vol. 27, MCA Records, 1980).

23. Armstrong in Richard Meryman, *Louis Armstrong: A Self-Portrait* (New York: Eakins Press, 1971), 41.

24. A long account of Armstrong's marijuana arrest is contained in a letter from Armstrong to Max Jones, c. 1969, in Jones and Chilton, op. cit., 113–116; His problems with the gangsters of Chicago and New York is most completely covered in Robert Goffin, *Horn of Plenty: The Story of Louis Armstrong* (New York: Allen, Towne & Heath, 1947).

25. Louis Armstrong (as told to David Dachs), "Daddy, How The Country Has Changed!," *Ebony*, May 1961, 81.

26. J.A. Rogers, "Jazz at Home," *Survey Graphics* 6, no. 6 (March 1925), 665.

27. Alain Weill et Jack Rennert, *Paul Colin; Affichiste* (Paris: Denoel, 1989); Phyllis Rose, *Jazz Cleopatra: Josephine Baker in Her Time* (New York: Vintage Books, 1989); Bricktop with James Haskins, *Bricktop*, (New York: Atheneum, 1983).

28. According to Armstrong, the first person to call him Satchmo was Percy Brooks, the editor of *Melody Maker* magazine, but others recall the name was used earlier. For the most thorough analysis of the issue, see Jones and Chilton, op. cit., 45–48.

29. Donna M. Cassidy, "Arthur Dove's Music Paintings of the Jazz Age,"*The American Art Journal* 20, no. 1 (1988), 5–23; Amy Bailey, *Misha Reznikoff; Paintings from the 1930s & 1940s*, (Amherst: Hester Art Gallery, University of Massachusetts, 1992); Hank O'Neal and Dan Morgenstern, *The Art of Pee Wee Russell and George Wettling* (Wilkes-Barre, PA: Sardoni Art Gallery, Tilkes College, 1986).

30. Statement by Stuart Davis, August 1950 in *The Fine Art of Jazz: A Stuart Davis Centennial Celebration*, ed. Earl Davis, (New York: privately printed, 1991), 13.

31. Louis Armstrong (with music section edited by Horace Gerlach)*Swing That Music*, (London: Longmans, 1936; reissued New York: Da Capo Press, 1993); Louis Armstrong, *Satchmo: My Life in New Orleans* (New York: Prentice-Hall, 1954).

32. Louis Armstrong, "Why I Like Dark Women," *Ebony*, August 1954, 61.

33. Among the many jazz performers who at one time or another lived in the New York City borough of Queens are Cannonball Adderly, Count Basie, Tony Bennett, Buck Clayton, John Coltrane, Ella Fitzgerald, Milt Hinton, Billie Holiday, Lena Horne, Milt Jackson, Mezz Mezzrow, Buddy Rich, Jimmy Rushing, Clark Terry, Rudy Vallee, Fats Waller, and Cootie Williams.

34. Richard Meryman, "Louis Armstrong Interviewed by Richard Meryman," *Life*, 15 April 1966, 93.

35. Barbara Haskell, *Ralston Crawford* (New York: Whitney Museum of American Art, 1985); J. Lee Anderson, "The Painter as Photographer," *The Mississippi Rag*, August 1990; Lee Friedlander, *The Jazz People of New Orleans* (New York: Pantheon Books, 1992).

36. Armstrong, "Daddy, How the Country Has Changed!," op. cit., 85

37. Felix Belair, *New York Times*, 6 November 1955, 1.

38. George Padmore, "A Holiday Honored Satchmo Armstrong," *The Crisis* (England), June-July 1956; Gilbert Millstein, "Africa Harks to Satch's Horn," *New York Times Magazine*, 20 November 1960.

39. Letter from Coretta Scott King to Lucille Armstrong, 8 July 1971, Louis Armstrong Archives, Queens College, City University of New York.

2 Louis Armstrong and African-American Culture

Richard A. Long

Born in 1901 in New Orleans, Louis Armstrong was to come to consciousness in a divided milieu characterized by a larger white American world and a circumscribed African-American one. The ethos of the Progressive movement—optimism, good feeling, and prosperity—characterized the new century for most white Americans. The African-American world faced a more somber reality: the continued institutionalization of prejudice and oppression. The history and culture of the African-American community was to continue existing in uneasy symbiosis with the larger American reality. Through a delineation of this distinct African-American history and culture, I propose to illuminate the astonishing career of Louis Armstrong.

A succession of overlapping cultural epochs characterize African-American history and culture.[1] The first of these, the folk-rural, had its origins in plantation society and survived well into the twentieth century. At the end of the Civil War, a parallel culture identified with city dwellers, the folk-urban, begins to evolve in the great cities of the north, to which large numbers of blacks from the rural South are beginning to emigrate. The trans-urban phase of African-American culture, which covers the period between the two world wars, derives from the intensified migration to cities, north and south, after World War I and the creation of such massive ghettos as Harlem and Bronzeville. The trans-African epoch was stimulated by advances in communication, which created a global electronic village, through which African-American culture consciously responds to Africa and to the African diaspora.

The rising young star of Chicago's Black Belt was photographed c. 1928 by Woodard Studios, whose pictures of local celebrities were often used in the black newspapers and magazines of Chicago. Historic New Orleans Collection, William Russell Collection.

Born into the folk-urban culture of New Orleans, where a distinct *citadin*[2] group, the Creoles of color, played an important role, Louis Armstrong achieved artistic triumph and fame in the 1920s in the trans-urban world of Chicago and New York and was a dominant presence in the cultural life of America throughout the 1930s. Armstrong's central role was partially eclipsed by new musical figures and styles in the 1940s and 1950s, but with the development of television and jet travel in the late 1950s Armstrong's appearances and reception in Africa in 1957 and 1960 assured him pioneer status in the trans-African epoch.

At the time of Armstrong's birth, the overwhelming majority of African-Americans in the rural South were participants in folk-rural culture, which has its origins in the plantation society of the Upper and Middle South (Maryland, Virginia, and the Carolinas) during the eighteenth century. In the nineteenth century it spread with the plantation system into the Deep South, along with the expansion of cotton farming. Slave narratives and traveler's accounts provide glimpses of this culture, particularly from the 1830s on.[3] Plantation agriculture was the defining parameter of the highly regulated lives of bondsmen and bondswomen; the changing seasons and farming chores were the primary framework for daily life. During the entire period of the slave trade, approximately 470,000 Africans from west and central Africa were transported to North America.[4] In succeeding generations cultural memory of Africa and the trauma of the

Top: The Perdido neighborhood (middle left) of New Orleans where Armstrong was raised. Photograph by Charles Franck, 1920s. Historic New Orleans Collection.

Bottom: Entitled *From Mulatto to Negro*, George François Mugnier's 1890 photograph shows the diversity of the African-American/Creole community of New Orleans. Louisiana State Museum.

Top: At the time of Armstrong's youth, most African-Americans lived in the rural south. *Comin' From Market Near Baton Rouge* (c. 1885) shows one of the cotton plantations along the Mississippi. The David Warner Foundation, Tuscaloosa, Alabama.

Right: Arkansas cotton pickers photographed by Ben Shahn for the Farm Security Administration, late 1930s. Photographs & Prints Division, Schomburg Center for Research in Black Culture, The New York Public Library, Astor, Lenox and Tilden Foundations.

middle passage (the leg of the triangular trade route that brought slaves from West Africa to the Americas) became increasingly vague but the continuous uprooting caused by the internal slave trade, with its southerly and westerly drift, kept alive a sense of gnawing anguish:

Of his earliest years Armstrong says, in his autobiography *Satchmo*:

> When I was born my mother and father lived with my grandmother, Mrs. Josephine Armstrong (bless her heart!), but they did not stay with her long. They use to quarrel something awful, and finally the blow came. My mother moved away, leaving me with grandma.[5]

Although he grew up in the city of New Orleans, Louis Armstrong had roots in folk-rural culture through his mother, Mary Albert, who came to the city from Boutte, Louisiana, a sugar cane–growing area. That Armstrong was himself acquainted with Boutte from at least one visit is revealed by an anecdote, which he told on several occasions, about being sent to fetch a bucket of water from the pond and being frightened by an alligator.[6] Such links between the folk-rural and folk-urban cultures were common in Armstrong's generation.

Armstrong's journey to Chicago in 1922 paralleled that of many southern blacks following World War I. The spirit of the Great Migration is captured in Langston Hughes' poem and an accompanying drawing by Aaron Douglas from their publication *Weary Blues* (1926). Art & Artifacts Division, Schomburg Center for Research in Black Culture, The New York Public Library, Astor Lenox and Tilden Foundations. Photograph: Manu Sassoonian.

I was all eyes looking out of the window when the train pulled into the station. Anyone watching me closely could have easily seen that I was a country boy.

Louis Armstrong, *Satchmo*, 1954

On De No'thern Road

Bound No'th Blues

Goin' down de road, Lord,
Goin' down de road.
Down de road, Lord,
Way, way down de road.
Got to find somebody
To help me carry this load.
Road's in front o' me,
Nothin' to do but walk.
Road's in front o' me,
Walk . . . . and walk . . . . . and walk
I'd like to meet a good friend
To come along an' talk.
Road, road, road, O!
Road, road . . . . road . . . . road, road!
Road, road, road, O!
On de No'thern road.
These Mississippi towns ain't
Fit for a hoppin' toad.

Langston Hughes

Stokely Webster, *Chicago Rail Yard* (1933). Illinois State Museum, Gift of the Artist.

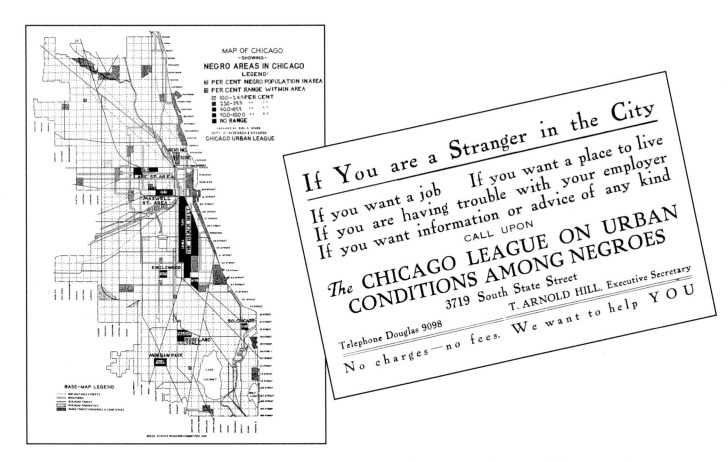

Armstrong settled on Chicago's South Side, a rapidly growing district centered around 35th and State Streets, that is sometimes called "Bronzeville" or the "Black Belt." Chicago Urban League Records, Special Collections, The University Library, The University of Illinois at Chicago.

Right: Armstrong arrived in the city with friends and a job. The Chicago Urban League distributed flyers offering to help new arrivals with bleaker prospects. Arthur Aldis Papers, Special Collections, The University Library, The University of Illinois at Chicago.

Perhaps the most fundamental feature of folk-rural life was the character of its religion: Christianity, tinctured by the African background and group expression. African religion, manifested chiefly in ritual involving music and dance, was tolerated among black populations in many parts of the Americas, but Anglo-Protestants in the United States censured such practices in a religious context. Nevertheless, religious expression in folk-rural culture was marked by emotional intensity. African spirit possession was transmuted to possession by the Holy Spirit; concerted singing was accompanied by movement; and the spiritual was born and nurtured in plantation religion. Although spirituals were primarily religious in function, they were also used as agents of relaxation and reflection in social gatherings. The primary function of work songs was to provide rhythmic accompaniment and enhancement of group tasks. The impact of European music on the folk-rural culture came chiefly through hymnody; however, strong African elements pervaded this music and were to persist and influence the music of the later cultural epochs. That hymnody was not absent from the experience of Armstrong is affirmed by his own recollections of early childhood:

> In those days, of course, I did not know a horn from a comb. I was going to church regularly for both grandma and my great grandmother were Christian women, and between them they kept me in school, church, and Sunday school. In Church and Sunday school I did a whole lot of singing. That I guess is how I acquired my singing tactics.[7]

Music was at the core of Black Belt life. More than 20,000 people attended a 1926 benefit for the black musicians union at Chicago's Coliseum which featured Armstrong and other recording stars. This full page advertisement appeared in the *Chicago Defender*. Newspapers and Current Periodicals Division, Library of Congress, Permission *Chicago Defender*.

Chicago's black publications received national distribution and played a crucial role in publicizing Armstrong and other Chicago celebrities. This short-lived publication was titled *Heebie Jeebies* (November 1925), also the name of one of Armstrong's best known records. Chicago Historical Society.

Winold Reiss's *Dawn in Harlem* was featured in the "Harlem: Mecca of a New Negro" issue of the popular magazine *Survey Graphics* (March 1925). By the 1920s New York had established itself as the capital of African-American culture. The DeWoody Collection.

Following emancipation, the migration toward cities in the north and south brought into being the folk-urban culture. The cityward movement continued until World War II.[8] The preexisting black population of the cities, which we have called *citadin*, had minimal rural ties. Hence a two-tiered urban black population can be traced from this point, and by the late nineteenth century distinct class lines, based on an urban or rural origin, had been established. The folk-urban culture was essentially the folk-rural ethos, including religion, music, and familial patterns, transposed to an urban context, where it underwent confrontation, accommodation, and some assimilation. Blues as a poetic-musical form can best be appreciated as such a transposition. On the other hand, the spiritual—or at least the most jubilant variety of spiritual—metamorphosed from the spirited hymnody of the folk-rural tradition into gospel music, which reached maturity only in the trans-urban era.

At the time of Armstrong's birth, the folk-urban embraced only a minority of black Americans. One and a half million African-Americans lived in the towns and cities of the South and another half million in northern cities; perhaps seven million still lived in the rural South. At the 1900 census, the black population of New Orleans was 77,714; Washington, D.C., Baltimore, Philadelphia, and New York each had comparable populations.

A few years before the birth of Louis Armstrong, a classic study of folk-urban life, W.E.B. Du Bois's *The Philadelphia Negro* (1899), was published. Du Bois depicted the layering of Philadelphia's *citadin* culture with its roots in the eighteenth century, and

Jacob Lawrence, *Harlem Rooftops* (1943). Hirshhorn Museum and Sculpture Garden, Smithsonian Institution, Gift of Joseph H. Hirshhorn, 1966. Photo: Lee Stalsworth.

the maturing folk-urban culture of the more recent arrivals. While Du Bois's study still depicts realistically African-American city life around 1900 and is quite useful as a key to such other cities as Baltimore and Washington, D.C., its paradigms are less applicable to Armstrong's New Orleans, where the *citadin*/folk-urban juncture was complicated by the historical roots of the Crescent City.

At the time of its incorporation into the United States following the Louisiana Purchase of 1803, New Orleans was a French-speaking city, although it had been a Spanish territory for several decades before Napoleon's brief repossession. A large immigration from Haiti (St. Domingue), following the Haitian Revolution of 1792, had enormous cultural and social impact on New Orleans. The Haitian immigrants were white and mulatto (*gens de couleur*) planters, professionals, and artisans, along with their mulatto and black slaves. They fled a plantation society that had a tripartite caste system—consisting of whites, free people of color, and slaves—and had recognized kinship linkages among the higher echelons of the first two groups. This structure was transferred to New Orleans and, although it was in continual conflict with Anglo-American two-caste system, remained strong there until the end of the nineteenth century. The folk-urban cultural community that developed in New Orleans following the Civil War tended to conform to this tripartite pattern.

In the New Orleans of Armstrong's time, the Creoles of color lived "downtown," holding onto their distinct *citadin* culture and to the French language (which was destined to be lost), while mainly

Text inside the map illustration includes labels such as: CONNIES INN · LAFAYETTE THEATRE · CLUB HOT-CHA · Harlem Moon · SMALL'S PARADISE · YEAH MAN · LOG CABIN · TILLIES · THEATRICAL GRILL · GLADYS' CLAM HOUSE · SEVENTH avenue or heaven · SAVOY BALLROOM · COTTON CLUB CAB CALLOWAYS BAND · RADIUM CLUB · LENOX avenue · A NIGHT-CLUB MAP OF HARLEM

By 1929 Armstrong was a featured attraction in Harlem's thriving nightclub scene. This *Night-Club Map of Harlem* (1932) was made by E. Simms Campbell whose illustration feature "Harlem Sketches" was syndicated to African-American papers around the country. Courtesy Elizabeth Campbell Rollins.

English-speaking blacks with their folk-rural ties and emerging folk-urban institutions lived "uptown." This social divide and its musical implications shaped New Orleans, the crucible of jazz, as Berendt recounts in *The Jazz Book:*

> The Creole Negroes had made French culture their own. Many were wealthy businessmen. Their main language was not English but "Creole," a French patois with admixtures of Spanish and African words.... It was an honor to be a Creole. Jelly Roll Morton took great pains to make clear that he was a Creole and that his real name was Ferdinand Joseph La Menthe.
>
> ...The "American Negroes" constituted the black proletariat of New Orleans. The Creoles looked down on them...
>
> Consequently, there were two very different groups of New Orleans musicians, and the difference found expression in the music. The Creole group was more cultured; the American had more vitality. The main instrument of the French group was the clarinet, which has a great tradition in France. This old French woodwind tradition remained alive well into the thirties in the playing of the leading Swing clarinetists....[9]

It is perhaps paradoxical that the defining tradition of early jazz, a music whose roots are firmly set in the folk-urban, arose from the collaboration of the often antagonistic Creoles and African-Americans of New Orleans. The raw materials of jazz—including band traditions, sophisticated syncopation, and a blues aesthetic—

Through new media like the phonograph, Armstrong and other African-American musicians secured their place as leaders of the black community. Photograph by Russell Lee for the Farm Security Administration, 1939. Photographs & Prints Division, Schomburg Center for Research in Black Culture, The New York Public Library, Astor, Lenox and Tilden Foundations.

existed in such other places as Memphis, St. Louis, and New York City.[10] But New Orleans provided more public occasions for experimentation, rivalry, and public appreciation in its range of events that required the music of marching and seated bands.

Armstrong lived "uptown," but his exceptional talents gained him acceptance with all the city's musicians. *Satchmo*, Armstrong's richly detailed autobiography of his early years, offers a lively picture of folk-urban New Orleans but seldom alludes to the rivalries and tensions between Creoles and Blacks, an omission probably explained by Armstrong's genial personality and his total absorption in music. Armstrong focuses on the musical milieu in which he grew up and evokes it with exuberance:

> There were many different kinds of people and instruments to inspire me to carry on with my music when I was a boy. I always loved music, and it did not matter what the instrument was or who played it so long as the playing was good. I used to hear some of the finest music in the world listening to the barroom quartets who hung around the saloons with a cold can of beer in their hands, singing up a breeze while they passed the can around. I thought I was really somebody when I got so I could hang around with those fellows—sing and drink out of the can with them. When I was a teen-ager those old-timers let me sing with them and carry the lead, bless their hearts. Even in those days they thought I had something on the ball as a ragtime singer, which is what hot swing singing is today.[11]

Left: Athletes were also cultural heros of the black community. Jack Johnson, the heavyweight boxing champion from 1903 to 1915, was an acquaintance of Armstrong. Photofest.

Right: Armstrong and members of his band greet the heavyweight boxing champion Joe Louis, c. 1948–1949. Courtesy Institute of Jazz Studies, Rutgers University.

Racial segregation became institutionalized by the end of nineteenth century, and a Louisiana law mandating segregation in railway carriages became the test case on its constitutionality. In its opinion the United States Supreme Court in *Plessy vs. Ferguson* (1896) found it "reasonable" that the state force Homer Plessy, a man of color, to sit in a carriage designated for non-whites, thus rendering a profound blow to New Orleans' tripartite social system.[12]

The basic sociopolitical theme of the folk-urban epoch was the controversy between Booker T. Washington (1858–1915), a former slave who founded Tuskegee Institute, a vocational school (1881), and W.E.B. Du Bois (1868–1963), a prolific writer active in the 1909 founding of the National Association for the Advancement of Colored People (NAACP) and other groups calling for equal rights for blacks. Washington's public acquiescence to segregation and disenfranchisement and his promotion of vocational education for blacks, expressed in a speech in Atlanta in 1895, in his autobiography *Up From Slavery* (1901), and in other actions and writings met eloquent opposition from Du Bois in the essay, "Of Mr. Booker T. Washington and Others" (*The Souls of Black Folks,* 1903), and in his work as editor of the NAACP's magazine *The Crisis* (founded 1910). Like the majority of his contemporaries, rural and urban, the young Armstrong was naturally far from being caught up by the terms of the controversy. Du Bois's call for voting rights, the right to a liberal arts education, and economic opportunity—equality, in short— would probably have seemed a fantastic expectation to Armstrong. In the pages of *Satchmo*, instances of white oppression, arbitrary

Left: William E. B. Du Bois, a founder of the NAACP and other groups calling for equal rights for blacks, painted by Winold Reiss, c. 1925. National Portrait Gallery, Smithsonian Institution.

Right: African-American political leaders of Armstrong's generation included Booker T. Washington, a former slave who founded the vocational school Tuskegee Institute. This 1915 photograph is by Arthur Bedou who also took the earliest surviving pictures of Armstrong. Tuskegee University Archives. Photo: Hawkins Studio.

imprisonment, and outright cruelty are recorded in a matter-of-fact manner with virtually no expression of indignation.

The Great Migration that followed World War I initiated a new cultural epoch, the trans-urban, for which Chicago serves as an exemplar. The continued decline of agriculture in the South convinced the populations mobilized to serve in the war to believe the persistent propaganda of a northern haven from southern oppression, which was promulgated by the black newspaper, *The Chicago Defender.* The black population of many northern cities increased dramatically: Chicago's grew from 44,000 in 1910 to 109,000 in 1920. Comparable growth occurred in such cities as Detroit and Gary, Indiana. In spite of this and the dramatic growth in such older cities as New York, Philadelphia, Baltimore, and Washington, 80 percent of the black population was still found in the South in 1920. Folk-rural, folk-urban, and the newly emerging trans-urban cultures all coexisted.

Louis Armstrong's personal odyssey reflects this cultural phenomenon. In 1922, at the age of 21, he left New Orleans for Chicago, joining more than one hundred thousand blacks, who were creating in that city a hustling, bustling trans-urban culture. In *Satchmo,* Armstrong recounts the journey by train, which parallels the experience of so many of the migrants who had preceded him and that of thousands who were to follow.

> When I got on the train I found an empty seat next to a lady and her three children, and she was really sticking. What I mean by

"sticking" is that she had a big basket of good old southern fried chicken which she had fixed for the trip. She had enough to last her and her kids not only to Chicago, but clear out to California if she wanted to go that far.[13]

Already a virtuoso trumpeter, he joined King Oliver's band, which was then composed of the musicians John and Baby Dodds, Honoré Dutray, Bill Johnson, Lil Hardin, and band leader Oliver, who summoned him to Chicago. Lil Hardin, the pianist, was to become Armstrong's second wife and new mentor. King Oliver's band was already attracting musicians, black and white, as listeners. Armstrong ends his autobiography with a description of his first night on the bandstand in Chicago: "I had hit the big time, I was up North with the greats. I was playing with my ideal, the King, Joe Oliver. My boyhood dream had come true at last."[14]

The trans-urban, which is characterized by the close interconnection and virtual simultaneity of experience in all the major urban centers, is the product of numerous factors, most resulting from technological developments. The shared reality of trans-urban culture was stimulated by the rapid growth and networking of the Negro press, illustrated by the establishment of the Associated Negro Press (headquartered in Chicago), and the flourishing of other such national organizations—fraternal orders, professional associations, and religious groups—and the easy access to their annual meetings available to members throughout the United States by rail and automobile.

The commercial phonograph, introduced in the 1920s, was increasingly affordable and so both stimulated and unified popular culture, an indicator of the trans-urban. Armstrong's recording career began in 1923 with King Oliver's band. In less than a decade he had already achieved status as one of the preeminent recording artists of the day; the only African-American recording artist of comparable status was Bessie Smith.[15]

Armstrong's records were the basis of his fame to most whites and to people living abroad. But to the African-American public, recordings were adjunct to his live performances or, at least, to reports of his concerts and of his real, or assumed, life-style, which the Negro press, one of the anchors of trans-urban culture, chronicled in detail. Armstrong's peripatetic life was avidly reported: from 1929 to mid-1932, when he made his first trip to England, he appeared across the United States in New York, Chicago, Detroit, Philadelphia, and California.[16] He was also featured in the Broadway show *Hot Chocolates*, which opened the 1929–30 Broadway season. His association with the Fats Waller-Andy Razaf song "Ain't Misbehavin' " began with this show.[17]

By the 1920s the language of jazz had penetrated to the core of culture, not only in the United States but also in Europe, and so the entire decade was identified by it, the Jazz Age. For African-American culture, the term "Harlem Renaissance" has come into

Although Armstrong generally avoided political issues, in 1957 he spoke his mind when Governor Orville Faubus ordered state troopers to stop the "The Little Rock Nine" from integrating an Arkansas high school. Because he was not known for political discourse, Armstrong's remarks had maximum impact. Photographs & Prints Division, Schomburg Center for Research in Black Culture, The New York Public Library, Astor, Lenox and Tilden Foundations.

THE LITTLE ROCK NINE

use to embrace the artistic, ideological, political, and social currents of the period.[18] The popularity of the term is unfortunate in that it obscures the participation of the other metropolitan centers, especially Chicago, in this first decade of the trans-urban phase. Alain Locke's *The New Negro,* published in 1925, became the example of the period. In the title essay Locke captures the buoyancy of the period:

> The tide of Negro migration, northward and cityward, is not to be fully explained as a blind flood started by the demands of war industry coupled with the shutting off of foreign migration, or by the pressure of poor crops coupled with increased social terrorism in certain sections of the South and Southwest. Neither labor demand, the boll weevil, nor the Ku Klux Klan is a basic factor, however contributory any or all of them may have been. The wash and rush of this human tide on the beach line of the northern city centers is to be explained primarily in terms of a new vision of opportunity, of social and economic freedom, of a spirit to seize, even in the face of an extortionate and heavy toll, a chance for the improvement of conditions. With each successive wave of it, the movement toward the larger and the more democratic chance—in the Negro's case a deliberate flight not only from countryside to city, but from medieval America to modern.[19]

Armstrong succumbed to the lure of New York in 1924. His New York sojourn was an *annus mirabilis* for Armstrong: he joined Fletcher Henderson's Orchestra and recorded with it, as well as

Norman Rockwell's illustration, *The Problem We All Live With*, showing the integration of New Orleans schools, was featured on the cover of *Look* magazine (1963). The image captured the cruel injustice that inspired Armstrong to speak out earlier against resistance to integration in Little Rock. Printed by permission of the Norman Rockwell Family Trust. Copyright © 1964 the Norman Rockwell Family Trust.

with Clarence Williams' Blue Five (which included Sidney Bechet), Ma Rainey, Clara Smith, and Bessie Smith. Nevertheless, Chicago to which he returned at the end of his New York year, offered the production and technical talent for his Hot Five and Hot Seven recordings and allowed him to collaborate with Earl Hines who also made Chicago his home. A jazz man par excellence, Armstrong was the embodiment of a distinct cultural moment, however labeled. His association with Chicago helped establish that city's eminence as a trans-urban center.[20]

Armstrong's achievements by the end of the 1920s elevated him to the status of a culture hero, especially among African-Americans. The traits, ideas, and personalities that embody images of a group are captured in a culture hero who enjoys, in consequence, the esteem and even veneration of his peers. Louis Armstrong was the first really monumental culture hero, of the trans-urban era. By 1931, when he first appeared in a film, Armstrong was one of the most famous African-Americans; his recordings and performances enjoyed international acclaim and he was acknowledged as a sartorial model whose fashion style set the trend among young blacks. (At one point, a hairstyle known as the "Louie Armstrong," though hardly approved by the polite, was sported by boys and young men.) Armstrong was instrumental in popularizing and sometimes creating words and expressions that were picked up by his musical colleagues and extended to a large public. Terms credited to Armstrong include *jive, scat, mellow,* and such terms of address as *pops, cat,* and *daddy.*[21] Two other jazz

The other woman in Jack's life is his mother, Mallie Robinson. Here she's visiting Jack and Rachael at St. Albans.

Armstrong's views on current events can sometimes be gleaned from collages he made in the 1950s and 1960s out of newspaper and magazine clippings. This collage of news photos of the baseball player Jackie Robinson pays tribute to another pioneer of American integration. Louis Armstrong Archives, Queens College, City University of New York.

musicians approached Armstrong's stature as a culture hero in the early 1930s: Duke Ellington (1899–1974) was widely known and admired as a band leader and composer, and Cab Calloway (b. 1907) was known as a band leader and a vocalist, in the latter capacity owing some debt to Armstrong.

As a culture hero, Armstrong was not antipathetic to white America, unlike boxer Jack Johnson (1876–1946), the heavyweight champion from 1903 to 1915, whose frequent defeat of white boxers provided a salutary release for oppressed blacks. In the wide, cross-racial acclaim that he elicited, Armstrong anticipated the cultural status of two athletes who emerged later in the thirties, Joe Louis (1914–1981) and Jesse Owens (1913–1980). For African-Americans, these two symbolized black prowess against Nordics; for white America, each symbolized American triumph over Nazi truculence.

Culture heroes who expressed firm political views in the 1930s and 1940s suffered negative consequences. Actor-singer Paul Robeson's (1898–1976) status, which had been elevated during the 1930s among both white and black Americans, was diminished by his engagement in political discourse following World War II. Many blacks who agreed with his condemnation of America's racial status quo were dubious about some of his pro-Soviet positions.

The magnitude of Armstrong's presence in the African-American consciousness and, more precisely, in the culture of the 1930s reposes primarily on the fact that jazz was, in one form or another, emphatically the music of trans-urban culture. Jazz was relayed to its audience through recordings, personal appearances at

dances and in vaudeville houses, late-night radio broadcasts, and film shorts—many seen only by black audiences. This black musical culture was paralleled by the jazz-influenced popular music of white America. Armstrong, the most dynamic public personality of the jazz era, was also its paramount instrumentalist and vocalist.

At the beginning of the 1940s one-third of the African-American population lived in the rural South, another third in the urban South—participants largely in a folk-urban culture—and the final third in northern cities, which were entering a second phase of the trans-urban. These demographic realities, frequently overlooked when generalizations are made about African-American culture, were disrupted by World War II, which set in motion a variety of significant population and social changes. Black migration from the South again intensified, but now the destination was often the far West. Black participation during the war in the armed forces and defense industry was much greater than in World War I. Although one-third of African-Americans still lived in the rural South at the outbreak of World War II, by five years after the war only 10 percent resided in the rural South, effectively ending folk-rural culture; folk-urban culture now completely melded into the trans-urban, while *citadin* culture also became a relic.

At war's end, the struggle for parity in American society invigorated demands for the ending of segregation and discrimination, which led to challenges in the courts, the legislatures, and the streets. In 1954 the unanimous decision by the U.S. Supreme Court in a landmark school segregation case, *Brown vs. Board of Education*

When I first saw her, the glow of her deep brown skin got me deep down...Lucille was the first girl to crack the high-yellow color standard used to pick girls for the famous Cotton Club chorus line. I think she was a distinguished pioneer.

Louis Armstrong, *Ebony*, August 1954

In 1942 Armstrong's married Lucille Wilson, a dancer he had met three years earlier at the Cotton Club. It was Armstrong's fourth marriage, but one that lasted: he spent the rest of his life with Lucille. Louis Armstrong Archives, Queens College, City University of New York.

(of Topeka, Kansas), that separate educational facilities were "inherently unequal" effectively reversed the court's 1896 decision in *Plessy vs. Ferguson*. In reaction to the court's decision, further litigation and group action was planned. Subsequent stages of what was now discerned as a Civil Rights movement included the Montgomery bus boycott of 1955, which led to the emergence of the Reverend Martin Luther King, Jr. (1929–1968), as a leader, and the Little Rock school crisis of 1957, which brought forth Armstrong's first public utterance on race relations and civil rights.

Armstrong was on the verge of making a U.S. government–sponsored tour to Russia in September 1957 when he learned from news reports that black high school students had been prevented from attending Central High School in Little Rock, Arkansas. Angrily announcing that he was canceling the planned tour, Armstrong denounced the U.S. government in the process and became the object of considerable hostility from whites as a result.[22]

Armstrong's personal star had been dimming among African-Americans, even though he was working as much as ever. The jazz music that he had come to personify was no longer mainstream, in black or white America. World War II marked a distinct shift in music taste. In the 1930s, jazz, which descended from the New Orleans tradition, was the mainstream music of African-Americans, who nevertheless cherished other music as well: the traditional spiritual, blues, then-emerging gospel, as well as sentimental parlor music, and standard hymnody. The status of jazz remained high throughout the war period, but the traditional venues for public

Louis and Lucille backstage at the Howard Theatre, Washington, D.C., 1942–1943. Louis Armstrong Archives, Queens College, City University of New York.

performances of jazz, the dance hall and vaudeville house, were already threatened.

Bebop, that great divide between serious and popular jazz, began in the early 1940s. New rhythmic, melodic, and harmonic ideas were developed in small club settings. Following the war, purely instrumental listener's jazz, variously called modern, progressive, or bop gained popularity, though the popularity was limited to audiences in New York and other large cities. In the popular taste jazz orchestras were superseded by singers. Some of the most popular singers were versed in traditional jazz but performed, often, in styles different from the established idiom of jazz. These and other musical figures, who became known to and were admired by the post-1940s generation, constituted a new mainstream music for African-Americans, one best known as soul.[23]

Armstrong, in common with many of his generation, professed little comprehension of and liking for the new listener's music, which nevertheless derives from his achievement and that of his great contemporaries. On the other hand, the soul generation found him and these same contemporaries quaint relics. Blues and jazz, including modern jazz, were effectively marginalized in African-American culture by the 1960s; at the same time, they were finding a wider, if limited, audience in white America and internationally.

Armstrong, as the outstanding exemplar of the jazz tradition, found himself increasingly lionized worldwide, but his stature diminished among African-Americans. Some African-Americans descried in Armstrong's film roles, and even his stage demeanor, elements of buffoonery offensive to racial dignity. The field of public entertainment with its Buckwheats, Stepin Fetchits, and Amoses and Andys, offered an abundance of deplorable characterizations. By the late 1940s, Louis Armstrong had been increasingly amalgamated with these emblems of embarrassment by a public either unaware of or uninterested in his musical eminence.

Armstrong's expression of indignation in 1957 at the Little Rock school crisis was welcomed and viewed as a gesture of rehabilitation by many, although it was not calculated on Armstrong's part. His African tours also provided a base for a new relationship with the African-American public. African consciousness reentered the African-American scene with decolonization in Africa and gave rise to a new epoch of African-American culture, the trans-African,

EBONY

A JOHNSON PUBLICATION

KING COLE'S
SECOND HONEYMOON

WHAT WAC'S
DO FOR LOVE

WHY I LIKE
DARK WOMEN
By Louis Armstrong

AUGUST 1954 30c
CIRCULATION OVER 500,000

characterized by concern and deep sentiment for Africa and the African diaspora.[24]

Armstrong made a well-publicized trip to pre-independence Ghana, then known as the Gold Coast, in 1956. He returned to Ghana in 1960 on an extensive African tour, which included concerts in Nigeria, central Africa, and Kenya. New technology brought this tour and Armstrong's enthusiastic reception by Africans to the attention of a worldwide community. Many of the Africans who enthusiastically greeted Armstrong were probably not aware of his historical role, but they responded positively to his performance and his personality. He was for them a successfully, talented, and gregarious son returning from a distant land.

Soon after their marriage, the Armstrongs bought a house in Corona, Queens, a quiet suburb of New York City away from Manhattan. Lucille's family lived in Corona, and Queens was the home of other jazz musicians like Clarence Williams and Dizzy Gillespie. Louis Armstrong Archives, Queens College, City University of New York.

Louis and Lucille on the cover of *Ebony* (August 1954), the most widely read magazine on black life. In an article entitled "Why I Like Dark Women," Armstrong expressed his racial pride and challenged the prejudice that equated beauty with light skin. Courtesy Institute of Jazz Studies, Rutgers University. Reprinted by permission of *Ebony* Magazine, ©1954 Johnson Publishing Company, Inc.

His African journeys put Armstrong in the advance guard of thousands of African-American who were to make a homeward journey, and he thereby became a tutelary presence in the trans-African epoch of African-American culture. As confirmation of his status in the African world, he was named a laureate at the First World Festival of Negro Arts, held in Senegal in April 1966. The poet-president of Senegal, Leopold Sedar Senghor, had, during his student years in Paris in the 1930s, come to regard jazz as a major cultural expression of the African spirit and was an enthusiastic admirer of Armstrong and Duke Ellington.[25] Armstrong was not present at the Festival, but Ellington and his orchestra performed there.

Armstrong's death in 1971 was the occasion for a global expression of grief and adulation. His life began at the outer limits of a socially marginalized group, the African-American, in a section of the country where they were perennially at risk. From his earliest years he was sustained and empowered by the richness of his culture. His genius, a gift of the gods, was nurtured and nourished in a quintessential African-American cultural milieu and his creativity found its first expression there. He, more than any other individual, was fated to symbolize during his seventy years of life the African-American contribution to the world's musical discourse, a contribution that, more than any other, characterizes the music of the twentieth century.

Ambassador Satch

After World War II, Armstrong acquired a new identity: Ambassador Satch, spreading goodwill for America and promoting jazz around the globe.

America's secret weapon is a blue note in a minor key. Right now, its most effective ambassador is Louis (Satchmo) Armstrong. . . . American jazz has now become a universal language.

Felix Belair, *New York Times*, November 6, 1955

Top: Armstrong and disk jockey Willis Cannover whose popular Voice of America program, "This is Music, USA," featured jazz and brought Armstrong to audiences behind the Iron Curtain, June 28, 1955. Courtesy Institute of Jazz Studies, Rutgers University.

Left: "The Ambassador of Jazz" is shown with a tuxedo and suitcase on a stock concert program used during his national and world tours in the 1950s and 1960s. Louis Armstrong Archives, Queens College, City University of New York.

Right: A souvenir photograph from the Walker Hill Photo Shop shows Armstrong in traditional Korean Dress, 1953. Walker Hill was a resort popular with American military officers stationed in South Korea. Louis Armstrong Archives, Queens College, City University of New York.

"This is a Diplomatic Mission of Outmost Delicacy. The Question is, who's the best man for it—John Foster Dulles or Satchmo?" A cartoon by Misha Richter, *The New Yorker* (1958). Prints and Photographs Division, Library of Congress. Drawing by Richter; ©1958, 1986 The New Yorker Magazine, Inc.

SATCHMO THE GREAT

STARRING LOUIS ARMSTRONG and EDWARD R. MURROW with Leonard Bernstein · W. C. Handy

Produced by EDWARD R. MURROW and FRED W. FRIENDLY · Released thru United Artists

His lyrical praise of the simple things of life was typical of his genius, as it was reminiscent of his unswerving attachment to his African ancestry... He will forever be remembered for his peerless contribution to contemporary music, and for his refinement of the very essence of traditional African rhythm.

Major-General Yakubu Gowon, Nigerian head of state, 1971

The documentary film *Satchmo the Great* by Edward R. Murrow and Fred Friendly captured Armstrong's visit to the Gold Coast in 1956 when the country was celebrating its emergence from colonial rule and rebirth as the free nation of Ghana. Armstrong and his music, symbols of the worldwide vitality of African culture, were enormously popular there. Courtesy John Kisch Separate Cinema Collection.

ARMSTRONG AKWABA !

At the Gold Coast city of Accra, Armstrong was met by throngs of people carrying signs reading *Akwaba!* ("Welcome!"). Louis Armstrong Archives, Queens College, City University of New York.

Armstrong is carried on the shoulders of an enthusiastic crowd at Leopoldville, Congo (now Kinshasa, Zaire). In 1960 the U.S. State Department sponsored Armstrong's visit to the Congo, then engulfed in a civil war. Louis Armstrong Archives, Queens College, City University of New York.

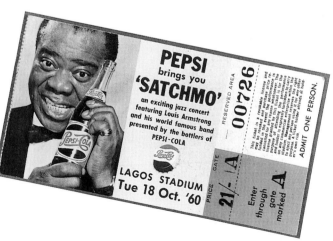

The U.S. State Department was not alone in recognizing Armstrong's importance in Africa; American businesses sought his sponsorship. In an innovative advertising ploy (which is now common), Pepsi-Cola sponsored the first leg of Armstrong's 1960 tour of West Africa to promote new bottling plants in Nigeria and Ghana.

Top: In 1961 Armstrong visited Egypt, which was then ruled by Gamal Abdel Nasser and part of the United Arab Republic. A photograph of Louis and Lucille by the Sphinx is captioned "Love from the First Sight." Louis Armstrong Archives, Queens College, City University of New York.

Left: A ticket to Armstrong's 1960 concert at Lagos Stadium is emblazoned with an advertising slogan: "Pepsi brings you Satchmo." Chicago Historical Society.

Right: Armstrong performs in an African costume during the tour of West Africa sponsored by Pepsi-Cola. Louis Armstrong Archives, Queens College, City University of New York.

Top: Ambassador Satch visits a hospital orphanage for homeless children outside Cairo, January 28, 1961. Louis Armstrong Archives, Queens College, City University of New York.

Bottom: This carved-wood relief of African musicians hung in Armstrong's home. The work of a Nigerian artist, it was probably given to him on one of his African tours. Louis Armstrong Archives, Queens College, City University of New York.

NOTES

1. For a fuller explication of these cultural epochs, see Richard A. Long, *The African Americans* (New York: Crescent Books, 1993, reprint of 1985 edition).

2. *Citadin*, a term borrowed from the French noun relating to urban populations and their culture, is sometimes used to describe the growing urban-based segment of the black population. The existence from the mid-eighteenth century of an urban black population created an articulate voice for African-American culture in the United States and shaped most of the institutions of pre-twentieth-century black America.

3. Of particular interest are the oral testimonies collected from surviving slaves in the 1930s by the Federal Writers' Project. See George P. Rawick, *The American Slave: A Composite Autobiography* (Westport, Conn.: Greenwood, 1972). The oral narratives supplement but do not replace valuable testimony in the succession of "emancipatory narratives" beginning with the much reprinted *Narrative of the Life of Frederick Douglass* (1846).

4. In *The Atlantic Slave Trade: A Census* (Madison: University of Wisconsin Press, 1969), Philip Curtin proposed this estimate. For other aspects of the folk-rural, see the following scholarly accounts: Eugene D. Genovese, *Roll Jordan, Roll: The World the Slaves Made* (New York: Pantheon Books, 1974); Herman Gutman, *The Black Family in Slavery and Freedom, 1750-1925* (New York: Pantheon Books, 1976); John W. Blassingame, *The Slave Community: Plantation Life in the Antebellum South* (New York: Oxford University Press, 1972); Dena J. Epstein, *Sinful Tunes and Spirituals: Black Folk Music to the Civil War* (Urbana: University of Illinois Press, 1977); Albert J. Taboteau, *Slave Religion: The Invisible Institution in the Antebellum South* (New York: Oxford University Press, 1978).

5. *Satchmo: My Life in New Orleans* (New York; Da Capo, 1959, reprint of 1956 edition), 8.

6. This story appears in Gary Giddins, *Satchmo* (New York: Doubleday, 1988), 55. Armstrong, however, in his own *Satchmo* makes no reference to a childhood experience of the folk-rural.

7. Armstrong, *Satchmo* (1959), 11.

8. See Daniel M. Johnson and Rex R. Campbell, *Black Migration in America: A Social Demographic History* (Durham, N.C.: Duke University Press, 1981) for a good overview.

9. Joachim E. Berendt, *The Jazz Book*, trans. by H. and B. Bredigkent with Dan Morgenstern (Westport, Conn.: Lawrence Hill, 1982), 9. An insider's view of the Creole-Black encounter and its significance in jazz history is provided by the story of Jelly Roll Morton edited by Alan Lomax, *Mr. Jelly Roll* (New York: Grove, 1956, reprint of 1950 edition).

10. James Weldon Johnson's novel *The Autobiography of an Ex-Coloured Man* (1913) provides considerable insight into African-American musical culture, both in its folk-rural and folk-urban aspects. In *Phylon* 32 (1971), a special issue devoted to Johnson, his value as musical observer is revealed in an important article by Wendell P. Whalum, "James Weldon Johnson's Theories and Performance Practices of Afro-American Folksong," 383–395.

11. Armstrong, *Satchmo* (1959), 111.

12. Frequently overlooked in discussions of this case is the fact that the railroad was also opposed to the legislation and supported Plessy's appeal.

13. Armstrong, *Satchmo* (1959), 229.

14. Gary Giddins, *Satchmo*, 240.

15. For Armstrong's record, film, radio and television output, see Hans Westerberg, *Boy from New Orleans* (Copenhagen: Jazzmedia, 1981).

16. Max Jones and John Chilton, *Louis, The Louis Armstrong Story* (New York: Da Capo, 1988, reprint of 1971 edition) provides a summary itinerary of Armstrong, "Travellin' Man," 287–297. See also the chapter entitled "Louis in Britain," 157–188.

17. Armstrong subsequently appeared on stage in *Swingin' the Dream* (1939). Armstrong was associated in the public mind with two other Broadway

shows, *The Threepenny Opera* and *Hello Dolly*, because of his hit recordings of "Mack the Knife" from the former and the title song from the latter.

18. Two collections dealing with the Harlem Renaissance in its larger dimensions are *The Harlem Renaissance Reexamined*, edited by Victor A. Kramer (New York: Arno Press, 1987) and *Black Music in the Harlem Renaissance*, edited by Samuel A. Floyd, Jr. (New York: Greenwood Press, 1990).

19. Alain Locke, *The New Negro* (N.ew York.: Atheneum, 1968, reprint of 1925 edition), 6. The term "New Negro" was frequently employed by Marcus Garvey, leader of a movement stressing black pride and African redemption. The term "Negro Renaissance," which may be attributed to Alain Locke, is modeled on the then-current terms "Irish" or "Celtic Renaissance" used to describe the cultural movement associated with William Butler Yeats and Lady Gregory.

20. The fullest account of a trans-urban community, comparable in importance to Du Bois's *The Philadelphia Negro*, is the study of Chicago by Horace Cayton and St. Clair Drake, *Black Metropolis* (New York: Harper and Row, 1962, rev. ed., original edition, 1945), 2 vols. The authors state in their conclusion, 755:

> The story of the growth of Black Metropolis between the Civil War and the Depression is, with minor variations, the story of the Negro in New York, Detroit, Philadelphia, Pittsburgh, and a number of other cities in America's northeastern and east-central industrial areas. During the Second World War it became the story, too, of San Francisco and Los Angeles as Negroes streamed to the West Coast to help man the arsenal of democracy. Negroes in America are becoming a city people, and it is in the cities that the problem of the Negro in American life appears in its sharpest and most dramatic forms. It may be, too, that the cities will be the arena in which the "Negro problem" will be finally settled.

It is a matter of interest, however, that this comprehensive study devotes no attention to the role of secular music in the life of the people of Bronzeville, despite the anthropological orientation of author Drake.

21. Giddins, *Satchmo*, 74. All these terms appear in the *Dictionary of American Slang*, edited by Harold Wentworth and Stuart Berg Flexner (New York: Crowell, 1960), where Armstrong is often quoted or referenced in the entry. The Dictionary's bibliography includes Armstrong's *Satchmo* and Dan Burley's *Original Handbook of Harlem Jive* (New York: privately published, 1944), but it omits Cab Calloway, *The New Cab Calloway's Hepsters Dictionary: Language of Jive* (New York: C. Calloway Inc., 1944).

22. See Giddins, *Satchmo*, 160–165.

23. Phyl Garland, *The Sound of Soul* (Chicago: Regency, 1969) shows soul's filiations from jazz and blues, and its affiliations with gospel and rock. Garland, as editor of *Ebony*, produced for its pages a number of insightful articles on black American music both before and after 1969.

24. This African consciousness was not new, or even a rebirth, so much as a reinvigoration, because African consciousness was a strain in *citadin* culture in the nineteenth century. Both Booker T. Washington and Du Bois showed considerable concern for Africa, Du Bois being active in the early Pan-African movement. Following World War I, Du Bois organized a series of Pan-African conferences, and Jamaica-born Marcus Garvey led a popular movement, one of whose tenets was African redemption.

25. Senghor, Aimé Cesaire, and Léon Damas are considered the initiators of the vindicationist movement known as negritude. They were inspired by the example of the Harlem Renaissance, especially Alain Locke's compendium *The New Negro*. Their activities and publications in turn inspired the creation of the Society for African Culture and its journal *Présence Africaine*. The Society of African Culture, under its secretary Alioune Diop, was the organizer of the Festival, which was considered a crowning event of the cultural agenda of negritude.

3 Louis Armstrong and the Development and Diffusion of Jazz

Dan Morgenstern

Through Louis Armstrong and his influence jazz became a truly twentieth-century language.
    –Gunther Schuller[1]

Though he was never billed as the King of Jazz, Louis Armstrong is the sole legitimate claimant to that title. Of course, there would have been the music called jazz, but how it might have developed without Armstrong is anyone's guess because he was the key creator of its mature working language. More than two decades after his death and nearly three-quarters of a century since his influence became widespread through the medium of phonograph records, there is not a single musician playing in the jazz tradition who does not make daily use, knowingly or unknowingly, of something invented by Louis Armstrong.

Those who recall Armstrong only as the world-famous, genial entertainer whose face, smile, and gravelly voice were instantly recognizable may find it hard to comprehend that this man was a revolutionary artist—one of the handful of radical visionaries who changed the face of art in the twentieth century. He made jazz a vehicle for unprecedented freedom of creative expression, for musical imagination within a uniquely balanced, democratic framework. Armstrong's genius transformed what had been an interesting, even fascinating folk and dance music into a genuine and vital art.

Armstrong's influence does not end with jazz. The way popular singers, from Bing Crosby to Harry Connick, Jr., phrase and breathe stems from Armstrong's liberating approach to melody, tone production, and rhythm. American instrumentalists (including symphonic brass and wind players) have learned to expand the range and expressive power of their instruments from Armstrong's

James Kriegsmann's double image of Armstrong in the spotlight was done for a Cotton Club brochure, c. 1939. Louis Armstrong Archives, Queens College, City University of New York.

Left: Among the most accomplished of Armstrong's New Orleans contemporaries was the saxophone player Sidney Bechet, seen here around 1920. Frank Driggs Collection.

Right: The beginning of Armstrong's professional career in the 1920s coincided with a time of unprecedented opportunities for black musicians playing music originated by African-Americans. One of the era's most popular recording stars was blues singer Bessie Smith. Photograph by Edward Elcha, 1924. Frank Driggs Collection.

unprecedented flexibility and range as a trumpeter; he created a new kind of virtuosity. And the composers of what is now known as "The Great American Songbook" consciously or unconsciously made use of the discoveries Armstrong passed on to the mainstream of jazz.

Armstrong accomplished all this in the most natural and unassuming manner, for he was the most natural of men. He was blessed with a perfect physique for playing the trumpet—that most demanding of all instruments—and with an ideal disposition for coping with the hard work of being a professional musician and the psychic stress that a black performer of his generation had to endure. He was even equipped to cope with success, regarded by some as the ultimate American dilemma.

Childhood and Early Training

Duke Ellington, who truly understood Armstrong's musical message and made marvelous use of it, eulogized him with characteristic pithiness: "I loved and respected Louis Armstrong. He was born poor, died rich and never hurt anyone on the way."[2] Poor was an understatement: Armstrong was born in a shack in the worst section of New Orleans. For many years it was thought that his first job was selling newspapers, but in his final year of life, Armstrong revised earlier accounts of his biography, writing that he first went to work at seven for a Jewish family, the Karnofskys, who had a thriving little business buying and selling junk, including stone coal, which he and one of the sons sold from a wagon:

Jazz was embraced by all Americans. This early 1920s photograph shows Bix Beiderbecke, a trumpet player strongly influenced by Armstrong, whom he first saw performing on a Mississippi riverboat and later in the cabarets of Chicago. Courtesy Institute of Jazz Studies, Rutgers University.

When I would be on the junk wagon...I had a little tin horn, the kind that people celebrate with—I would blow this long tin horn without the top on it, just hold my fingers close together. Blow it as a call for old rags-bones-bottles or anything that the people and kids had to sell. The kids...loved the sound of my tin horn... After blowing the tin horn so long I wondered how would I do blowing a real horn—a cornet was what I had in mind. Sure enough, I saw a little cornet in a pawn shop window—five dollars. My luck was just right, with Karnofsky loaning me on my salary...(The horn) was all dirty, but was soon pretty to me.[3]

This revision also overturns another long-held notion:

I kept that horn for a long time, I played it all through the days of the honky tonks. People thought that my first horn was given to me at the Colored Waifs Home for Boys (the orphanage). But it wasn't.[4]

He did, however, apparently receive his first formal music instruction at age twelve or so in the Waif's Home—more a reform school than an orphanage to which he was committed more than just once for minor scrapes with the law. In the Home's band, he played first tambourine, then alto horn, bugle, and at last cornet. The boy practiced constantly, and his teacher, Peter Davis, soon realized that he had an exceptionally gifted pupil and gave him special attention. On the outside, young Louis had been musically active in a quartet that sang in the streets for pennies; he appears to have been its star, also excelling at what is now called break dancing.

By Armstrong's own accounts, his first idol was Joseph "King" Oliver (1885–1938), whose sobriquet was an indication of his stature in the Crescent City's lively musical life. After his release from the Home, he ran errands for Oliver's wife in return for lessons (probably not much more than a few pointers). Like Peter Davis, however, Oliver soon recognized a special talent and became the closest thing to a father the boy was to know. He played duets with Louis, and after a while sent him out on jobs he couldn't fill himself, also imbuing his young charge with a philosophy of music that "Little Louis," as he was by 1917 known in musical circles, summed up decades later as "always playing that lead. I used to run all over the horn, playing those figurations—something like what they call bop now. But King Oliver taught me to play that lead."[5]

That, of course, was hindsight—there were long periods in Armstrong's career when he played plenty of "figurations." But in the end, he did return to "that lead," and Oliver's is the only discernible influence on Armstrong's playing as we know it, though some old-timers claimed that cornetist Buddy Petit, who never made records, had a strong impact on his melodic conception.

In 1919 Oliver left town for Chicago and bequeathed to Little Louis one of his best jobs, that of cornetist with Kid Ory's band. Ory (1886–1973), a Creole, was one of the finest trombonists in New Orleans. Louis soon came to the attention of Fate Marable (1890–1947), bandleader on the biggest of the popular Mississippi River–excursion steamers. Though Marable, a well-schooled pianist, insisted that his bandsmen be good readers, he took a chance on Armstrong, whose exceptional ear stood him in good stead while he

CRAZY BLUES

By PERRY BRADFORD

MAMIE SMITH AND HER JAZZ HOUNDS

Get this number for your phonograph on Okeh Record No. 4169

PUBLISHED BY
PERRY BRADFORD
MUSIC PUB. CO.
1547 BROADWAY, N. Y. C.

NEW ORLEANS HOP SCOP BLUES

Words and Music by
GEO. W. THOMAS

CLARENCE WILLIAMS
MUSIC PUBLISHING CO., INC.
1547 BROADWAY, NEW YORK

Left: The success of Mamie Smith's 1920 recording of "Crazy Blues" paved the way for other black artists in the record business. Historic New Orleans Collection, William Russell Collection.

Right: The entrepreneurial talents of New Orleans-born musician Clarence Williams made him a formidable power in the early world of jazz. An early supporter of Armstrong, Williams hired him for many recordings sessions in the mid-1920s. Historic New Orleans Collection, William Russell Collection.

took reading lessons from the band's mellophonist, Davey Jones. He was a quick study and soon had no trouble learning the new tunes the band was expected to play each week or so. This band included a number of musicians with whom he would later work closely: Johnny Dodds (1892–1940) on clarinet and his younger brother Baby (1898–1959) on drums; bassist Pops Foster (1892–1969); and banjoist Johnny St. Cyr (1890–1966). The steamer took the Marable band's music as far north as Davenport, where young Bix Beiderbecke (1903–31) first heard Louis. Jack Teagarden (1905–64) also first encountered his future idol and boss on the boats.

We know Armstrong's playing at this time only from what other musicians have related. Sidney Bechet (1897–1959), four years older, confirmed that Louis started to play around age ten, and also recalled that the kid stunned him a bit later by playing the famous "High Society" clarinet solo on cornet. This anecdote reveals that a very young Armstrong (Bechet left New Orleans in 1917) already had the technique to execute such a multinoted passage, which would have challenged the foremost concert-band cornetists of the day, as well as such leading jazz lights as Oliver and Freddie Keppard (1889–1933), whose later work on records includes nothing at such a level of execution.

Reliance on recordings is at once jazz's blessing and curse. Without recorded evidence, it would be impossible to construct a sensible history of the music, but the annals of jazz history are filled with legendary musicians and orchestras who never encountered a recording device. Armstrong's later music was well docu-

mented, but the first decade of his music has been lost because he did not get to record until March 31, 1923—some seven months after he went to Chicago at King Oliver's beckoning to join the King's Creole Jazz Band at the Lincoln Gardens.

First Recordings

The year 1923 was a watershed in jazz recording. Black bands and singers had been recording for some time: in late 1913 James Reese Europe's band was the first that was remotely jazz related; Mamie Smith's 1920 "Crazy Blues" started the business of so-called race records, recordings made specifically for the African-American market, which turned out to be considerable. The first real jazz records, by the white New Orleanian Original Dixieland Jazz Band, were made in 1917. Kid Ory, who had moved to California, made records there in 1922, which hardly circulated outside that state. But in 1923, King Oliver, Bessie Smith, and Jelly Roll Morton all made their first records—a major breakthrough, artistically speaking.

Oliver's Creole Jazz Band is identified in jazz history as a "true" New Orleans band, but musically it had evolved from the parent style. From the testimony of musicians and fans who heard the 1922–24 Oliver band live, its most potent attraction was the unique two-cornet team. Oliver and Armstrong worked out fancy double-cornet breaks that seemed to be miraculously harmonized and synchronized on the spot—something hinted at on such records as the two 1923 versions of "Snake Rag." Though these breaks seemed purely spontaneous to the listeners, they were in

Armstrong's career was fueled by the technological changes that were transforming the entertainment business. By the 1920s phonograph records enabled the stars of the era to reach unprecedently large and geographically diverse audiences.

fact worked out in a most ingenious way: at a given point in the preceding collective band chorus, Oliver would play what he intended to use as his part in the break, and Armstrong, lightning quick on the uptake, would memorize it and devise his own second part—which always fit to perfection.

Armstrong played his first recorded solo, on "Chimes Blues," during the first Oliver studio session. It sticks close to the attractive melody, but in its sound, phrasing, and swing stands out like a little gem in a plain setting. On "Tears," a tune by Armstrong, his solo breaks are the strongest indicators of the future in all his work with Oliver. Armstrong's lead and solo parts on both versions of "Riverside Blues" hint at the majestic quality his playing would acquire.

By early 1924 Armstrong had married the band's pianist and best reader, Lil Hardin, who was sure that Oliver had hired her man to keep him under wraps as a potential rival to his crown. Eventually, she succeeded in cutting Armstrong loose from his putative father. In a charming recorded memoir, "Satchmo and Me,"[6] she describes how, after she had left the band, she would hear Louis whistling as he approached their house on his way home from work, expressing beautiful musical ideas. She asked him why, since he could imagine such things, he did not play them on his horn. Soon he did, of course, and also began to show gifts as a composer.

"Tears" was an Armstrong composition and Armstrong was also cocomposer, with Oliver, of "Dippermouth Blues," which contains Oliver's most famous solo. It is not unthinkable

A Victrola produced in the 1920s by the Victor Talking Machine Company. Courtesy Institute of Jazz Studies, Rutgers University.

A big event for me was buying a wind-up Victrola [in 1918]. Most of my records were the Original Dixieland Jazz Band...They were the first to record the music I played.

Louis Armstrong, *Life*, April 15, 1966

Opposite
Top: Recordings including "West End Blues" (1928) and "Georgia Grind" (1926), by Armstrong's Hot Five and Hot Seven, the first made under his own name, established the trumpeter's national reputation. Courtesy Institute of Jazz Studies, Rutgers University.

Bottom: Armstrong and King Oliver are credited as the composers of "Sugar Foot Stomp," recorded by Fletcher Henderson & His Orchestra when Armstrong was a member in 1925. Courtesy Institute of Jazz Studies, Rutgers University.

that at least the outline of this three-chorus solo was conceptualized by the younger man; in any case, "Dippermouth" was one of Louis's early nicknames. The recently discovered lead sheet of "Weather Bird Rag" confirms Armstrong as its sole author, though Oliver shares composer credit on the band's recording. Armstrong deposited the sheet, written in his hand, in 1923 in the Library of Congress' copyright files and on January 18, 1924—less than a month after Louis's last recording date with Oliver—registered "Cornet Chop Suey," which would first be recorded more than two years later, by Louis's own Hot Five. These pieces were not Armstrong's first compositions, although apparently they were the first he registered. In 1918, while still in New Orleans, he sold outright his piece "I Wish I could Shimmy Like My Sister Kate" to bandleader-publisher A. J. Piron for $50. The tune became a big hit. He also had bad luck with two of his greatest compositions, both standards of traditional jazz: "Muskrat Ramble" and "Struttin' with Some Barbecue." The latter, though clearly Armstrong's in every phrase, was claimed by his by-then ex-wife Lil; when his manager wanted to countersue, Louis told him that she needed the royalties more than he did. As for "Muskrat Ramble," it came as a great surprise when Louis told me, in a 1965 interview, that it was he and not trombonist Kid Ory who had composed this fetching and durable piece in the classic New Orleans idiom. "Ory named it, he gets the royalties. I don't talk about it," he said.[7]

Was Armstrong performing "Cornet Chop Suey" as early as 1924? Very probably, but not with the Oliver band as it has come down to us on record, nor with the New York dance band of Fletcher Henderson (1897–1952), his next important musical berth.

Henderson Days

In 1921, while touring with singer Ethel Waters, Henderson had first heard Armstrong and tried to hire the trumpeter for Waters's small group. When he established his own, much bigger band and had a permanent, well-paying job at the Roseland Ballroom on Broadway, he tried again to lure Armstrong to the big town. With Lil's help, it worked.

Henderson's music was far removed from the lilting New Orleans rhythms of King Oliver; though the band contained some gifted players, and at least one who could play real blues, trombonist Charlie "Big" Green (c.1900–36), its arrangements, designed for the white clientele of Roseland, were rhythmically stiff and the players—Green aside—were stilted in their phrasing. As Armstrong begins to contribute to the band's recordings, his solos—often no longer than eight, twelve, or sixteen bars and seldom a full chorus—stand out, not like gems in a fitting setting as with Oliver, but as poetry in a sea of doggerel. Even as accomplished a saxophonist as Coleman Hawkins (1904–69) sounds like a stumblebum after Armstrong.

By the time Armsrong leaves the band fourteen months later,

Armstrong's records were first marketed to African-American audiences and advertised in black publications. This 1930 notice in the *Amsterdam News* announced the release of "Song of the Islands." Newspapers and Current Periodicals Division, Library of Congress, Permission *The New York Amsterdam News*.

Armstrong's music soon demonstrated its cross-racial appeal. A 1930 record catalogue for general audiences featured Armstrong's hit "Peanut Vendor!" next to music by the Yale Collegians. Frank Driggs Collection.

the changes that have been wrought in it are substantive; a case in point is arranger-saxophonist Don Redman's setting of Armstrong and Oliver's erstwhile "Dippermouth Blues" as "Sugarfoot Stomp," the rhythm evened out to an Armstrongian 4/4 feel, the section phrasing much smoother, and Armstrong's three-chorus tribute to his ex-leader set in a fitting context. That solo, played on open horn (Oliver used a plunger mute) reveals the pupil's rhythmic and tonal superiority to the teacher. Armstrong performs other noteworthy solos with Henderson, and the gradual improvement in Coleman Hawkins's playing during Armstrong's tenure is remarkable.

The finest recorded work by Armstrong during his first New York period is on his accompaniments to blues singers (often with Henderson at the piano), and on a series of small-group performances, most of them recorded under the supervision of Clarence Williams. The New Orleans–born pianist, music publisher, and entrepreneur was by then in his second year of producing race records for OKeh and was a leading figure in this growing field. His own groups recorded as the Clarence Williams Blue Five; Armstrong also appeared on the rival Gennett label with a similar non-Williams group known as the Red Onion Jazz Babies.

What was most special about the Williams Blue Five (or Red Onion) recordings was the occasional teaming of Armstrong with the only other horn player then capable of giving him real competition—fellow New Orleanian Sidney Bechet, who'd been to Europe and had added the soprano saxophone to his formidable clarinet. When these two, the only true jazz virtuosi of the day, get together

on the two versions of "Cake Walking Babies From Home," sparks fly. On the OKeh version, more exciting than the Red Onions', they engage in actual rivalry, each man soloing and presenting a sequence of slashing breaks. It's almost a draw, but Armstrong's superior rhythm wins; even Bechet, a powerful swinger, cannot match Armstrong's subtle juggling of almost subliminal note values. Like a tightrope walker, he never makes a wrong move.

Among the blues singers with whom he collaborated, Bessie Smith stands out, of course. She herself presumably preferred to work with cornetist Joe Smith (who rejoined Henderson's band shortly before Armstrong left), and from her point of view she may have been right—Smith was a perfect foil whereas Armstrong was her equal. Yet his fills and obligatos consistently enhance her singing. As far as he was concerned, Bessie was the greatest. "Everything I did with her, *I like,*" he said.[8]

Armstrong already considered himself a singer, and this was one of the reasons for his leaving Henderson. Though the few near-spoken breaks at the end of one of two takes of Henderson's "Everybody Loves My Baby" are Armstrong's first recorded vocal efforts, he seldom sang with the band in person, and there were no other recorded vocals. This still rankled Armstrong years later. During my last visit to his home, in December 1970, he was in a feisty mood. Fletcher wouldn't let him sing, he said, because his gravel voice actually embarrassed the "dicty" (stuck up), high-toned bandleader—though Fletcher did let Armstrong do a Bert Williams imitation! (It wasn't the last time Henderson missed the boat: ten years later, he turned down a chance to hire Ella Fitzgerald.)

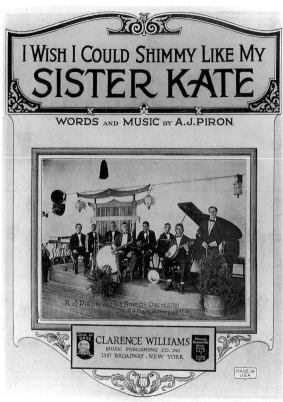

I WISH I COULD SHIMMY LIKE MY
SISTER KATE

WORDS AND MUSIC BY A.J.PIRON

A. J. PIRON AND HIS NOVELTY ORCHESTRA
A. J. Piron standing with cello

CLARENCE WILLIAMS
MUSIC PUBLISHING CO. INC.
1547 BROADWAY, NEW YORK

Although Armstrong is best known as a musician and performer, he was also an accomplished composer. A. J. Piron is credited on this sheet music as the author of the hit "I Wish I Could Shimmy Like My Sister Kate," but, in fact, the tune was written by Armstrong in 1918. It was common practice at the time for songwriters to sell their work outright to publishers. Hogan Jazz Archives, Howard-Tilton Memorial Library, Tulane University, New Orleans, Louisiana.

On His Own

Soon Armstrong returned to Chicago where his wife had a band at the Dreamland Ballroom. She prepared a banner to welcome him that read "The World's Greatest Trumpet Player," and although Louis was embarrassed, nobody questioned the claim. Before long, he was doubling with a big band headed by Erskine Tate (1895–1978) at the prestigious Vendome Theater, the Southside's first-run movie palace, where the stage shows included such popular classical features as the intermezzo from *Cavalleria Rusticana*, as well as jazz specialties. Opera was nothing new to Armstrong, who recalled that around 1918, a "big event for me was buying a wind-up Victrola. Most of my records were the Original Dixieland Jazz Band... They were the first to record the music I played. I had Caruso records, and Henry Burr, Galli-Curci, Tetrazzini—they were all my favorites. Then there was the Irish tenor, McCormack—beautiful phrasing."[9] The New Orleans of Armstrong's youth was filled with music of all kinds; a local favorite was the French Opera, where the Creole Bechet was taken as a child. (Armstrong never attended the French Opera, and had anyone close to him wanted to take him, they couldn't have afforded it.)

Popular music in the early decades of this century was still rooted in the "classics." Concert bands, which always featured cornetists and/or trumpeters as their star soloists, had repertories that included paraphrases of favorite operatic arias. Ragtime was rooted in the classical piano tradition, and its star performers could play the sort of operatic paraphrases that Liszt had specialized in. The popular works Armstrong performed at the Vendome also included special scores written for silent pictures and such overtures as "Poet and Peasant"; he soon perfected his sight-reading and turned into a full-fledged virtuoso of the trumpet, which he had taken up to match horns with Tate's lead trumpeter, dropping his stubby little cornet. The trumpet's greater range and brilliance also suited his musical development.

In 1925 Armstrong began to record as leader of his own group, the Louis Armstrong Hot Five, an activity that significantly influenced the future of jazz. This group was strictly a studio combination—it performed in public only once, at a benefit concert, during its two-year existence. Armstrong was the youngest member of his own band, which included his wife Lil (two years his senior) on piano, his former boss, Kid Ory, on trombone, and two riverboat and Oliver bandmates, Johnny Dodds, clarinet, and Johnny St. Cyr, banjo. The absence of bass and drums was less an artistic or economic decision than a technical one—the OKeh company was still recording acoustically in late 1925 in Chicago, and these two instruments did not record well. By May 1927, the Hot Five had become the Hot Seven, with the addition of Baby Dodds on drums and a tuba player to the now-electrical recordings.

Traditional-minded jazz commentators have argued that

Armstrong's wife Lil Hardin encouraged him to compose and helped Armstrong write down his musical ideas. She submitted the written scores to the copyright office in Washington, D.C., thus registering "Cornet Chop Suey" in 1924. Music Division, Library of Congress, Permission Louis Armstrong Educational Foundation, Inc.

these Armstrong groups wrecked the wonderful collective New Orleans style, but this manner of ensemble playing was on its way out, squeezed by larger dance bands and the rise of the saxophone, among other factors—including the changing repertory. The success of the Hot Five/Seven actually helped to keep the New Orleans style alive for a while longer, though the emphasis was on solos and Armstrong's clearly was the dominant musical voice. Even though this group did not represent the context in which he was playing day by day (or rather, night by night), it gave Armstrong his first opportunity to play extended solo passages on records and to display fully his powerful lead work.

The Virtuoso

The more room Armstrong gave himself on these records the better were the results, and with such masterpieces as "Big Butter and

When Armstrong returned to Chicago in 1935 after his second European tour, he hired a new manager, Joe Glaser, the owner of the Sunset Cafe. It would become a lifelong relationship. Bill Mark's photograph shows Armstrong and Glaser in 1949. Louis Armstrong Archives, Queens College, City University of New York.

Egg Man," "Wild Man Blues," "Potato Head Blues," and "Hotter Than That," the revolutionary young Armstrong is clearly displayed. With solos such as these, he created a vocabulary of phrases that would echo in the music for decades, even unto this day—in the work not only of such older players as Ruby Braff (b. 1927) but also Wynton Marsalis (b.1961) and other young neo-traditionalists (or post-modernists). Armstrong now proceeds with utter fearlessness and freedom, crossing bar lines, extending the working range of the horn, mastering breaks and stop time and other rhythmic devices, and creating lovely melodies and phrases that linger in the mind and stir the emotions. Hundreds upon hundreds of musicians, not only in America but wherever jazz records were sold, studied these solos, learning them note for note—to sing if not to play, for the technical demands, not to mention the rhythmic and harmonic ones, were well beyond the capacity of most. In 1927 the Chicago music publisher Melrose put out a book of Armstrong solos and breaks.[10]

Armstrong's phraseology now began to enter the mainstream of jazz; it would remain a cornerstone at least until the advent of bebop—and a close analysis of Charlie Parker's vocabulary will show that he, too, was steeped in Armstrong, willy-nilly.

Armstrong also sang on the Hot Five/Seven discs, at first in a premicrophone style that sounds bucolic compared with his later work but already reflects his playing. It is probably more accurate that Armstrong sings like he plays than vice versa, there being so many trumpetlike aspects to the voice, among them "using dentals, labials and gutturals as he would use tonguing in a cornet solo, and enlivening the vowel colors with abrasive flutterings of the throat."[11] Armstrong's singing had a profound effect on his listeners. On the 1926 "Heebie Jeebies," he claimed that he dropped the lyric sheet while recording and spontaneously substituted scatting for the words; chances are that this was a bit of deliberate legend-making, given that there are earlier recorded examples of this vocal procedure. But it was this record that made scatting catch on, with (among others) the Paul Whiteman Rhythm Boys, which included the young Bing Crosby (1903–77).

The old Hot Five/Seven bowed out with a December 1927 recording date. A new Hot Five (really Seven), sometimes known as the Savoy Ballroom Five, made its debut the following June. It included members of the band with which Armstrong was now working at Chicago's Savoy Ballroom, led by Caroll Dickerson. A much more modern unit than its predecessor, its second star was pianist Earl Hines (1903–1983), a key representative of a new breed of players to whom the Armstrong vocabulary was second nature. Also featured was Armstrong's New Orleans buddy, drummer Zutty Singleton (1898–1975), perhaps the best player on his instrument in 1928. The other members of the group were merely competent. Don Redman (1900–64), then musical director of McKinney's Cotton Pickers, provided some excellent arrangements and frequently augmented the group on alto saxophone.

Glaser shared Armstrong's ambition of reaching the largest possible audience. An updated, sophisticated look, new musical arrangements, and a heavier emphasis on entertainment helped solidify Armstrong's place as one of America's most popular performers. Publicity photographs by Maurice, taken in 1938, show Armstrong as leader of Louis Russell Orchestra and alone. Top: Frank Driggs Collection; bottom: Courtesy Institute of Jazz Studies, Rutgers University;

The most famous of the new Hot Five sides is "West End Blues," a jazz landmark due mainly to Armstrong's dazzling introductory cadenza. This masterful creation, with its "spectacular cascading phrases,"[12] has often been imitated but never successfully; its rhythmic pitfalls are not really negotiable, and reading transcriptions won't help the player much. Armstrong also offers a sublime, wordless vocal and trumpet conclusion, and Hines delivers a first-rate solo.

The "West End Blues" cadenza is a dramatic example of opera's influence on Armstrong, though it is purely instrumental. Musicologist Joshua Berrett, who has made a study of Armstrong's relationship to opera,[13] has traced the cadenza's genealogy to its 1924 germ-cell appearance in a break behind singer Margaret Johnson's "Changeable Daddy of Mine,"[14] showing that it is not as gloriously spontaneous as it sounds, but was the result of years of refining an idea that was spectacular even in its embryonic form.

The Hot Five/Seven/Savoy Ballroom Five stage of Armstrong's recordings ends with further masterpieces, among them "Beau Koo Jack," with an Armstrong invention in the conclusion that quickly found its way to transcription for trumpet sections in bands, and "Muggles," with its two choruses of blues in two tempos. These, however, were surpassed by a piece performed by Armstrong and Hines alone, "Weather Bird." (In 1928 the "Rag" of the original title was dropped as old-fashioned.)

The piece, already mentioned, comes from the Oliver Creole Jazz Band repertory. The Armstrong-Hines duet is among the all-

In 1937 Joe Glaser and Louis Armstrong sign a contract for Fleischmann's Yeast Hour, a radio program. Hired as a temporary replacement for singer Rudy Vallee, Armstrong became the first African-American to host a national radio program. Louis Armstrong Archives, Queens College, City University of New York.

time masterpieces of recorded jazz, stunning in its almost symbiotic teamwork and joint virtuosity. In his seminal book *Early Jazz*, Gunther Schuller devotes nearly three pages of analysis to this piece, stating that "the cohesiveness of this performance is at a level we usually attribute to consciously premeditated composition. When we realized that it is the result of spontaneous creation born of the passing moment, we can only marvel at the musicianship displayed."[15] But years of listening has led me to a different conclusion: that this is by no means an unpremeditated "first" spontaneously created in the studio. Three strains structure "Weather Bird Rag," and there is no way Hines could have familiarized himself with its structure on the spot. A far more likely scenario is that the two, then inseparable friends who often got together to play without others on hand, had "fooled around" with the piece until they felt ready to record it. They certainly made it sound fresh, but there can be little doubt that they knew where they were going.

The Hot Five era extended from November 12, 1925, to December 12, 1928—almost exactly three years, within which the activity of recording represents only about three weeks. During this period, Armstrong also recorded with various singers, mostly of the blues but also of popular songs; with other leaders; and, on only three occasions, with actual working bands. The recordings made with working bands included Erskine Tate; a 1927 session by Louis Armstrong and his Stompers, the band he led at the Sunset Cafe, from which just one side has survived, not issued until 1942; and two 1928 sides by Caroll Dickerson's band from the Savoy.

These few glimpses are sufficient evidence that the music of the Hot Five was a far cry from what Armstrong was playing outside the studio. All three bands have a typical 1920s approach to orchestral jazz, with the earliest (Tate) being the least formulaic and most explosive. In any event, these few records only dimly illuminate what Armstrong himself and other contemporaries have described. For instance, pianist Art Hodes recalled hearing Armstrong improvise for half an hour on "Poor Little Rich Girl," a sophisticated Noel Coward tune, at the Sunset. Nothing remotely like that survives for us to hear, but along with other testimony it indicates that the switch from New Orleans–type jazz originals to popular songs of the day took place much earlier in his *working* repertory than in his recordings. Such late Hot (or Savoy Ballroom) Five pieces as "Squeeze Me," "Save It Pretty Mama," and "Basin Street Blues," all by black songwriters, reflect this change.

Into the Limelight

The breakthrough recording for Armstrong took place during a brief visit to New York in March 1929. He joined the Luis Russell band on a Jimmy McHugh-Dorothy Fields song, "I Can't Give You Anything But Love," performing it at a very slow tempo. He opens with a muted trumpet solo (Armstrong seldom used a mute, and when he did, from 1926 on, it was never anything but a straight mute, the kind that least alters the tone) backed by chords from the band and sings a passionate vocal. Then, after a trombone break, he constructs an arialike open-horn solo ending with a climb to the top.

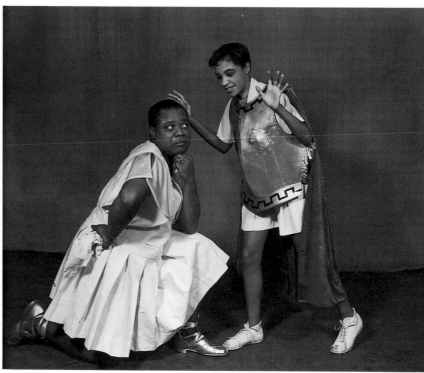

Left: In 1939 Armstrong returned to Broadway in *Swingin' the Dream*, a jazz version of Shakespeare's *Midsummer Night's Dream*. The ambitious production lasted only fifteen performances, but it was well documented in production photographs by Vandamm Studios. Billy Rose Theater Collection of The New York Public Library for the Performing Arts, Astor, Lenox and Tilden Foundations.

Right: Louis Armstrong and Maxine Sullivan in *Swingin' the Dream*. Photograph by Vandamm Studios. Billy Rose Theater Collection of The New York Public Library for the Performing Arts, Astor, Lenox and Tilden Foundations.

That ballad was also an innovation in jazz recording: nearly the first time that a black artist sang a standard pop song. Only Ethel Waters and the McKinney's Cotton Pickers' vocalist George Thomas had done so before and their voices had a far less African flavor than Armstrong's. On that same morning, Armstrong had made another kind of breakthrough: recording an impromptu blues, "Knocking a Jug," with a racially integrated group.

A few months later Armstrong came to New York to stay and was soon booked into Connie's Inn. This Harlem nightspot was the chief rival of the Cotton Club and, like it, a venue for elaborately staged floor shows, specially written and choreographed and featuring singers, dancers, and specialty acts. As luck would have it, the 1929 edition of Connie's revue, dubbed "Hot Chocolates," was so good (with a score by Fats Waller and Andy Razaf) that it moved to Broadway, where it earned rave reviews and a respectable run.

Initially, Armstrong was featured only in the pit band, standing up during the entr'acte, playing and singing the show's prime hit, "Ain't Misbehavin'," which had already been introduced by the romantic male lead. Soon Louis was moved up on stage for "Ain't Misbehavin'" and also given a spot in a vocal trio billed as "One Thousand Pounds of Rhythm," which included Waller and the show's female lead, Edith Wilson. After each night's show, Louis taxied uptown to lead his band—still the Dickenson crew from Chicago—at Connie's. He was in such demand that for a while he also did a spot in the late show at the Lafayette Theater, next door to Connie's. "Had to get my sleep coming through the park in a cab," he recalled years later. "I was only 29 years old [in fact, he was 28]. Didn't exactly feel I had the world at my feet, but it was very nice that everyone was picking up on the things I was doing, and all the bandleaders wanted me. Pretty soon I had to get in front of my own band. Nothing else I could do."[16]

"Ain't Misbehavin'" was Armstrong's first real hit record, backed with another song from *Hot Chocolates*, "Black and Blue." Armstrong turned this song, which in the show was a dark-skinned lady's lament about losing in the game of love to lighter rivals, into what has long been regarded as a "protest song." (Indeed, as such, it [and Armstrong] are made emblematic of the hero's plight in Ralph Ellison's masterful novel *Invisible Man*.) By stripping that verse and singing the song in a male voice with such dignity and passion that he renders some of the lyrics' less fortunate turns of phrase as genuine poetry, Armstrong forever transformed the song, adding some majestic opening and closing trumpet flights for good measure.

The success of this 1929 record established the pattern for Armstrong's recordings through the next two decades. Henceforth, his material would be popular songs, often of high quality and sometimes written specifically for him, with a smattering of novelties. He would record almost exclusively with his own big bands, which had a very specific task: to back the leader's playing and singing. Record buyers wanted Armstrong, and most of his bands served competently in their self-effacing role.

Armstrong had a significant impact on the jazz repertory: he turned many Tin Pan Alley tunes into jazz evergreens. He had a special relationship with Hoagy Carmichael (1899–1981), who shares the vocal on the first recording (1929) of his "Rockin' Chair" with Louis. In 1931 Armstrong found inspiration in Carmichael's masterpiece, "Star Dust"; cut a definitive version of "Georgia On My Mind" (Ray Charles was not the first African-American to put his distinctive imprint on this song); and made "Lazy River" (a collaboration between Carmichael and New Orleans clarinetist Sidney Arodin) his own for keeps—this piece remained in the Armstrong repertory to the end. The studio recording of "Jubilee," written for a 1937 film, ranks among Armstrong's greatest works of the decade. The charming "Ev'ntide" was another Carmichael special for Armstrong, who immortalized it.

Armstrong showed a special affinity for songs by Jimmy McHugh and Dorothy Fields, starting with "I Can't Give You Anything But Love." Both "Exactly Like You" and "I Can't Believe that You're in Love with Me" were three years old when Louis recorded them in 1930; they have been jazz standards since. "On the Sunny Side of the Street" entered the working Armstrong repertoire before he first recorded it in Paris in late 1934; one of his sincerest imitators, trumpeter-singer Taft Jordan (1915–83), beat him to it by almost a year. (From 1929 on, record companies tried to groom rivals to the OKeh label's Armstrong: Brunswick featured the fleet and inventive Jabbo Smith (1908–91); Vocation had the lesser-known Ruben

Reeves (b. 1905); and Victor showcased the brilliant New Orleanian Henry "Red" Allen (1908–67). Not one proved viable competition, creatively or commercially, though Allen showed a remarkable grasp of Armstrong's musical essence.)

As early as 1930, Armstrong pioneered in what the record industry would later call "crossovers." At the special request of Jimmie Rodgers, accurately described as the father of country music, Louis and Lil joined him in recording "Blue Yodel No. 9," incidentally the last in a string of brilliant blues accompaniments by Armstrong that had begun with Ma Rainey in 1923. Louis also "crossed over" to Hawaiian music, recording (with three violins added to the Luis Russell band, then accompanying him) "Song of the Islands." With his version of "The Peanut Vendor," a Cuban rhumba, Louis can be said to have initiated Latin jazz.

This last was recorded in Los Angeles, where Armstrong appeared at Frank Sebastian's New Cotton Club, a nightclub catering to the movie colony, during his lengthy 1930 stay. The young drummer in both bands that Armstrong fronted in Los Angeles was Lionel Hampton (b.1908), who credits the trumpeter with getting him started on the vibraphone, which he plays on the memorable recording of Eubie Blake and Andy Razaf's "Memories of You." Other key recordings from this California sojourn include "You're Driving Me Crazy," which directly inspired arranger Eddie Durham's "Moten Swing," based on the chords of the Walter Donaldson song and considered the anthem of Kansas City Jazz; "Sweethearts on Parade," which constitutes a kind of summation of Armstrong's art-

Al Hirschfeld's lively expressive lines effectively capture the jazz spirit of *Swingin' The Dream*. © Al Hirschfeld. Reproduced by special arrangement with Hirschfeld's exclusive representative, The Margo Feiden Galleries Ltd., New York.

Hirschfeld's caricature of Armstrong, costar Benny Goodman, and a finger-snapping William Shakespeare originally appeared as the *Playbill* cover for the *Swingin' the Dream*. © Al Hirschfeld. Reproduced by special arrangement with Hirschfeld's exclusive representative, The Margo Feiden Galleries Ltd., New York.

Melrose Bros. Music Company transcribed Armstrong's improvised solos and in 1927 published a book of sheet music that made his secrets available to all musicians. Historic New Orleans Collection, William Russell Collection.

Many of the greatest hot men we have today, men who have made enviable reputations as recording artists, will tell you that they conceived many of their tricks and ideas from the Armstrong style of playing.

Publisher's Note, Introduction to *Louis Armstrong's 125 Jazz Breaks for Hot Trumpet*

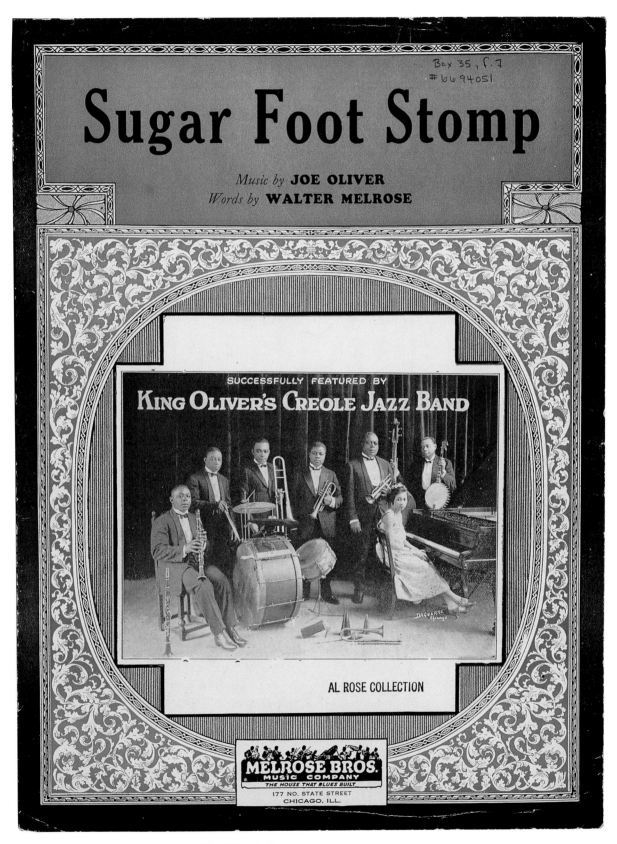

Armstrong is shown as a member of King Oliver's Creole Jazz Band on the cover of the sheet music for "Sugar Foot Stomp," published by Melrose Bros. Music Company in 1927. Although he was coauthor of the tune, the credit is given solely to Oliver. Hogan Jazz Archives, Howard-Tilton Memorial Library, Tulane University, New Orleans, Louisiana.

In late 1939 Armstrong starred at the Cotton Club, which had recently moved from Harlem to Broadway. Francis Feist provided the designs for the costumes and stage set. Museum of the City of New York.

istry, vocal and instrumental, at this point of his career; and "Ding Dong Daddy From Dumas," with its remarkable stop-time breaks, including one that contains the riff later expanded into the bebop classic "Salt Peanuts."

Back to New Orleans

In Chicago in early 1931 Armstrong (and his new manager, Johnny Collins) formed the first Armstrong big band proper, that is, a band that was not a preexisting entity fronted by the trumpeter, but a specially assembled crew. This group included several New Orleanians and was later frequently described by its leader as the happiest band he ever led. With it, he visited his hometown for the first time in nine years. He received a triumphant welcome, including a parade (not an honor commonly accorded blacks in 1931) and had a cigar (the Louis Armstrong Special) and a baseball team (Armstrong's Secret Nine) named for him. He became the first performer of his race to do his own announcing on radio when a redneck announcer refused to introduce him on opening night at the Suburban Gardens ballroom. The cracker was fired, but Louis had been so effective that he continued to fill the role for the duration of the three-month–long engagement.

Before and after this historic visit, which included a sentimental journey to the Waif's Home, Armstrong recorded some of his biggest hits to date with this "happy" band. Among them: his theme song, "Sleepy Time Down South," and the humorous novelty "I'll Be Glad When You're Dead, You Rascal, You," which, though recorded

Armstrong's name appears in lights on the marquee of the Oriental Theatre in Chicago, c. 1940. Louis Armstrong Archives, Queens College, City University of New York.

by many others, became permanently identified with Armstrong.

There was also room for trumpet specialties like "Chinatown," with its "battle between the trumpet and the saxophones"—no other instrumental virtuoso created such miniature skits within which to frame his flights—and "New Tiger Rag," in which he announces that it will take eight choruses to catch the big cat. In Armstrong's live performances of the venerable "Tiger" from this period, he would offer as a climax as many as two hundred high Cs, topped by some Fs. This kind of display of course gave rise to grumblings from the budding aesthetes of jazz; Armstrong himself later disowned such acrobatics, saying he was just trying to impress his fellow musicians (which he certainly did!). During this period Armstrong first recorded Gershwin ("I Got Rhythm," which would become the anthem of jazz) and Arlen ("Between the Devil and the Deep Blue Sea," extant in two takes, of which the slower contains a muted trumpet passage that in its mastery of melodic double time presages Charlie Parker).

The Depression years 1931–32 were the absolute nadir for the record business in the U.S. That Armstrong did so much work in the studios at this lean time speaks volumes for his popularity, growing apace among blacks and whites.

To Europe

In July 1932 Armstrong made his first appearances in Europe, performing in England. Many jazz-related Americans had performed in Europe before, starting in 1919 with the white Original Dixieland

A poster from around 1940. New
Orleans Jazz Club Collections,
Louisiana State Museum.

A new dance of the Swing era was the Lindy Hop, more often called the Jitterbug. William H. Johnson captures its frantic energy in *Jitterbug V* (1941–1942), one of a series of his paintings showing Jitterbug dancers. National Museum of American Art, Smithsonian Institution, Gift of the Harmon Foundation.

Richard Merrill shows Armstrong in performance around 1940. With faster film and portable flash units, photographers could now regularly capture performers in action. Louis Armstrong Archives, Queens College, City University of New York.

My heart gets a chill

I feel such a thrill

My feet won't keep still

When they swing that music!

—"Swing That Music"

by Horace Gerlach and Louis Armstrong

Jazz Band and the black Southern Syncopated Orchestra, led by Will Marion Cook and featuring young Sidney Bechet (who would spend much of the 1920s touring all over Europe with various bands, including his own). But Armstrong was the first jazz artist to appear there as an individual star, not as a band leader or band member. He did not bring his own accompanists but was first featured with a group of black musicians of various nationalities (including some from the U.S.) assembled for him in Paris, and then, in another Armstrong "first," at the helm of a band made up of some of Britain's best white jazzmen.

Reception was mixed—enthusiasm from musicians and jazz fans (who were numerous in England by 1932) and puzzlement (and sometimes outrage) from the general public. Among the more amusing sidelights was the request by a delegation of musicians to examine Armstrong's trumpet to ascertain that it, and his mouthpiece, had not been doctored in some odd fashion. His virtuosity was still not quite credible.

His first three-month European visit made it clear to Armstrong that there were important people who took his music seriously and that (though London and the British hinterlands of 1932 were hardly free of prejudice) there were lands where racism was not a constant factor.

Back home, Armstrong toured with a new "Hot Chocolates," revue, far from the first in quality, accompanied by Chick Webb's band, with which he recorded in December. By then, he was increasingly plagued by lip problems (he used the pressure system,

Adolf Dehn's drawing *Jazz Babies* (1927).
Mrs. Adolf Dehn.

Top left: *Rockin' in Rhythm*, a drawing by
Charles H. Alston, 1940s. Harmon
Foundation, National Archives. (200S-HN-
ALS-C-5)

Top right: Miguel Covarrubias's lithograph,
The Lindy Hop (1936). The Metropolitan
Museum of Art, Harris Brisbane Dick Fund,
1940, 40.92.8.

and the abundance of high notes was taking its toll),
but the date produced fine results. He was under a
new contract, with Victor, then the most prestigious
record label, and their famed Camden studios captured his awesome sound better than any previous
recordings.

By January 1933, a new band had been
assembled in Chicago, in some ways the best of the
Armstrong big bands yet. The brilliant young pianist
Teddy Wilson (1912–86) made his recording debut in
this group, and the Johnson brothers—Keg (1908–67)
on trombone and Budd (1910–84) on tenor sax—were
first-rate soloists. Recording sessions over three con-
secutive days were taxing on the embouchure, but
Armstrong is in brilliant form on such wonderful Arlen tunes as
"World on a String" and "I've Got a Right to Sing the Blues" and
creates a new and very special "Basin Street Blues."

Three months later, a two-day recording stint brings us the
unique "Laughin' Louie," which must be heard to be appreciated.
Like his good friend Fats Waller, Louis combined comedy and music
in a very special and inimitable manner. The piece concludes with
an unaccompanied trumpet solo on a classical theme that displays the
fullness, warmth, and range of his sound at this time to perfection.[17]

In 1933 Armstrong returned to Europe. He opened in London in August, at the helm of a band that included several musicians from the previous year's Paris-based group. Relations between

Sailors dance to the music of a jukebox in
Ralph Van Lehmden's oil painting, *Saturday
Night Swing* (c. 1945). Courtesy Michael
Rosenfeld Gallery, New York.

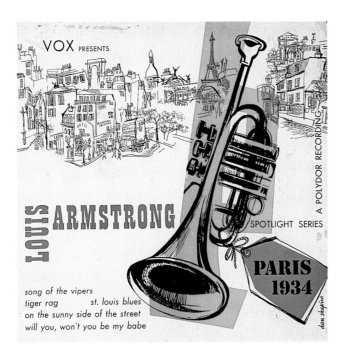

The first record albums, sets of 78 rpm records packaged together, were issued in the 1940s. The ambitious new packaging included stylish visuals on the album covers.

Top left: "Louis Armstrong's Hot 5," (Columbia Records; Jim Flora, Illustrator), 1941. Courtesy Institute of Jazz Studies, Rutgers University.

Top right: "King Louis—Hot Jazz Classics" (Columbia Records; Steinweiss, Illustrator), 1940. Courtesy Institute of Jazz Studies, Rutgers University.

Bottom: "Louis Armstrong—Paris 1934" (Polydor Records; Dan Shapiro, Illustrator), 1947. Courtesy Institute of Jazz Studies, Rutgers University.

Left: The July 19, 1940, issue of *Harlem Tattler* featured a photograph of Lindy Hoppers by Marvin and Morgan Smith on the cover, and in an article entitled "Special Jive" by Louis Armstrong inside. Courtesy Institute of Jazz Studies, Rutgers University.

Right: Claude Clark's painting *Downbeat* shows both the dance and fashion style of Philadelphia around 1944-46. Harmon Foundation, National Archives. (273-HN-CL-100)

the trumpeter and his manager, Johnny Collins, had long been strained. They now came to a head, and Armstrong fired Collins, who retaliated by leaving with Armstrong's passport—a clue to the man's mentality. Now managed by the British band leader and entrepreneur Jack Hylton, Armstrong toured Denmark, Sweden, Norway, and Holland. By a stroke of luck, the Danes were shooting a musical film at the time of Armstrong's visit and decided to film a set of three tunes by him and his band in a straightforward performance on a concert stage, without gimmicks. The sequence is perhaps the best Armstrong on film because it was filmed "live," not with the customary synchronized sound. Since he never did anything exactly the same way twice, Armstrong in dubbed sound is not quite right. A partial transcription of a concert broadcast from Sweden also survives. Because Armstrong would not visit a recording studio again until a full year later, documentation of these performances is very important.

Armstrong's reception in Copenhagen, was the most enthusiastic he had yet received. A crowd estimated by the unhyperbolic Danes at some ten thousand awaited his arrival at the main train station on October 19, 1933. There was a band, a sea of flowers, and a motorcade. Not until after World War II would he again experience a comparable public demonstration of affection, and he was very moved and surprised—at first, he thought the crowd was waiting for someone else.

From April to October 1934 Armstrong took the longest vacation of his life. He rented an apartment in Paris and enjoyed the

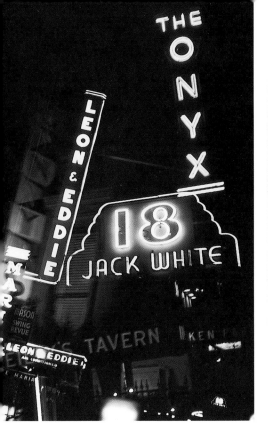

companionship of fellow Americans there, as well as such locals as Gypsy guitarist Django Reinhardt, who idolized Louis. (It was an Armstrong record, "Dallas Blues," that led Django to jazz.) With yet another manager—N. J. Canetti, who had ties to the record industry—Louis reorganized a band. This time, they made records in Paris, followed by a series of concerts at the Salle Pleyel in early November. (At the first of these concerts he had to take so many curtain calls that he'd changed into his bathrobe by the time he came back on stage for the last bow.) They performed in Belgium, Switzerland, and Italy, and then Armstrong quarreled with Canetti and abruptly decided to return home, arriving in New York in late January 1935.

Clearly Armstrong had experienced problems with managers. Collins was an unsavory character. Even though he had extricated his client from potentially serious trouble with gangsters (in 1931, while appearing in Chicago, Armstrong was visited in his dressing room by a notorious gunman who at gunpoint ordered him to return promptly to New York; Collins spirited Louis and the band off on an impromptu southern tour), Collins was probably a small-time gangster himself. When he was dismissed, he threatened that Louis would never work in his homeland again. Conversely, Canetti claimed breach of contract when the trumpeter suddenly left Europe, though he later apologized.

Upon his return to the U.S., Armstrong had planned to again tour with Chick Webb's band, but Collins prevented this, claiming exclusive rights to Louis's professional services. To make matters worse, Lil, from whom Louis had been estranged since

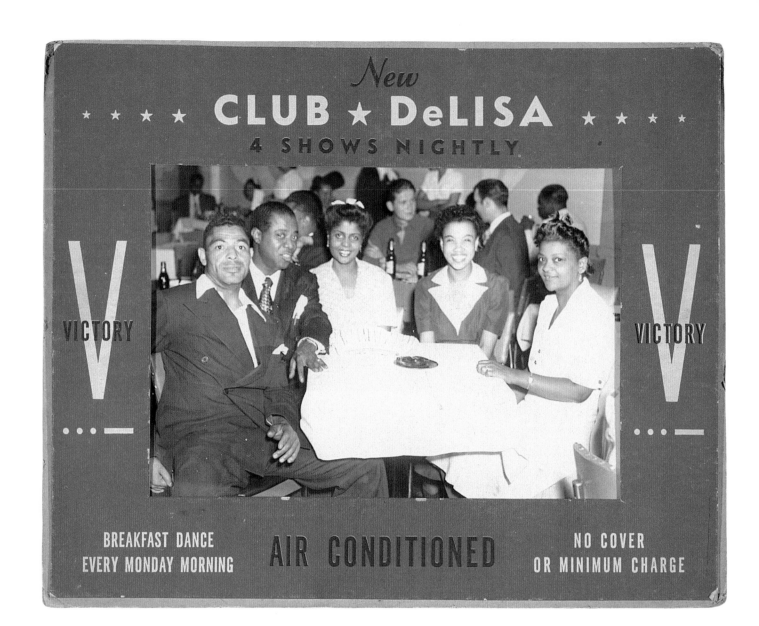

By the 1940s, photographers were a staple in jazz clubs, replacing the portrait sketch artists that had been popular in the 1920s and 1930s. At the Club DeLisa in Chicago, Armstrong joins his wife Lucille, "adopted" son Clarence, and other friends, c. 1943. Armstrong had been looking after Clarence, the child of his cousin Flora Miles, since her death in 1925. Louis Armstrong Archives, Queens College, City University of New York.

Jazz Is In (c. 1949) was painted by George Wettling, a jazz drummer who often played with Armstrong. Wettling learned painting from Stuart Davis in exchange for drum lessons. Collection of Hank O'Neal and Shelly Shier.

The All Stars

The late 1940s was an era of changes for jazz. Small clubs replaced larger theaters as jazz venues, and big swing orchestras gave way to small combos. As part of the trend, Armstrong disbanded his orchestra and formed the septet, Louis Armstrong All Stars.

Left: In 1948 Earl Hines, Armstrong's old Chicago friend and former Hot Five bandmate, joined the All Stars. Jack Teagarden's relationship with Armstrong also dated back to the 1920s. In a jazz world increasingly polarized between the new direction of bop and the traditional New Orleans/Chicago sound, Armstrong's All Stars were the leaders of the traditional wing. Courtesy Institute of Jazz Studies, Rutgers University.

Right: Photographer Robert Parent shows the original members of the All Stars in concert in Boston, 1947. Left to right: Dick Cary, Velma Middleton, Jack Teagarden, Armstrong, Barney Bigard, Big Sid Catlett, and Arvell Shaw. Courtesy Don Parent.

1929, sued him for sizable back maintenance. For the record, it was claimed that Louis was suffering from lip problems when questions arose about his prolonged inactivity, but problems with Collins, and perhaps the gangsters from the past as well, were the real reason.

Enter Glaser

At this low ebb in his career, Armstrong turned to an old acquaintance from Chicago. Joe Glaser, manager of the Sunset Cafe when Louis had starred there, proved to be the right man at the right time. Glaser came from a well-to-do family; his parents had wanted him to study medicine, but he preferred to hang out at the racetrack and enjoyed Chicago's flourishing night life. The Sunset was owned by relatives, who installed him as a manager. After the end of Prohibition, Glaser seems to have been at loose ends, so when Armstrong, whose artistry he admired, came to him for advice, the time was right for him as well. On the spot, the two men decided that Glaser would henceforth personally manage Armstrong. The relationship was unique; a handshake sufficed, and nothing was ever signed. Glaser took a desk in the offices of Rockwell-O'Keefe, a booking agency; Tommy Rockwell had worked for OKeh Records during Armstrong's tenure there, and indeed was responsible for his coming to New York in 1929. At first, Armstrong was Glaser's sole client. By June, he was back in front of a band, returned to New Orleans for another ballroom booking and warm welcome, with yet another parade, then proceeded to break attendance and salary records at Harlem's still-new Apollo Theater. A long-term booking at

Left: The changing personnel of the All Stars, seen onstage in Accra, Gold Coast (Ghana), in 1956, included veteran New Orleans clarinetist Edmond Hall and trombonist Trummy Young. Frank Driggs Collection.

Right: Singer Velma Middleton first joined Armstrong's big orchestra in 1942. Her stint with Armstrong's All Stars lasted until her death in 1961. Frank Driggs Collection.

Connie's Inn was obtained, and arrangements were made for Louis to front, once again, the Luis Russell Band. This time, the collaboration stuck (until late 1942); it also inaugurated a contract with Decca Records.

The Decca recordings began auspiciously with another Jimmy McHugh song, "I'm in the Mood for Love," and an interpretation of "You Are My Lucky Star" that contained a startling trumpet solo. The "new" Louis Armstrong of the Swing Era, introduced on these records, was a much more controlled and sober musician than the one heard prior to the second European stay. Along with more measured cadences came an almost majestic phraseology— utterly relaxed and rhythmically secure. The tone, burnished and mellow, was also imbued with new maturity. These new developments did not preclude flights of high-range fancy or startling ideas: "Lucky Star," for instance, was rendered in double time and the solo takes an oblique approach to harmony.

The singing, too, was "new"—insofar as Armstrong now took greater care to convey lyrics clearly. To be sure, he still throws in the "mamas" and the hummed or scatted asides and fills of yore. But his diction has a new clarity —without, however, a trace of affected "correctness." This is Louis's own voice, as always the most natural medium, but with a new discipline.

The Decca repertory was in the main oriented toward the desires of song publishers. Because Louis now was entering a new phase of popularity, however, he could be a bit more choosy than other artists, black or white. Louis also began to write songs again;

*Oh the Mardi Gras
The memories of Creole tunes
that filled the air
I dream of oleanders in June
and soon I'm wishing that I was there...
Do you know what it means
to miss New Orleans?*

Do You Know It Means to Miss New Orleans sung by
Louis Armstrong in the movie New Orleans (1947).
Lyrics by Eddie DeLange and music by Louis Alter.
Used by permission of Shapiro, Bernstein & Co., Inc
and The Songwriters Guild of America.

Top: During the years after World War II,
interest in the origins of jazz boomed.
Armstrong was increasingly associated with
New Orleans, the city where both he and jazz
were born. The connection received
worldwide exposure when Armstrong was
invited to be King Zulu at the 1949 Mardi Gras.
Photograph by Leonard Feather. Courtesy
Institute of Jazz Studies, Rutgers University.

Bottom: The Zulu Social Aid and Pleasure
Club was the first African-American group
to participate in New Orleans' Mardi Gras.
New Orleans Jazz Club Collections,
Louisiana State Museum.

ZULU SOCIAL AID
AND PLEASURE CLUB
—PRESENTS—
LOUIS ARMSTRONG
and his Esquire All Star Band

1949   1949

KING ZULU
Sunday, February 27th, 1949
BOOKER T. WASHINGTON
AUDITORIUM
DOORS OPEN 7:00 P. M.

his composition "Old Man Mose" was a hit record both for him and
for Eddie Duchin in 1936. Also in 1936 "Swing that Music" was
launched to coincide with the publication of his first book, the
rather heavily ghosted (but not uninformative) "autobiography" of
the same title. The song became a jazz standard. "If We Never Meet
Again" was an attractive Armstrong ballad.

An unusual 1937 collaboration between Louis (music) and
Ben Hecht (words) on the song "Red Cap" celebrated the members
of A. Philip Randolph's Sleeping Car and Pullman Porters' Union,
then the most powerful predominantly black union in the U.S. The
now largely forgotten Hecht was a man of many parts—novelist,
playwright, screenwriter, muckraking journalist, film director, and
political activist. "Red Cap" was his only known encounter with
jazz. It is a charming song that should be better known.

Louis also revisited some of his landmark recordings.
Best among these is the 1938 "Struttin' with Some Barbecue,"
with an excellent arrangement (by Chappie Willet) and a trumpet solo—first stating the melody with matchless accents, then
transforming it into something new and startling, and concluding
with a cadenza in which fingering and tonguing combine
uniquely. (In a late 1950s *Down Beat* panel on Armstrong,
trumpeters as stylistically and aesthetically polarized as Bobby
Hackett and Maynard Ferguson both cited the Decca "Barbecue" as a special favorite.)

Decca experimented with bringing together various
contract artists—a kind of precursor of the LP-era "sam-

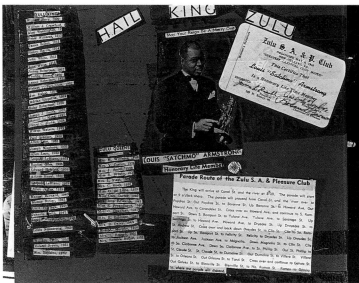

Left: Armstrong (center) wears King Zulu's traditional straw skirt and exaggerated blackface makeup. Photograph by Don Perry. New Orleans Jazz Club Collections, Louisiana State Museum.

It's been my lifetime ambition to become King of the Zulus some day...Even when I was a kid, I'd black my face [for Mardi Gras], pick up on some old raggedy clothes, and burlesque somebody.

Louis Armstrong, 1953

Right: A collage by Armstrong celebrates his role as King Zulu. Louis Armstrong Archives, Queens College, City University of New York.

pler." Sometimes the results were excellent: Louis and the Mills Brothers had several memorable encounters producing a little masterpiece with "Darling Nellie Gray." At other times, the pairings were a bit far-fetched, for instance, when Louis joined Andy Iona and his Islanders "On A Little Bamboo Bridge." Louis was also teamed with the Lynn Murray Mixed Choir to sing some spirituals, which produced a recorded document of racial stereotyping: on "Going to Shout All Over God's Heaven" the white chorus repeatedly sings "hebben," and Louis responds each time with a clearly articulated "heaven."

One of Louis's Decca milestones was the 1938 "When the Saints Go Marching In." The record was a hit, but it is seldom noted that this tune's entry into the jazz repertory dates from its release. It became the anthem of traditional jazz.

Clearing the Way

World War II took its toll on Armstrong's band, as it did on all the big orchestras. The recording ban imposed in 1942 by the musicians' union did not prove helpful to jazz and contributed to the already rising popularity of singers vis-à-vis big bands. Armstrong, typically, did a record number of engagements at military installations during the war, although these jobs did not pay as well as civilian ones, and travel and accommodations were often problematic. But Armstrong and Glaser shared a patriotic spirit; the trumpeter was especially keen on entertaining black men and women in uniform.

Glaser, meanwhile, had become an empire builder. He had established his own talent agency, Associated Booking Corporation,

The growing interest in the history of jazz was expressed in the work of visual artists. Palmer Hayden's *Basin Street* (1943) celebrates New Orleans with a combination of modern images and traditional motifs. Harmon Foundation, National Archives. (200-HN-HAY-P-7)

and expanded his roster from one to dozens of clients. Armstrong always came first, but Glaser was now the leading booker of black musical talent in the U.S., and thus in the world. While Armstrong gladly left everyday business matters and even most personnel and salary decisions to Glaser and his staff, he was far from a passive leader. For example, Armstrong himself hired one of the outstanding members of his 1944 band, tenorist Dexter Gordon (1923–90). He heard him at a Los Angeles jam session and invited him to join the band then and there, according to Gordon himself.[18] When Gordon eventually told him he wanted to quit, Armstrong immediately offered him a substantial raise.[19] The picture of Louis Armstrong as someone who let others run his band is distorted.

From 1945 on, bebop, later called modern jazz, gradually became dominant. Initially, as his hiring of Gordon (the premier modern tenor-sax stylist) indicates, Armstrong was not hostile toward the "new sounds," as its proponents soon called them. But bebop was as much an attitude as a music, and that attitude, too complex to analyze in detail here, triggered a war of words between traditionalists and modernists.

Ironically, the advent of modern jazz coincided with a rising interest in pre-Swing music, specifically New Orleans style. The resurgence of interest in early jazz was symbolized by the rediscovery of Bunk Johnson, a legendary New Orleans trumpeter who had left music around 1931 and was rumored to have played in Buddy Bolden's band. Johnson was also credited with having taught young Louis Armstrong, a bit of revisionist history that Louis did not

Raymond Steth's lithograph *Evolution of Swing* traces the history of jazz from the work songs of the old South to the modern sound of Swing carried to the nation through radio. Thè Metropolitan Museum, Gift of the Works Progress Administration, 1943, 43.46.54.

protest until after Johnson's death in 1949. Then Louis corrected the record: Bunk had been too busy drinking port wine and chasing women to pay attention to a kid wanting to learn to play trumpet, he said. Bunk did have a lovely tone, and little Louis had enjoyed listening to him. But his teacher? King Oliver, not Bunk.

Moldy Figs and Boppers

Bunk was a symbol; the traditional movement would have happened without him. In fact, the seeds were sown as early as 1938, when Tommy Ladnier (1900–39), Sidney Bechet, and Mezz Mezzrow (1899–1972) recorded in New York under the aegis of visiting French critic Hugues Panassie. The resultant music was a deliberate attempt—the first such—to recreate pre-Armstrong New Orleans jazz. By 1946, there were traditionalist revival bands, made up of mainly young white musicians, in both the U.S. and Europe.

The traditionalists were soon dubbed "moldy figs" by the moderns, to whom Armstrong increasingly became a symbol of the past—if not entirely from a musical standpoint, then certainly from a social one. Jazz journalists on both sides fanned the fires. Stung by the boppers' accusations of Uncle Tomming, the man who had so long been idolized by his fellow musicians and opened so many doors for jazz now spoke of "the modern malice" and warned that young trumpeters would quickly ruin their embouchures by attempting to follow in Dizzy Gillespie's musical footsteps. (Louis exempted Dizzy himself from criticism. They were then neighbors and on good personal terms, and their wives had been dancers together in nightclubs years before.)

Left: In the 1940s and 1950s photographers documented what remained of the original world of New Orleans jazz. Ralston Crawford's photographs of a 1958 funeral procession with the Eureka Brass Band are among more than 10,000 of his photographs documenting the city's musical traditions. Hogan Jazz Archive, Howard-Tilton Memorial Library, Tulane University, New Orleans, Louisiana.

Right: The second line (people following the procession) dance to the music on the way back from the cemetery. Photograph by Ralston Crawford, 1958. Hogan Jazz Archive, Howard-Tilton Memorial Library. Tulane University, New Orleans, Louisiana.

Them oldtime drummers [at New Orleans funerals], they just put a handkerchief under the snare on their drum and it go tunk-a, tunk-a, like a tom-tom effect. And when that body's in the ground, man...everybody gets together and they march back to their hall playing "When the Saints" or "Didn't He Ramble"...and they rejoice, you know, for the dead.

Louis Armstrong, *Life*, April 15, 1966

Ironically, Louis himself and his own big band were not at all immune from "modern" influences. On his first record issued after the recording ban was lifted, in early 1945, long-lined, harmonically complex trumpet playing characterizes both the sinister "Jodie Man" and the beautiful "I Wonder," a rhythm-and-blues ballad composed and recorded by the short-lived singer-pianist Cecil Gant. In a more traditional vein, Armstrong is in wonderful form on a V Disc date from a month before, which brought him together with Jack Teagarden and Bobby Hackett, and was a kind of preview of the Armstrong All Stars.

Such encounters with smaller groups not only offered an interesting contrast to Armstrong's everyday big-band work but also pointed toward the future. Armstrong was prominently featured in the 1947 film *New Orleans*, a rather hokey script about New Orleans at the time of Storyville's closing. Armstrong headed a band made up of Crescent City veterans Kid Ory, Bud Scott, and Zutty Singleton, performing traditional material—as well as the film's hit song, "Do You Know What It Means to Miss New Orleans." At the end, Louis is seen at Carnegie Hall with his 1946 big band, but the film's musical message clearly was that the good old days had been the golden ones.

The making of this film provided an opportunity for the critic, record producer, songwriter, and promoter Leonard Feather to organize a record date in Los Angeles that surrounded Louis with some of the players from the film's small group. It was a delightful session, with Armstrong in a relaxed mood on "Sugar" and "I Want a Little Girl," vocally and instrumentally.

Lee Friedlander's portraits of Crescent City musicians capture the aging face of New Orleans Jazz and the new respect for their historical roles which recharged the careers of many veteran musicians in the 1950s.

Top: Edmond Hall played with Armstrong's All Stars (1958). Courtesy Fraenkel Gallery, San Francisco.

Bottom: Johnny St. Cyr played banjo with Armstrong's Hot Five (1958). Courtesy Fraenkel Gallery, San Francisco.

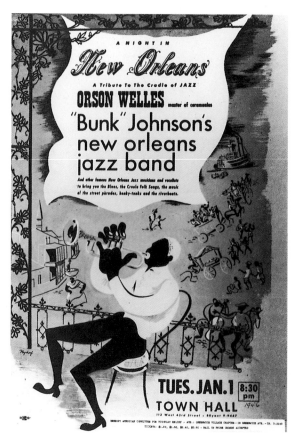

Left: The revived interest in traditional jazz was symbolized by the rediscovery of Bunk Johnson, the legendary New Orleans trumpeter who had once inspired Armstrong. In the early 1940s Johnson sent his portrait to Armstrong and thanked him for aiding his comeback. Louis Armstrong Archives, Queens College, City University of New York.

Right: A handbill for Bunk Johnson's concert at Town Hall, New York, January 1, 1946. Moorland-Spingarn Research Center, Howard University, Washington, D.C.

Feather kept nudging Louis and Glaser to present the trumpeter in New York in a small-group setting. (Like most critics, Feather hated Louis's big band, and though he was a champion of bebop, he also greatly valued Armstrong.) Eventually, Louis agreed, with the proviso that it be a two-part concert, with his big band also performing. The event took place at Carnegie Hall on February 8, 1947. Armstrong appeared with a working sextet led by a fellow New Orleanian, clarinetist Edmond Hall (1900–67), in a program of tunes long identified with Louis, among them "Lazy River," "You Rascal, You," "Muskrat Ramble," "Struttin' with Some Barbecue," and "Dippermouth Blues." Though Big Sid Catlett (1910–51) was brought in to beef up the big band, and Billie Holiday (1915–59) made a cameo appearance in the second half, the press (both jazz and lay) waxed ecstatic over the small group and panned the big band.

End of the Big Band

Asthetics aside, the big band had fallen on lean days. The asking price for the band had gone down to $750 for a one-nighter, less than half the going rate of a few years before, and although Louis was loathe to let sixteen men go, the handwriting was on the wall.

A concert at New York's Town Hall on May 17, 1947 (actually concerts, because a second event at midnight had to be added, so great was the demand for tickets) that included no trace of the big band proved decisive in eliminating the large ensembles from Armstrong's performance repertory. Jack Teagarden, Bobby Hackett, Sid Catlett, and other friends were featured. There was a recording device on the premises. What one hears is Armstrong in magnificent form, clearly inspired by the love that surrounded him, on the bandstand and in the packed house.

The big band was put on notice, and Glaser and Louis began to make plans for a small group. Three weeks later, Teagarden, Hackett, and some others joined Louis in the Victor studios for a session that produced a lovely first recording of Louis's own "Someday." When this group, called Louis Armstrong All Stars, made their debut at Billy Berg's Los Angeles club in August, a new chapter in the Louis Armstrong saga had begun.

The All Stars

Glaser had not been idle. First, seeing how well Louis and Jack Teagarden worked together, he had persuaded the trombonist-singer to get rid of *his* big band—a veritable millstone around Jack's neck which had gotten him deeply into dept. Clarinetist Barney Bigard had worked with Louis on the film, *New Orleans*; though he'd left Duke Ellington in 1942 to venture out on his own, he had most recently been a sideman in Kid Ory's band. It did not take much persuasion to make him join. Percussionist Big Sid Catlett was doing well free-lancing on 52nd Street and in the recording studios, where some recent associates had included Charlie Parker and Dizzy Gillespie, but he loved Louis and was ready to give him that special beat once again. On piano, the nod went to Dick Cary, who had been involved in the Town Hall concert, sketching out arrangements, doing a fine job as accompanist and occasional soloist, and generally making a good impression. Louis knew who he wanted on bass: a youngster who had been in his big band long enough to impress the leader with his solid time, big sound, and showmanship. Arvell Shaw (b.1923) was the baby of the All Stars, but in age only. The girl singer, as they said then, was also a given: Velma Middleton (1917–61) had been in Louis's big band since 1942, and they had a special relationship, working and personal.

It only took a while for the All Stars to find their groove. A concert recorded live in Boston in December 1947, and eventually issued on Decca, presents a mixture of individual features, en-semble numbers, Armstrong-Teagarden and Armstrong-Middleton duets, and evergreens from the Armstrong annals. This pretty well defined the musical profile of this most durable group, which lasted until the end of Armstrong's life.

The initial success of the All Stars was great when compared to the final years of Armstrong's big bands, but the group was not an overnight smash. There were ample bookings in leading jazz clubs and a first visit to Europe in the winter of 1948, for a star turn at the world's first international jazz festival in Nice. By then, the All Stars had become even more so: one of Joe Glaser's prime clients had decided to give up *his* big band, and thus Earl Hines was reunited with his old friend from the Chicago years.

Musically this reunion did not quite draw the sparks one

Left: Armstrong is reunited with Hot Five veterans Johnny St. Cyr and Kid Ory on the *Mark Twain,* a recreated Mississippi riverboat at Disneyland, 1962. Courtesy The Walt Disney Archives.

Right: Gene Johnson, *Design for Frontierland, Rivers of America (with Mark Twain),* 1983. © Disney, Loaned by Walt Disney Imagineering.

might have hoped for, though Hines was even more brilliant at the keyboard than he had been in the 1920s. Years of big-band work had clearly affected all the players in the group, and in a sense it was more a collection of soloists than a band with a style of its own. When Louis played lead, however, there was a special sound and feeling. There was never any doubt that he was in charge. In fact, as the drummer who replaced the ailing Catlett, the powerful Cozy Cole, once stated, Louis was active in the All Star performances "at least 80 percent of the time." He was featured on his own specialties, partnered the two other vocalists, led the ensembles front and back on the other instrumentalist's features, and did all the announcing.

Working Hard

As the All Stars settled into their routine, it became clear that this was one of the hardest-working bands in jazz history. Louis had been consumed by the work ethic all his life, and Glaser was a man to whom turning down a solid booking was a crime against nature. Consequently, the more in demand the All Stars became, the more they worked.

The public was blissfully unaware of how tired the All Stars might be when they hit the stage, because when Louis Armstrong hit, he put on a show that never let his audience down. "We got to keep it moving," he would say periodically, and keep it moving he did. Certain things, after the first few years, became set. Thus the opener—after the theme, "Sleepy Time Down South"—was always "Indiana," a fast-paced instrumental. From then on, until the

closing "Sleepy Time" reprise, the order would be whatever the leader felt was right under the specific circumstances—he had an acute sense of what an audience wanted. The band's repertory was always large, much larger than that of most organized jazz groups. While there were many warhorses, surprises were also frequent. Armstrong, a past master at pacing, ensured there were no dull spots, even when the sidemen were not of the highest caliber.

Personnel Changes

Personnel was surprisingly stable during the All Star's first decade. Catlett left in 1949 for health reasons. Earl Hines wasn't cut out for a sideman role (after all, he'd led his own bands from 1929 on) and had accepted it solely with Armstrong. Teagarden gained so much exposure from his All Star tenure that he would have been foolish not to seize the opportunity to front a similar group of his own, as he did from August 1951 until his death; reunions with Louis were frequent and always warm. The new permanent trombonist was Trummy Young (1912–84), who stayed for twelve years and was Armstrong's closest friend and strongest musical supporter in All Star history. Young was first replaced by "Big Chief" Russell Moore (1912–83), who stayed one year, and then by Tyree Glenn (1912–74), who stayed for six years—until the end. Hines's permanent replacement, Billy Kyle (1914–66), was another twelve-year man; unfortunately, sudden death ended his tenure. Bigard, the charter clarinet, remained until late 1956. His successor, Edmond Hall, was the best clarinet in All Star history; after him came the able but somewhat bland Peanuts Hucko (b.1918) and the excellent Buster Bailey (1902–67), then a succession of lesser lights; the final incumbent, Joe Muranyi (b.1928), knew what Armstrong represented and gave him all he had. Arvell Shaw left often, but always came back; among the other bassists, Buddy Catlett was the most gifted, Mort Herbert the most reliable. Drummers included Barrett Deems (b.1914), in for several key years and much better than the critics allowed, and Danny Barcelona (b.1929), who stayed from 1958 until the very end. No matter what the weak spots, the All Stars were held together by the leader, who in a very real sense could be the whole show when he had to.

That Armstrong sometimes did have to pull it all together was not proper but probably unavoidable. Great players who would have loved to work with Armstrong refused to risk their health by undertaking the All Star's notoriously grueling pace, even though the pay was good. The examples of Kyle and Bailey, who succumbed to the road—or at least so it seemed to their colleagues—were not encouraging. Perhaps even more poignant was the fate of Velma Middleton, whose devotion to Armstrong was legendary. She suffered a stroke during the All Stars' tour of Africa in 1961, and had to be left behind in a Sierra Leone hospital where she died three weeks later. Louis was an iron man, but at the 1959 Spoleto (Italy) Festival he fell ill, collapsing onstage. This bout with "indigestion" was almost certainly a heart episode, and although both patient

Left: A publicity photo by Popsie Randolph for the joint concert tour of Benny Goodman and Louis Armstrong in 1953. Frank Driggs Collection.

Right: Armstrong performing with Leonard Bernstein and the New York Philharmonic Orchestra, 1957. Frank Driggs Collection.

and doctors fluffed it off, it made front-page news throughout the world. Aside from China and the U.S.S.R., there was hardly a country in which the All Stars hadn't performed and made friends.

He was "Ambassador Satch," and mainly through his international popularity, jazz had become a valuable commodity in the cultural cold war. Because his example was such a diplomatic success, other jazz artists soon were hired by the U.S. State Department to make goodwill tours all over the globe.

Beyond the All Stars

The All Stars provided Armstrong's everyday musical environment, yet much of what the group might perform at a given moment was created outside of it. Starting in 1949, Armstrong frequently recorded with augmented All Star personnel, or without them entirely—with big bands, strings, choirs, and as in earlier days, in partnership with other stars. The All Stars' own records, many of them "live," almost never gained the popularity of such items as "Blueberry Hill," Louis's 1949 recording of a 1941 Gene Autry hit (which directly inspired Fats Domino's hugely successful 1956 version) or the 1951 "A Kiss To Build a Dream On," which was even more popular in Europe than at home. Armstrong's versatility encompassed the tender "La Vie En Rose" and from the film version of *Carousel*, "That's For Me," with a vocal that ranks among his finest. From his recordings with other stars, a remarkable "You Rascal, You" with Louis Jordan stands out; these two should have been paired more than once.

Perhaps Armstrong's ideal partner was Ella Fitzgerald, who was herself one of his greatest fans. Early gems from their first meeting on records (in 1944) include "Can Anyone Explain" and the sublime "Dream A Little Dream of Me." Their collaborations got under way in earnest when Norman Granz signed Ella for his Verve label, releasing the albums "Ella and Louis" and "Ella and Louis Again" in 1956 and 1957, followed by the lovingly produced and superbly packaged "Porgy and Bess" in 1957. Although Louis's trumpet was featured in these enterprises, the trumpet tour de force of this period was the four-LP "Autobiography," with recreations of 1920s and 1930s Armstrong masterpieces for Decca in 1956-57. Astonishingly, he managed in some of these recordings to surpass himself, as on "King of the Zulus" and "I Can't Give You Anything But Love." Even those critical voices that had dismissed Armstrong as a lasting creative force in jazz were silenced.

The All Stars also participated in two other notable recording ventures. Bringing together the two greatest names in jazz, Armstrong and Ellington, could have been even more impressive if it hadn't been planned and executed in haste. The two stars had briefly worked together on the 1961 film *Paris Blues*, which didn't utilize the Ellington band. Neither did this union: the All Stars (to which ex-Ellingtonian Barney Bigard had briefly returned) were joined by Ellington on piano. Though he was suffering from sore lips, Louis played as beautifully as he sang, learning tunes by Ellington he'd never heard before and making them his own. The pianist-composer Dave Brubeck (b. 1920) had conceived a kind of

Left: "Louis Armstrong's Own Original Tunes, Swing Song Folio, with Trumpet Solos," Clarence Williams Music Publishing Co., Inc., New York, late 1930s. Historic New Orleans Collection, William Russell Collection.

Middle: "Lights Out (Close Your Eyes and Dream of Me)," Shapiro Bernstein & Co., 1935. Frank Driggs Collection.

Right: "That Lucky Old Sun," Robbins Music Corp., 1949. Private Collection, New York.

jazz oratorio, *The Real Ambassadors*, with Armstrong as the centerpiece. Again he mastered unfamiliar material with astonishing speed, including a lovely version of "Summer Song." Joining in this effort were singers Carmen McRae and Lambert, Hendricks, and Ross.

Much more traditional were Louis's recordings with the hugely popular Dukes of Dixieland, whose New Orleans-born coleaders treated him with love and respect. The compatibility of the group and their music yielded much better Louis than might have been anticipated, but his embouchure, which sometimes impaired his performance, was in splendid shape.

An example of Armstrong's ability to transform unexpected material was his 1955 recording of Kurt Weill's "Mack the Knife," the theme from *The Threepenny Opera*, which became a big hit. Louis noted that his childhood experiences in New Orleans made it easy for him to capture Mack's unsavory essence. The success of such All Stars albums as music by W.C. Handy (which was universally hailed) or Fats Waller (for whose music Armstrong had a genuine affinity) was dwarfed by the totally unexpected success of Armstrong's version of the rather unsophisticated but good-natured title song from a new 1962 Broadway show, "Hello Dolly."

For the recording of this song, and to give proper early 1900s period flavor, a banjoist was added to the All Stars. Two sides (the flip side was "I've Got a Lot of Living to Do") were quickly made and had almost been forgotten by Louis when the disc (a single) was released by Kapp Records in early 1963, with overdubbed strings. It was one of those things that can not be planned or manufactured:

an instant smash hit, soon constantly heard on the radio, in the street, everywhere. It knocked the Beatles from the number one perch on the Top Forty List that they had occupied for months, and it gave Armstrong tremendous pleasure as well as plenty to put in his bank account. Not even Barbra Streisand could do as much with "Hello Dolly," as the 1969 film version of the musical, in which she and Armstrong appear together, demonstrated. Only he knew how to make that song sound good, and he was stuck with it from then on—which bothered him not one bit. Few popular artists are granted such luck late in their careers.

In 1966 Louis's recording of "What a Wonderful World" became a number one hit in England and the continent and did fairly well at home. Another title song from a Broadway musical, "Cabaret," also did well for Louis in the following year. In 1968 he proved once again that he could work wonders with unlikely material on an album of Walt Disney songs, notably the dark and oddly ominous "Chim Chim Cheree." Although his trumpeting was, by earlier standards, somewhat impaired on this album, the musical message was almost overwhelming.

By September 1968, Louis was seriously ill and hospitalized. In October 1969, he returned to the studios, recording (vocally only—the trumpet forbidden by doctors) the theme song for a new James Bond film, "We Have All the Time in the World."

The Last Rites

The time remaining for Louis was considerably less. Fortunately, this period was mainly characterized by a long overdue outpouring

Left: "Mack the Knife," Harms, Inc., Publishers, 1955. Private Collection, New York.

Middle: "Cool Yule," Bregman, Vocco, and Conn, Inc., Publishers, 1950s. Sam DeVincent Collection of Illustrated American Sheet Music, c. 1790-1980, Archives Center, National Museum of American History.

Right: "What A Wonderful World," Valando Music, 1967. Frank Driggs Collection.

of love and affection from the so-called jazz community, which for once acted as such.

In May 1970 a recording session brought into the studio (in addition to a large complement of playing musicians) Miles Davis, Ornette Coleman, Chico Hamilton, Tony Bennett, Eddie Condon, Bobby Hackett, Ruby Braff, and a bunch of jazz critics, who took on the roles of backup singers. The results were issued on the LP *Louis Armstrong and his Friends.*

For his seventieth birthday, *Down Beat* magazine gathered tributes from ninety musicians, covering the entire spectrum of jazz, including voices that decades before might not have been so positive. Perhaps most interesting were the statements of modernist trumpeters Kenny Dorham (1924–72), Cal Massey (1928–72), and Thad Jones (1923–86) that Armstrong had been the cause of their taking up the instrument, when most critics had claimed his active influence was over by the early 1930s.

At the Newport Jazz Festival in July, there was a night of musical tributes to Louis from trumpeters including Hackett, Ray Nance, young Jimmy Owens, Joe Newman, Wild Bill Davison, and Dizzy Gillespie. The Eureka Brass Band came up from New Orleans to march for Louis, and Mahalia Jackson (a hometown girl) duetted with him on "Just a Closer Walk with Thee." The event, including backstage and rehearsal sequences, was filmed, and interview passages with Armstrong were later inserted. (Portions of this material have been shown on television and at special jazz film events.) And, of course, his performance included "Hello Dolly."

Armstrong still was not allowed to play trumpet, though friends knew he was practicing at home. In September, when the All Stars were reactivated for a two-week Las Vegas stand, according to Joe Muranyi, at the first rehearsal Louis played like a man possessed, In October he flew to England for a charity concert, and in late December, after a rare Christmas celebration at home, he was back in Las Vegas. In February he and Bing Crosby were reunited for the last time on David Frosts television show, doing "Blueberry Hill" together. There was not much trumpet playing on the show, but in his dressing room, Louis warmed up, with a mute in the bell, on "Pennies from Heaven." Those present will not forget that.

The All Stars played their final engagement in March 1971 at the Waldorf Astoria's Empire Room. Before that two-week stint ended, Louis was clearly ill and then suffered a heart attack. Released in May, he recuperated at home. On his birthday he was seen on a television newscast with trombonist Tyree Glenn of the All Stars at his side. Frail but smiling, he ventured a few notes of "Sleepy Time Down South" and told the visitors (and, of course, the world at large) that he would be back to entertain them soon. In the early morning of July 6, Louis Armstrong died peacefully in his sleep.

The Living Legacy

Wynton Marsalis, a young trumpeter from Louis's hometown who achieved sudden fame by dint of his unique combination of great jazz and classical skills, began to change the perception of the master among contemporary jazz musicians. By his example of performing Armstrong's music and insisting that the jazz tradition be honored by more than words, Marsalis brought some even younger trumpet acolytes to study Louis Armstrong.

As if there had not been enough Armstrong "firsts" during his lifetime, he made a posthumous encore. In the 1989 film *Good Morning, Vietnam*, the disc jockey hero plays many records, among them Armstrong's 1966 recording of "What a Wonderful World." The artist's name is not mentioned nor is his face seen. There is no trumpet—just that voice. On the strength of this unannounced performance, the record, quickly reissued, "charted," as they say in the music business, staying on Billboard's Top 100 for six weeks and reaching the number thirty-three spot without benefit of promotion. Louis would not have expected it. You see, he didn't know that he was immortal.

NOTES

1. Gunther Schuller, *Early Jazz: Its Roots and Musical Development* (New York: Oxford, 1968), 85.

2. Duke Ellington, *Music Is My Mistress*, (Garden City, N.Y.: Doubleday, 1973), 236.

3. Gary Giddens *Satchmo* (New York: Doubleday, 1988). 63.

4. Ibid.

5. Interview with the author, Corona, N.Y., 15 July 1965. Audiotape. Jazz Oral History Files, Institute of Jazz Studies, Rutgers University, Newark.

6. Riverside RLP12-120 (New York; Ben Grauer Productions, 1959).

7. Dan Morgenstern, "Armstrong at 65," *Downbeat*, 15 July 1965, 18.

8. Richard Meryman, *Louis Armstrong–A Self-Portrait* (New York: The Eakins Press, 1971), 32.

9. Ibid.

10. *Louis Armstrong's 50 Hot Choruses for Cornet*, and *Louis Armstrong's 125 Jazz Breaks for Cornet*, (Chicago: Melrose Bros. Music Company, 1927)

11. Schuller, op. cit.

12. Ibid., 86.

13. Joshua Berrett, "Louis Armstrong and Opera," *Musical Quarterly*, 76 no. 2 (1992).

14. Berrett credits Lewis Porter with first pointing this out.

15. Schuller, op. cit., 126.

16. Meryman, op. cit., 40.

17. Interview with the author for *Satchmo*, videocassette in Masters of American Music Series, New York, 1988.

18. Ibid.

19. *Satchmo*, CBS Music Video, 1986 videocassette. Gordon was a member of Armstrong's band for about six months in 1944. He did not accept the offer of a raise because he was determined to join the Billy Eckstine Band.

4 Louis Armstrong: The Films

Donald Bogle

The 1947 film *New Orleans* is a dreary pedestrian mess. Although this story is supposedly about jazz's rise to mainstream acceptance, the real jazz innovators—Louis Armstrong and Billie Holiday—are neatly relegated to the sidelines while the plot follows the lives of the lead white characters, who are uniformly bland. Armstrong comes on for musical sequences and some playful comic dialogue, and Holiday is cast as a dippy maid named Endie who likes tinkering around at the piano and, so we are to believe, just happens to sing.

In a few key sequences in *New Orleans*, the nonsense ends and everything suddenly comes alive. In one, Holiday discards her maid's uniform and stands by a piano with a group of musicians, including Armstrong on trumpet, to perform "Do You Know What It Means To Miss New Orleans." Later the two reappear to perform "The Blues Are Brewing." These are sweetly rapturous moments. When they are free simply to do the thing they are best at—perform their music—Armstrong and Holiday are splendid together: an elegant, assured, luminous pair. And, of course, whenever Armstrong does take to his horn, backed by his orchestra, he's in top form.

Louis Armstrong's fine musical sequences in *New Orleans* may well redeem his checkered film career. While Holiday appeared only in this one feature film (and in the 1935 musical short *Symphony in Black*), Armstrong appeared in twenty-four American films from 1931 to 1969. In the 1950s and 1960s, he also performed on numerous television programs. Movies broadened his fame and enabled him to reach a huge audience that otherwise might have

Armstrong as the trumpeter to the devil in *Cabin in the Sky* (MGM Pictures, 1943). Louis Armstrong Archives, Queens College, City University of New York.

147

Left: Popular music's place in film was assured when *The Jazz Singer* (Warner Brothers, 1927) launched the era of sound. But with Al Jolson, the movie's star, playing a minstrel in blackface, the film also demonstrated the restrictive environment that black performers would encounter in Hollywood. Photofest.

Right: Having helped transform American music, dance, and comedy, African-American performers made their film debut in the all- black musical *Hearts in Dixie* (Fox, 1929). Courtesy John Kisch Separate Cinema Collection.

known nothing about either him or jazz. These films preserve some invaluable glimpses of his live performance. Although he was the most successful jazz musician ever to work in movies, Hollywood often did not serve Louis Armstrong well; his film work distorted his accomplishments and his place in cultural history.

For the mass audience, especially a later generation of African-Americans who did not experience Armstrong as a brilliant musical innovator during the 1920s and 1930s, his films and later television work have formed a deep impression and an image that still rankles sensibilities and remains a source of criticism and controversy. For many, his movie and television image is an all-grinning, all-mugging, ever-cheerful minstrellike figure who with unabashed glee performs corny, knuckle-headed routines—singing "Jeepers Creepers" to a horse or playing a character who can barely add two and two.

The screen image of that other jazz master Duke Ellington was a composed, controlled sophisticate, whereas the movies often seemed to have turned Armstrong into a misunderstood clown icon. Looking at his films today, it is sometimes hard to see the artist within the entertainer.

Yet audiences remain intrigued by Armstrong perhaps because each of his appearances is distinguished by his superb musicianship and killer energy, which when fused with his unwavering commitment to his work and one-of-a-kind enthusiasm, endow him with an almost mythic power and resonance. Love him or hate him, he is unfailingly mesmerizing.

Hollywood offered African-American performers a limited range of roles. As a servant tending to Shirley Temple in *The Little Colonel* (1935), Bill "Bojangles" Robinson's film persona was very different from his glamorous stage image. Photofest.

Armstrong's movie work falls into various categories. For the most part, he performed specialty acts: musical segments in feature films. He might unexpectedly appear in a nightclub setting where he would perform a number or two and then vanish as the plot proceeded. Such films were less damaging to Armstrong because he simply played the music that made him famous.

In others, Armstrong was cast in settings and situations that conformed to then-accepted notions (reassuring perhaps to white audiences) of the Negro as a nonthreatening, childlike figure or that otherwise distorted African-American culture and experiences. In such features as *Pennies From Heaven* (1936) and *Going Places* (1938), Armstrong was saddled with dim-witted dialogue and played stereotyped characters: easygoing, ever-helpful, rather naive, and genial fellows at the beck and call of a white hero.

In such short films as *A Rhapsody in Black and Blue* (1932), Armstrong the star performed his hits but again was sometimes entangled in stereotyped conceptions about African-American life.

Concert footage captured the best of Armstrong, as did the documentary *Satchmo the Great* (1957), in which audiences were granted a personal yet elusively brief look at the remarkable, heroic man behind the legend. These are among Armstrong's most compelling film appearances.

Armstrong began to work in the movies during the Depression, shortly after he made his first trip to the West Coast for appearances at Culver City's Cotton Club in 1930. Having made his reputation in New Orleans, Chicago, and New York, Armstrong was already an established

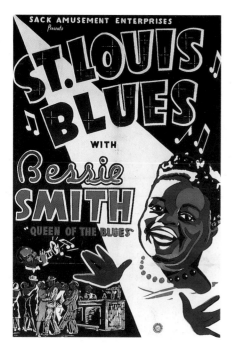

Top: Jazz music and dance were featured in the ten-minute film shorts that screened before the main feature. *St. Louis Blues* (Sack Amusement Enterprises, 1929) featured Bessie Smith. Courtesy John Kisch Separate Cinema Collection.

Bottom: Duke Ellington and his Cotton Club Orchestra were the stars of the short *Black and Tan* (RKO Radio Pictures, 1929). Courtesy John Kisch Separate Cinema Collection.

recording and nightclub star. It didn't take Hollywood long to take note, and within the next year, he appeared in his first film.

In a paradoxical way, he arrived in Hollywood at the absolute right moment: when the movies had just learned to talk and a call went out for black performers. In earlier decades, African-American actors and actresses had mostly been shut out of Hollywood. White actors in blackface were summoned to play important black characters in early shorts and in D. W. Griffith's 1915 *The Birth of A Nation*. But that situation changed when Al Jolson (1886–1950), in blackface, swung his arms, twisted his body, and sang "Mammy" in Warner Brothers' smash hit of 1927, *The Jazz Singer*. The sound of Jolson's voice flipped the movie industry on its head and effectively killed off the silent film. Audiences went mad for the new talkies. Across the nation, theaters were wired for sound. Studio executives in Hollywood, eager to cash in on the new medium, scrambled about for projects and new performers—with voices.

Since the early 1920s in urban centers around the country, black entertainers had transformed pop culture with race records, Broadway shows, and nightclub appearances. Black stars, including Ethel Waters, Duke Ellington, Florence Mills, Josephine Baker, Bessie Smith, and the comedy team of Flournoy Miller (1887–1971) and Aubrey Lyles (1884–1932), invigorated popular entertainment with their glamorous and individualized styles, their high flying energy, and their dazzling personas. The Negro as entertainer had entered the cultural mainstream with a unique rhythm and sound and was now an acceptable showbiz commodity.

None of this was lost on Hollywood, which in 1929 released two black musicals, *Hearts in Dixie* and *Hallelujah*. These films spotlighted such African-American talents as Nina Mae McKinney (1913–1967), Daniel Haynes (1894–1954), blues singer Victoria Spivey (1907–1976), Clarence Muse (1889–1979), and that much-maligned marvel of movement and sound Stepin Fetchit (b. 1902). That same year, a slinky Ethel Waters performed her magic on the silver screen with two numbers in *On With the Show*. A hefty sensual Bessie Smith starred in the short *St. Louis Blues*. In *Black and Tan*, Duke Ellington, suave as ever, even something of a romantic hero, cut a dashing figure opposite an iridescent Fredi Washington (b. 1903).

For critic Robert Benchley, black voices marked the salvation of American cinema.

> There is a quality in the Negro voice, an ease in its delivery and a sense of timing in reading the lines which make it the ideal medium for the talking-picture. What white actors are going to do to compete with it is their business. So long as there are enough Negroes to make pictures, and enough good stories for them to act in, the future of the talking-picture is assured.[1]

In this review of *Hearts in Dixie* for the Urban League publication *Opportunity*, Benchley also enthusiastically noted, "It may be that the talking-movies must be participated in exclusively by Ne-

In the musical short *A Rhapsody in Black and Blue* (Paramount Pictures, 1932), Armstrong is weighed down with a silly costume, soap bubbles, and a cardboard set. He rises above it all through the power of his music and knowing looks that mock the whole proceeding. Frank Driggs Collection.

groes, but, if so, then so be it. In the Negro the sound-picture has found its ideal protagonist."[2] That did not happen. When both *Hearts in Dixie* and *Hallelujah* failed to drum up business at the box office, Hollywood retreated from making films with all-black casts until 1936 when Warner Brothers took a chance on *Green Pastures*, which had already been a great popular and critical success on Broadway.

Yet after this initial explosion, a spot in the Hollywood market place of the 1930s was reserved for the Negro—and not just as a musical performer. Black actors and actresses finally had a chance to work with a degree of regularity. More often than not, though, they ended up playing comic servants: ditzy maids, baffled butlers, bug-eyed bootblacks, busboys, and waiters, who might perform an outlandishly funny antic or mangle the English language. Or they played faithful companions or loyal buddies to the white stars, be it Jean Harlow or Clark Gable, Bing Crosby or Marlene Dietrich, Will Rogers or Claudette Colbert.

Sometimes performers from the theater and clubs found their personas completely altered in the movies. During his years as a vaudeville headliner, dancer Bill "Bojangles" Robinson, who was Armstrong's favorite performer, was the consummate entertainer: supremely talented, dapper, polished, exuding always a cool, urbane savoir faire. In *Hooray for Love* (1935), Bojangles simply danced, but in his best-known movies, *The Little Colonel* (1935) and *The Littlest Rebel* (1935), he played an ever-loyal, tirelessly agreeable, submissive buddy to little Shirley Temple. Such movies robbed Bojangles of his autonomy and sleek control, much of his professional persona. In

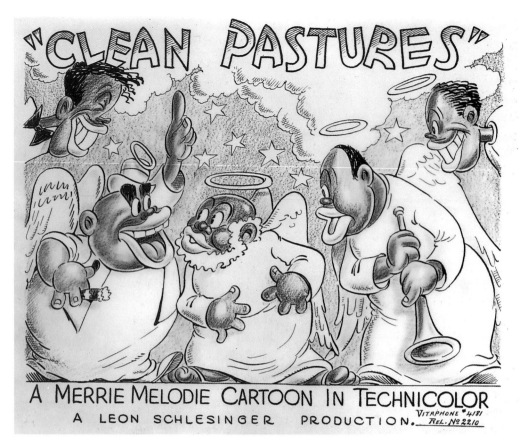

A MERRIE MELODIE CARTOON IN TECHNICOLOR
A LEON SCHLESINGER PRODUCTION. *Vitaphone #4181 Rel. Nº 2210*

Top: Armstrong's popularity in the 1930s is reflected in the many animated cartoons featuring his character. Animated versions of Armstrong and Fats Waller appeared in *Clean Pastures* (Warner Brothers, 1937), a takeoff on the hit Broadway play and movie *Green Pastures.* Wisconsin Center for Film and Theater Research.

Bottom: Armstrong, Cab Calloway, and Stepin Fetchit were the cartoon stars of *Swing Wedding/Minnie the Moocher's Wedding Day* (MGM Pictures, 1937), a cartoon based on Calloway's hit record. Courtesy Academy of Motion Picture Arts and Sciences. Permission Turner Entertainment Co.

character roles, Armstrong, too, was cast in much the same way—and with similar effects.

Other impressive African-American talents who worked in Hollywood in the Depression years included: Stepin Fetchit, Mantan Moreland (1902–1973), Butterfly McQueen (b. 1911), Willie Best (1916–1962), Hattie McDaniel (1895–1962), Clarence Muse, Theresa Harris, Madame Sul-Te-Wan (1873–1959), Eddie "Rochester" Anderson (b.1905), Louise Beavers (1902–1962), and even Paul Robeson.

Appalling as their servant roles were, the performers themselves were often highly individual talents who knew how to milk a line for all it was worth, who mastered the double take, and who audaciously stole scenes. Their offbeat, upbeat interpretive skills enabled them—sometimes intuitively, sometimes consciously—to transcend the distortions and shocking stereotypes and to deliver surprisingly ironic, quick-witted performances.

Interestingly, performers like McDaniel, Anderson, McQueen, and Robeson did have distinctive sounds: voices unlike any that had ever been heard before. Immediately recognizable, these voices caught the audience's ears and also established a trademark identity for each performer. Armstrong also had a unique voice and sound—gravelly, husky, scatty, optimistic, energetic, warm—that became a favorite during the talkie era.

That distinctive Armstrong sound was certainly displayed in his first film *Ex-Flame* (1931), which is now lost. Armstrong no

Top: In *Pennies from Heaven* (Columbia Pictures, 1936), Armstrong both acts and performs music. The show business magazine *Variety* noted, "Best individual impression is by Louis Armstrong...not as an eccentric musician but as a Negro comedian he suggests possibilities." Photofest.

Bottom: A storyboard shows the Haunted House Cafe in *Pennies From Heaven*. Armstrong's performance of "Skeleton in the Closet" was a highlight of the film, but it was enmeshed in racial stereotypes playing on the old notion of Negro superstition. Norman Z. McLeod Collection, Margaret Herrick Library, Academy of Motion Picture Arts and Sciences.

doubt was brought in along with his orchestra in the hope that they could jazz up the action and inject some much-needed energy in an otherwise tepid melodrama. Nothing could save *Ex-Flame*, on which the critics pounced. *The New York Times* panned the film's "mediocre direction and an embarrassingly old-fashioned psychology."[3] Armstrong was not even mentioned. In its review, *Variety* listed Armstrong in the credits and noted that the film had "a colored jazz orchestra" and that "the comedy is as slight as the orchestra leader made it." Otherwise it had nothing to say about him.[4] Not an auspicious debut.

A year later Armstrong was back in front of the cameras, appearing as himself in a black musical short (that has since become a classic simply because Armstrong is in it) called *A Rhapsody in Black and Blue*. Armstrong's above-the-title billing in the opening credits certified his stardom. The film's mix of domestic harangue, lively popular music, and a rigidly stereotyped set of images are, however, are an unfortunate setting for his talents.

A Rhapsody in Black and Blue opens with a record spinning on a Victrola™ while a man taps to the beat with drumsticks, clearly too caught up, so we soon realize, in the giddy excitement of listening to Louis Armstrong to be aware of anything else. That is, until his moment of musical bliss is interrupted by his wife—heavyset, dowdy, quarrelsome, and ready for a fight—who, upon entering the room, immediately berates him. She calls him a

American racism was manifest in the controversy surrounding Armstrong and Martha Raye's performance of "Public Melody Number One" in the film *Artists and Models* (Paramount Pictures, 1937). *Variety* (August 4, 1937) tut-tutted, "This intermingling of the races isn't wise...It may hurt her personally." The sequence was cut from the film in many Southern states. Raye photo: Photofest; Armstrong photo: Courtesy Academy of Motion Picture Arts and Sciences.

"great big hunk of unemployment" and warns "Looka here, it's the last time I'm going to tell you to kick your ear from that jazz box and jazz that mop around the floor." With little other choice, the husband soaks the mop in a pail of sudsy water, then begins mopping the floor. But once his wife leaves the room, he's back listening to the record.

The sequence conforms to the traditional stereotypes of African-Americans in films: the hardworking, long-suffering, crankily domineering black woman in conflict with her triflin', good-for-nothing, lazy man. This scene was played out repeatedly in movies of the time: *Judge Priest* (1934), in which the industrious Hattie McDaniel goes about her kitchen work while Stepin Fetchit sits around playing his harmonica, and perhaps most notably in *Show Boat* (1936) with McDaniel and Paul Robeson. The music itself is cast as both solace and something of the devil's doings: in *Show Boat*, after McDaniel scolds Robeson as "the laziest man that ever lived on this river," he wants merely to whittle but finds real relief from domestic tensions and obligations by singing "Ol' Man River."

In *A Rhapsody in Black and Blue*, Armstrong's music prevents the husband from fulfilling his responsibilities, but it also transports him away from it all. When the man persists in listening to the jazz box, the wife hits him over the head with the mop, and the poor guy passes out. Unconscious, he dreams of the court of Jazzmania where he emerges dressed as an emperor with an attendant. In this world, any wish or pleasure is immediately gratified. There to perform for the new monarch is the one and only Louis

In *Every Day's A Holiday* (Paramount Pictures, 1937), Armstrong leads a street parade in a rendition of "Jubilee." Louis Armstrong Archives, Queens College, City University of New York.

Armstrong, dressed in a leopard cloth and standing in a floor of suds, with his orchestra in the background. Grinning throughout and sometimes widening his eyes, mugging it up almost shamelessly, Armstrong performs "I'll Be Glad When You're Dead, You Rascal, You" and "Shine."

For contemporary audiences, some of the exaggerated expressions and movements seem a carryover from the nineteenth-century minstrel tradition, in which white males, made up in blackface with broad grins painted on their faces, mocked and cruelly caricatured the antics, movements, language, attitudes, and very rhythm of African-Americans. Some lyrics, too—"When you're laying six feet deep/No more chicken will you eat" (from "I'll Be Glad When You're Dead You, Rascal, You")—reinforce long-held stereotyped images of the Negro. In *A Rhapsody in Black and Blue*, Armstrong seems too obviously to be performing, almost as if he were on stage, without the subtlety and fluidity that film demands. But with undaunted energy and enthusiasm and a very knowing and shrewd manner that seems part-parody, he carries the material off.

He playfully works the lyrics. "I brought you in my home/You wouldn't leave my wife alone/I'll be glad when you're dead, you rascal, you," he sings in this tale of a man whose wife has taken a fancy to another, presumably a friend of his. Then he turns up some heat with the double entendre, "You bought my wife a bottle of Coca-Cola/So you could play on her Victrola/You old dog, you." It is a funny and surprisingly sexy song, performed with vigor and insight in an age when black male sexuality was far too great a

Opposite

Top: In *Going Places* (Warner Brothers, 1938), Armstrong sings "Jeepers Creepers" to a horse. The set-up is blatantly dopey, but Armstrong pulls it off by making it seem totally natural. He actually seems to communicate with the animal. The song was nominated for an Academy Award. Warner Brothers Archives, University of Southern California, Los Angeles, Permission Turner Entertainment Co.

Bottom: Armstrong performed "Mutiny in the Nursery" with Maxine Sullivan and the Dandridge Sisters in the movie *Going Places*. Courtesy John Kisch Separate Cinema Collection.

threat to be presented on screen. In one respect, his humor neutralizes any fears about black sexuality, but Armstrong's rendering creates a sly man of the world, far more knowledgeable than he may first appear, from what could have been a simple stereotype.

The lyrics of his second number, "Shine," repeat the image of the stoic, happy-go-lucky darky, unphased by problems and very much satisfied with his lot in life. "Just because my hair is curly/Just because my teeth are pearly/Just because I wear a smile," he sings, later adding, "Just because I'm glad I'm living/I takes all my troubles with a smile. . . .That's why they call me Shine."

When he puts the lyrics aside to take up his trumpet, he is transformed right before our eyes. For now his communication—intense, personal, demanding, imaginative, honest—is with his horn. His eyes close, and he's at one with his instrument. Part of Armstrong has forgotten the audience. In these moments, there is something so real, so pure, so sublime that he takes us with him as he transcends the sequence, the very nature and concept of the film itself, and makes us forget the hackneyed setting. Indeed he has left it behind and takes the viewer into his world where he is the true emperor.

The type of material, setting, and performance seen in *A Rhapsody in Black and Blue*—so jarring to audiences today—was a staple of old-style black theatre and ethnic comedy. (Maybe that's why the film was not greatly criticized when first released.) The early Williams and Walker all-black productions, Sissle and Blake's/Miller and Lyles' *Shuffle Along* as well as *Runnin' Wild*, *Chocolate Dandies* all made use of similar exaggerations. As did later such race movies—all black cast films independently produced outside of Hollywood and made especially for African-American audiences—as *Killer Diller* (1948), *Boarding House Blues* (1948), *Juke Joint* (1947) and *Boy! What A Girl* (1946). So, too, did such comics as Moms Mabley (1897–1975), Pigmeat Markham (1906–1981), and Dusty Fletcher when they carried on at the Apollo or some club on the old chitlin circuit. This fast-moving, rambunctious, sometimes raucous and rowdy style, characterized by eye pops, thick dialects, broad gestures, and stylized theatrical mugging, is far different in spirit from the uninformed and sometimes vicious mockery of the white minstrels who understood nothing about black cultural experience.

Black performers' intonations, inflections, double takes were pitched to a black audience (even when the audience was integrated) that understood and enjoyed the performances as entertaining social comment, far-flung parody, and on occasion pointed satire. When this material was transferred to mainstream movies, it was lifted out of its cultural context and lost a distinct set of cultural references as well as the recognition by the audience that these shenanigans were but *one* comment on but *one* aspect of the African-American experience.

Because this type of comic exaggeration (via the comic

157

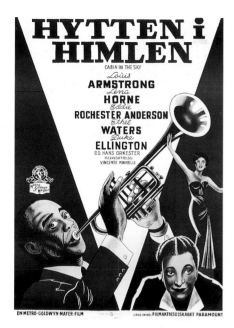

Although Armstrong only had a brief role in *Cabin in the Sky*, he got top billing on a Danish poster. Courtesy John Kisch Separate Cinema Collection.

servants) was just about the only depiction in Hollywood films of the black experience: shown without any counterbalancing image and without its cultural context, such antics made a shocking and inaccurate statement on black America. This aspect of black performers' work was no longer viewed as satire but perceived as a truth.

In some respects, Armstrong himself, as an early crossover star, was lifted out of a cultural context. At the start of his career, Armstrong's following was solely African-American. For that audience, he had talent to burn. An innovative musician, he could also get laughs with his highly personalized clownery. In the early years of Armstrong's career, black audiences did not greatly object to his mugging and the stylized persona he projected. After all, Armstrong's favorite comic Bert Williams went onstage in blackface and spoke with an exaggerated dialect. While Armstrong objected to the blackface tradition, he saw nothing wrong with ethnic humor and old-style ethnic images. Once his fame grew to the point where he was a favorite of integrated and finally white audiences, Armstrong remained true to the type of entertainment he had grown up with.

Perhaps Armstrong did not give enough serious thought to how another culture perceived him. For a large segment of the white audience, he was not simply entertaining and jiving it up (as he had initially been perceived by a black audience); instead, he represented an ever-enthusiastic, nonthreatening, friendly figure who did not challenge their assumptions on race or racial superiority—except when he played his instrument. This was to be the sour chord in Armstrong's film (and television) work, particularly in the post-World War II period.

Armstrong performed the song "I'll Be Glad When You're Dead, You Rascal, You" in another Hollywood short: Max Fleischer's 1932 Betty Boop cartoon named after the song. Armstrong appears with his orchestra in a brief live-action opening sequence. Once the animation begins, Betty Boop and her assistants Bimbo and Ko Ko are shown venturing onto the dark continent of Africa, which is populated by spear-chucking natives who seemed to grow right out of the bushes. At one point, Bimbo and Ko Ko sit in a cauldron with flames licking its sides surrounded by natives ready for a meal. In another scene, the two are pursued by a native whose head (with exaggerated thick lips, nose, and tongue) is shown in the upper corner of the screen; the face is an animated version of Armstrong's. As he sings the title song, shots of the animated Armstrong are interspersed with live-action shots of Armstrong's head, still in the upper corner of the screen. As he sings, the Bimbo and Ko Ko run off in fear.

Poor, curvaceous Betty is later tied suggestively to a pole while also surrounded by the hungry natives, one of whom carries a trumpet, all of whom are ready to feast on her. Once she escapes and runs off with her friends, she dodges the spears being thrown at her as music fills the background. The sequence suggests that

159

Louis Armstrong and His Orchestra—Trumpet King of Swing!

Armstrong performs "I Can't Give You Anything But Love" in *Jam Session* (Columbia Pictures, 1944). Courtesy John Kisch Separate Cinema Collection.

danger lurks not only in the savage natives (with their nasty phallic spears and pole) but also in the sexy, wicked song (and bandleader) that propels the action.

That Armstrong's image was animated and appeared in a cartoon indicates his popularity and widespread fame. White stars such as Gable and Garbo were satirized in cartoons. Few black stars were accorded such treatment. An animated Armstrong also appeared (along with animated versions of Fats Waller, Stepin Fetchit, Cab Calloway, and The Mills Brothers) in another cartoon called *Clean Pastures* (1937), a take off on the hit Broadway play and movie *Green Pastures*.

Depression-era movies often feature sequences in which characters from different stations, classes, and perspectives merge together in some shared experience, be it adversity or celebration. These scenes send a message to the audience that the very worst of times can be endured if people just stick together and offer one another a helping hand, that everyone has something to contribute. In the case of the Negro, that contribution might be some nifty homespun wisdom or some hilarious gaffe that alters a white character's point of view. Or it might simply be high spirits and optimism.

High spirits characterize Armstrong's appearance in the turn-of-the-century Mae West comedy *Every Day's A Holiday* (1937). He has little to do. In one sequence, he struts down the street with his horn, breezing past Mae West, who sits in a horse-drawn carriage with a gentleman friend. Others on the street perform somersaults and handstands. All seem giddy with excitement

Armstrong performs "When It's Sleepytime Down South" in a 1942 "soundie," a short-lived ancestor of the music video. Soundies were short films of musical performances, which could be played on special jukeboxes equipped with screens. Courtesy Institute of Jazz Studies, Rutgers University.

at the arrival of West. Armstrong adds energy and color to this street scene: a communal gathering that mixes races, classes, genders. Yet in this mix, racial lines remain in place. Armstrong can set the lively tone of the proceedings, but he's not going to hop into the car or the arms of Mae West.

In another communal celebration, Armstrong—dressed in white with a white helmet with plumes—joyously leads a street band parade in a rendition of "Jubilee." In both sequences, he's all energy and exuberance and terrific to watch. He does a dance step or two while playing his trumpet, with moves reminiscent of a New Orleans street–style funeral march. He accomplishes just what the filmmakers want: his energy really can send viewers soaring. In the "Jubilee" scene of *Every Day's A Holiday*, the Negro seems a part of society, not wholly removed in a world of his own.

In the comedy *Artists and Models* (1937), which stars Jack Benny and Ida Lupino, the Negro characters turn up only in a separate musical specialty sequence. The setting is Harlem, depicted as some faraway exotic land where high spirits reign; so, too, do an unbridled extrovertism and a sexually charged atmosphere. In the opening of this Harlem street scene, gunshots are heard and residents scatter. Climbing down a fire escape onto the street is white comedienne Martha Raye, dressed in a tight, sexy, satiny outfit and with her skin darkened. Armstrong appears alone, dressed like a gentleman dandy in suit and derby; as he blows his horn, its sound moves through the street like an all-consuming mist. As an ersatz red-hot mama, Martha Raye sings a warning "to

Louis Armstrong and Billie Holiday lend musical credibility to *New Orleans* (United Artists, 1947), a Hollywood pseudohistory about jazz's rise to mainstream acceptance. Photofest.

lock your door/draw your blind/why, you're in danger of the strangest kind." Raye swings her hips, shakes her shoulders, and contorts her body in an attempt to approximate the style of a black woman. With her burnt-cork complexion and caricatured sexy moves, the sequence has both a minstrel quality and a cartoonish sexuality.

The lyrics warn of the power of the music (and of course, the artist who performs it), which is "gonna sneak right up upon you/and kind of put the finger on you/so look out for Public Melody Number One." A G-man announces, "Let's start raiding every rhythm den" as if the music—jazz—is an epidemic overtaking these people of the street, but a smooth, growly Armstrong advises, "Ain't no use hidin'/I'm going to take you ridin'/Look out for Public Melody. . ."

In pure pop terms, the sequence uncovers fears about the powers of the musician. Armstrong himself emerges as both Rhythm Lord and Rhythm Outlaw. In its images of African-Americans scurrying about, eager for music, ready for dance, wary of the law, "Public Melody Number One" makes clear its lopsided, misconceived notions about race and cultural difference. The world of the dark others is isolated from the white characters and from the plot of the movie itself. In this world, the black characters (unlike the white characters in the rest of the film) are not defined by work or relationships but by their response to this uninhibited music. Yet the music itself is true and pure and authentic. Armstrong's rapport with his trumpet elevates him. While we may reject the setting as so much distorted nonsense, we cannot reject him.

The critic for *Variety* expressed concern about the teaming of Armstrong and Martha Raye:

Photojournalist Phil Stern captures Armstrong performing with New Orleans musicians Zutty Singleton, Kid Ory, and Bud Scott on the set of *New Orleans*. © Phil Stern Foto.

There are a couple of misguided sequences, one of which may react negatively to the future of Martha Raye whom the studio has developed into sizeable b.o. It's that 'Public Melody Number One' sequence, with Louis Armstrong tooting his trumpet against pseudo-musical gangster idea...While Miss Raye is under cork, this intermingling of the races isn't wise, especially as she lets herself go into the extremest manifestation of Harlemania torso-twisting and gyrations. It may hurt her personally.[5]

Of course, the critic seemed oblivious to the effect the stereotyped sequence might have on Armstrong's career. The very idea of inter-racial minglings, let alone couplings, was very much a topic of concern and controversy.

In his two important character roles of the 1930s, *Pennies from Heaven* (1936) and *Going Places* (1938), Armstrong, was cast as comic, rather dim-witted servant figures. Like other Depression-era films, the romantic comedy *Pennies from Heaven* dramatizes the plight of ordinary people enduring hard times but determined to survive through pluck and ingenuity. The hero Larry Poole, played by Bing Crosby, is a wandering troubadour of sorts who, recently released from prison, sets out to make something of himself. He converts an old house, said to be haunted, into a restaurant/nightclub that will specialize in serving chicken dinners. Crosby tries to turn adversity to his advantage by putting signs—designed like skeletons—along the highway to advertise the club. Although plucky, Crosby clearly needs all the help he can get.

One morning as Crosby stands outside the house while workers are busy trying to restore it, there appears—almost as if out of nowhere—a character named Henry, played by Armstrong. Neatly (almost nattily) dressed in a hat, sweater, open white shirt, and slacks, Armstrong's Henry is deferential as he greets Crosby with a "Good morning, Mr. Poole." Crosby wants him to perform at the new club. The two then exchange a round of dialogue that firmly locks Henry in place as a not-very-bright but quite accommodating fellow, the perfect ally and undercover servant figure for the hero:

> "You see I got the boys together and I told them you wanted us to play the music at the restaurant. And for that we'd get ten percent of the business," says Henry. "And that's where the trouble started."
>
> "Oh, well, Henry," asks Crosby, "don't you think ten percent is enough?"
>
> "Well, yes. And no," Henry says. "Maybe it's enough. And maybe it's too much. But you see, Mr Poole, there's seven men in the band. And none of us knows how to divide ten percent up by seven. So if you could only make it seven percent."
>
> Bing laughs, "Seven percent. Henry, it's a deal."
>
> Relieved and enthusiastic, Henry exclaims, "Oh, thank you, Mr. Poole, I told them cats you'd do the right thing."

Henry's loyal desire to help is revealed in another sequence built around the chickens. In an exchange confronting the question of how Crosby will feed his restaurant customers with two hens, Henry suggests he and his boys are willing to act as chicken thieves.

Not long afterward Armstrong performs his primary function in *Pennies from Heaven*: dazzling entertainment in a sequence in which race is part of both text and subtext. Inside the Haunted House Cafe, Armstrong, dapper in suit and tie, performs "Skeleton In the Closet." As he sings, Armstrong bugs his eyes overtime. When Armstrong blows his trumpet, the camera pans the restaurant packed with patrons. Then a skeleton dances in the audience. And a ghost pops up from a dinner table. That old debbil music sure can conjure up dem spirits! The choice of material ("Skeleton in the Closet") and the setting (the Haunted House Cafe) obviously play on familiar racial stereotypes: the old notions of Negro fear and superstition, and the image of the frightened Negro in the haunted house.

At the same time, *Pennies from Heaven* has no interest in Henry. We do not learn where he comes from, how he lives, what he is all about. Henry's presence and definition are basic and true to Hollywood's formula for dealing with Negro characters as little more than convenient marginal figures, who can help advance the plot or add tone and texture. Foremost, Henry provides some comic relief, lends his support to the hero, assuages any notions of Negro anger or dissatisfaction or threat, and finally provides the film's musical highlight.

Despite all this, how does Armstrong himself do?   Frankly, he acquits himself very well. Of *Pennies from Heaven*, *Variety* wrote: "Best individual impression is by Louis Armstrong, Negro cornetist

Although the film *Glory Alley* (MGM Pictures, 1952) is set in contemporary New Orleans, Armstrong plays a character who clearly harks back to an earlier time. Frank Driggs Collection.

and hi-de-ho expert. Not as an eccentric musician but as a Negro comedian he suggests possibilities. He toots his horn to a nice individual score, plus his band chores."[6] Armstrong handles it all with charm and reserve. Even when it appears as if Henry is about to go off to steal some chickens, Armstrong displays some initiative and the wherewithal to, like the hero, survive. The film itself may not give a hoot about Henry's existence apart from his relationship with the hero, but Armstrong is able to suggest another life. Once Henry leaves the screen, he does not leave our thoughts.

In the racehorse comedy *Going Places*, Armstrong—as the groom Gabe—again played a helpful, friendly comic fellow. Much of the movie's humor itself revolves around a racehorse, often reckless and uncontrollable, except when he hears the song "Jeepers Creepers." Naturally, it falls to Armstrong's Gabe to sing or plays the tune at precisely the right moments to calm the horse.

Gabe first turns up at an empty racetrack where he tries unsuccessfully to lead the racehorse, which runs off. Two white men who loiter about are amazed at the horse's breakneck speed. Armstrong reappears with a trumpet as he plays "Jeepers Creepers," one of the men calls out to Gabe,

> "Hey, Uncle Tom. In case you don't know it, your horse is running away."
>
> Gabe responds, "If there's anything that can stop that horse, it's this here trumpet."
>
> "You mean he's afraid of the trumpet?" the man asks.

SATCHMO THE GREAT

STARRING
LOUIS ARMSTRONG and EDWARD R. MURROW with Leonard Bernstein · W. C. Handy

Produced by EDWARD R. MURROW and FRED W. FRIENDLY · Released thru United Artists

Armstrong performs with the New York Philharmonic in Fred Friendly and Edward R. Murrow's feature film documentary, *Satchmo the Great* (United Artists, 1957). With sequences shot on four continents, the film captures Armstrong's transition from entertainer to cultural icon. Courtesy John Kisch Separate Cinema Collection.

"Oh, no, sir," Gabe says. But he sure likes this song. And I calls it by his name 'Jeepers Creepers.'"

"Jeepers Creepers! Uncle Tom is kidding us," says the second.

"Oh, no, sir, I ain't," Gabe says earnestly.

Of course, Armstrong's congenial Gabe shows no objection whatsoever to the racist address, "Uncle Tom." The film has no desire to create a character who might question or become angry about such a matter.

Shortly after this encounter, he is filmed singing "Jeepers Creepers" to the horse! It's a blatantly dopey but also, dare we admit it, vastly enjoyable sequence. Armstrong pulls it off because, splendidly self-contained and seemingly oblivious to what anyone might think, he actually seems to be communicating with the animal.

The big musical sequence in *Going Places* is the "Mutiny in the Nursery" number. Standing on the grounds of a palatial inn, Armstrong and his band perform and are soon joined by Maxine Sullivan (b. 1911) as a maid who just happens to sing, the Dandridge Sisters (Dorothy [1922-1965] and Vivian Dandridge [1921-1991] and their friend Etta Jones), and a lineup of musical extras. It's a lively, jaunty sequence replete with a play on nursery rhymes and high spirits. Some cockeyed semblance of a black community (albeit an escapist musical one) emerges briefly in this sequence. It provides Armstrong with a valid context: during this scene he is not some displaced personage without cultural connections as he is through most of this film and *Pennies from Heaven.*

166

SATCHMO THE GREAT

STARRING LOUIS ARMSTRONG and EDWARD R. MURROW with Leonard Bernstein · W. C. Handy

Produced by EDWARD R. MURROW and FRED W. FRIENDLY · Released thru United Artists

Satchmo the Great documents Armstrong's visit to the Gold Coast (Ghana) where 100,000 people attended his concert in Accra. Courtesy John Kisch Separate Cinema Collection.

How is Armstrong as an actor? Well, here as in *Pennies from Heaven*, he comes to acting without the experience or training of his contemporaries, who over the years mastered distinct comic personas. Stepin Fetchit perfected a stylized comic nihilism. Willie Best created a half-awake, half-asleep lazy mass of befuddlement. Mantan Moreland managed to be quick on his feet both with and without dialogue. Hattie McDaniel and Eddie "Rochester" Anderson (especially in his movies with Jack Benny) were known for their self-assurance and cocky outspokenness. Like these performers, Armstrong reveals that he understands a thing or two about playing to an audience and, aware of the effects and force of his personality, he's convincing precisely because of the shrewd manner in which he projects that personality rather than because of any gift for developing a character. (The roles are so skimpily written that there is really nothing to develop.)

Part of his effect, perhaps part of his charm, is the way in which he seems to operate in a sphere of his own. Like so many other black performers of the period, he has a persona strong enough to suggest for us another life apart from the seemingly benign yet racist world of the film—a life that the film unfortunately has no desire to dramatize, explore, or explain. There remains an irreducible part of Armstrong the actor, as there is of Hattie McDaniel and Eddie Anderson, that cannot be touched; there is a part of himself that he keeps unto himself. It is Armstrong we enjoy even while we may detest the films.

In 1942 Armstrong appeared in four "soundies": short films

167

"GREAT!"
—N. Y. TIMES

"A CLASSIC!"
—N. Y. DAILY NEWS

JAZZ
ON A
SUMMER'S DAY
*love on
a summer's
night!*

"EMBARRASSINGLY
INTIMATE!"
—SATURDAY REVIEW

Their songs and music set the magical mood—
LOUIS ARMSTRONG • MAHALIA JACKSON • GERRY MULLIGAN
DINAH WASHINGTON • GEORGE SHEARING • CHICO HAMILTON
ANITA O'DAY • JACK TEAGARDEN • THELONIUS MONK
A FILM BY BERT STERN • A GALAXY ATTRACTIONS PRESENTATION • A UNION FILMS RELEASE

COLOR BY DELUXE

Left: In the 1950s Armstrong appeared in ten feature films including *Beat Generation* (MGM Pictures, 1959). Courtesy Academy of Motion Picture Arts and Sciences. Permission Turner Entertainment Co.

Right: Armstrong and his All Stars are the stars of Bert Stern's visually rich *Jazz on a Summer's Day* (1958), a documentary of the Newport Jazz Festival. Courtesy John Kisch Separate Cinema Collection.

that were played on jukeboxes with small monitors, precursors of today's music videos. With his orchestra he performed, in fairly straightforward fashion, "Shine," "Swingin' On Nothing" (a lively version done with his vocalist Velma Middleton), and "I'll Be Glad When You're Dead, You Rascal, You." The fourth of these soundies, "When It's Sleepy Time Down South," has familiar stereotypical imagery.

The next year, he accepted a small role in Vincente Minnelli's all-black musical *Cabin in the Sky* (1943). Based on the Broadway show, this musical fantasy—a tale of an all-black heaven and an all-black hell fighting for the soul of Little Joe Jackson—featured some of the most famous black performers of that era: Ethel Waters, Eddie Anderson, Lena Horne (b. 1917), Rex Ingram (1875–1969), John Bubbles Sublett (b. 1902), Butterfly McQueen, Ruby Dandridge (b. 1904), Mantan Moreland, Willie Best, and Duke Ellington.

Armstrong appears only once. In a Hotel Hades sequence, he plays one of the devil's henchman who, along with a crew of others, plots a way to get Hell's clutches on Little Joe. It might best be called a comic coon sequence. But it's a lively, ensemble piece in which the actors play off one another perfectly, each aware he has to punch his lines for all they're worth.

Armstrong briefly blows his trumpet and has a bit of dialogue. Hamming it up with Mantan Moreland, Willie Best, and Rex Ingram—black actors well versed in the art of scene-stealing—Armstrong confidently holds his own. Director Minnelli mainly

Armstrong is reunited with Bing Crosby in *High Society* (MGM Pictures, 1956). Frank Driggs Collection.

makes use of Armstrong's by-now famous playful personality. Without his particular high-spirited extrovertism, Armstrong's character wouldn't exist.

The difference between Armstrong and his contemporary Duke Ellington, who also performs in *Cabin in the Sky*, is clearly seen, even though the two have no scenes together. Elegantly turned out and seated at a piano, Ellington plays his music in high style—and, of course, maintains his urbane dignity (just as Count Basie did in films) by not playing the kind of jester role that Armstrong accepted.

World War II marked a shift in Hollywood's depiction of African-Americans. In the early 1940s, Walter White, the Executive Secretary of the NAACP, journeyed from New York to Los Angeles to talk with industry leaders about the movie image of African-Americans. He urged that the Negro be treated simply as a human being and that depictions of black Americans as serious, productive citizens be incorporated into the fabric of American society. During the war years, as black G.I.s in segregated units fought abroad for the freedom of others, Hollywood (in part because of efforts by the Office of War Information's Bureau of Motion Pictures) began to treat racial matters more sensitively and came to understand that it was prudent, at least as wartime propaganda, to portray America as a land of the free and home of the brave.

By the late 1940s, the old rigidly stereotyped comic servants were on their way out, to be replaced at the close of the decade by the intelligent and troubled black characters of Hollywood's Negro

Jazzman Red Nichols, played by Danny Kaye, is joined by the real Louis Armstrong in a film biography of Nichols entitled *The Five Pennies* (Paramount Pictures, 1959). Courtesy Academy of Motion Picture Arts and Sciences.

problem pictures of 1949, which explored America's racial tensions. *Home of the Brave* examined racism within the American military. *Pinky* focused on racial conflicts in the South. *Lost Boundaries* explored the covert racism of a small New England community. *Intruder in the Dust* also dissected explosive racism in the South. Now no longer carrying a tray or singing a happy tune and then receding to the sidelines, the bruised and brooding black characters of these films were the central protoganists.

Armstrong's movie appearances of the 1940s, even in musical sequences, sometimes reflected this change in perspective and attitude. In *Atlantic City* (1944), he appears in a musical sequence once again set in Harlem, but here Harlem is presented in a more restrained manner. After an exterior shot of the Apollo theater establishes the setting, a pretty young woman—a very young Dorothy Dandridge—sings and dances to a tune about Harlem on parade. In this phase of her career, before her ascension to full stardom in *Carmen Jones* (1954), Dandridge is flat-out cute and adorable and her performance is natural. Dandridge's short song introduces Armstrong. Well-turned out in a tuxedo, he's a pleasure to watch as he performs "Ain't Misbehavin'." Although a bit more subdued than in the past, he still mugs and works his eyes and smile. That same year in a black musical sequence in *Jam Session*, Armstrong performed the pop tune "I Can't Give You Anything But Love" in a similar fashion.

During this time, Armstrong's career was rejuvenated. The success of his Town Hall concert in May 1947, helped launch a new

Playing a jazz legend named Wild Man Moore, Armstrong gives authenticity to *Paris Blues* (United Artists, 1961), the fictional story of two expatriate American musicians, played by Paul Newman and Sidney Poitier, in Paris. Photojournalist Sam Shaw was the producer of the film. Copyright Sam Shaw.

wave of popularity for him. Many fans felt as if he had left pop to return home to jazz. That same year *New Orleans* was released, and in it the now legendary "Pops" was again working with jazz material. Although he does not have much of a role in the film, he's truly effective when he performs. It is moving to see him with Holiday. In those moments when he graciously introduces his band, which includes Kid Ory and Zutty Singleton, Armstrong is strangely humanized and personalized for us in a way that is far removed from the feeble plot mechanizations and distortions.

His career moved along at full steam during these years. *Time* ran a cover story on him in 1949. Three years later readers of *Down Beat* voted him "the most important musical figure of all time." He hit the top of the pop charts with such hits as "Blueberry Hill," "Mack the Knife," and in the 1960s, the smash of smashes, "Hello Dolly." The reactions of a younger generation, particularly to his image in film and television appearances, were, however, increasingly mixed.

Had Armstrong's movie work ended with *New Orleans*, the later impressions and reactions to him—from a new generation—might have been quite different. Perhaps his screen image would have been accepted (or tolerated) as part of a prewar perspective. Or his screen work might have been forgotten. But Armstrong continued working in films, with varying results and responses, into the turbulent 1950s and 1960s, which were marked by the struggle for civil rights and then the Black Power movement.

"Louis Armstrong as Satchmo the Jester was sometimes the source of embarrassment and confusion among some civil rights

A Mexican lobby card for *A Man Called Adam* (Embassy Films, 1966). Playing opposite Sammy Davis, Jr., Armstrong expanded his range as an actor in this drama about an old musician callously treated by a younger musician, who fears that one day he will face the same exploited fate. Courtesy John Kisch Separate Cinema Collection.

spokesmen and black college students," critic Albert Murray wrote, "but he always counterstated his clowning with his trumpet, which was never a laughing matter."[7] Murray was absolutely right about Armstrong's counterstatement: his musicianship. The problem was that this new audience, coming of age in the 1950s and 1960s, didn't listen to Satchmo play his horn. That audience might see him on television, but its ears were tuned to a new kind of popular music.

Armstrong's forceful stand on civil rights, precipitated by the Little Rock school crisis in 1957, might have altered his image. He told the press that Arkansas Governor Orval Faubus, who had barred black children from attending a school, was "a plow boy" and that President Eisenhower was "two-faced" and had "no guts." He then cancelled a U.S. Government–sponsored tour to Russia. "The way they are treating my people in the South, the government can go to hell," he said.[8] Still, for the new generation, Armstrong's entertainer image was not a politicized one.

Newsweek commented that few younger Americans were familiar with Armstrong's breathtaking work on such recordings of the 1920s as "Potato Head Blues" or "West End Blues." The later postwar generation "know him instead as the happy-go-lucky, gravel-voiced minstrel who shucked and jived his way through cornball hits like 'Hello Dolly.'"[9]

The young African-American audience of the 1950s and 1960s, now weaned on television sets in their living rooms, focused on the indelible visual emblems of Armstrong's showbiz persona: the grin, the eye pops, the mugging, the sweaty handkerchief, the perpetual high spirits, the all-too-friendly banter with his white costars. His movies of the late 1940s through the 1960s included *A Song Is Born* (1948); the Bing Crosby-vehicle *Here Comes the Groom* (1951), in which he performed but did not play a character; *The Sting* (1951), in which he sang one of his enduring pop hits "A Kiss to Build A Dream On"; *Glory Alley* (1952); *The Beat Generation* (1959); *When the Boys Meet the Girls* (1965); and *Jazz on a Summer's Day* (a record of the 1958 Newport Jazz Festival). In these, he usually made guest appearances.

In *Glory Alley* (1952), he played a character named Shadow Johnson, who clearly harked back to an earlier time. Set in New Orleans, the film focuses again on the white hero, coming of age, with Armstrong used again for intermittent laughs and serving, along with his music, as part of the backdrop.

Throughout the postwar years, he thus held onto his prewar image. He never saw any need to retailor his persona to fit a new set of political and social values and aspirations. For an age increasingly disdainful of anything that smacked of servitude or white patronizing, Louis Armstrong came across too often as a political anachronism.

When he appeared as himself in such biographical films as *The Glenn Miller Story* (1954) and *The Five Pennies* (1959, with Danny Kaye as jazzman Red Nichols), his musical numbers are often wonderfully performed. Armstrong's appearances, even at this late date, continued to widen the audience for jazz, enabling the music to win more and more mainstream acceptance. His presence also helped create an authentic jazz ambiance for these melodramas. His appearance can easily be construed as a tribute to his prominence in jazz, but for the African-American audience, he seemed to be used as a brilliant walk-on—still employed to enliven other people's movies. African-American audiences no doubt would have preferred seeing the great Armstrong in a film about black jazz artists, with perhaps even a story developed around him, no matter what his limitations as an actor.

Of *The Glenn Miller Story*, *Time*'s critic noted that "Louis Armstrong, playing a pie-eyed piper in one scat session, may make the audience wish for a few wild minutes that this were Armstrong's story and not Miller's."[10] Sadly, Hollywood did not yet realize that if any American musical artist deserved a film biography that traced his struggles, accomplishments, and extraordinary impact on the cultural landscape, surely it was Armstrong. Apparently, Orson Welles did understand, for at one time he had plans for an Armstrong biopicture. It is unfortunate that Welles's film never materialized because Armstrong needed to be put into perspective for the new generation (particularly the new black generation).

The Armstrong movie of the postwar era that was, at once, the most popular and ironically perhaps the most detrimental to his standing with young black audiences was *High Society* (1956). In it, he worked once more with his old friend Bing Crosby. The two sang a duet of "Now You Has Jazz." He also served as a type of chorus for the film, appearing at the opening and setting the stage for the story to follow and periodically commenting on the action, then closing the film with a rousing blast from his horn and the line, "End of story!"

His reviews were good. "While I thought now and then that Mr. Armstrong was being neglected," wrote the critic for *The New Yorker*, "I have to admit that I'd be inclined to give up any movie to listen to him line out a tune."[11] The reviewer for *The Christian Science Monitor* commented, "Jazz ensembles in Hollywood are usually treated like classical ballet: the camera lingers on them timidly for a few seconds, then flits away in panic for fear of boring audiences with an unfamiliar sight or sound. But the Armstrong All-Stars are given the preferred treatment they deserve in several full-length numbers, including a toe-tapping how-jazz-began sequence with Mr. Crosby."[12]

In contrast, the black movie audience of 1956—now having watched such actors as Dorothy Dandridge, Sidney Poitier (b. 1927), James Edwards (1918–1970), Ruby Dee who were dramatic, forceful, disdainful of any old clown routines, and so a direct challenge to outdated ideas about the Negro's accepted place and position in American society—thought that Armstrong in *High Society* seemed locked in a time warp.

Indeed the very image of the jazz musician had also undergone a significant change. By now, such titans of the bebop era as Dizzy Gillespie and Charlie Parker as well as that high priest of the "cool jazz" era Miles Davis had entered the consciousness of the cultural mainstream, refashioning a view of the jazz star as a serious, nonaccommodating artist. Being an entertainer was the very last thing any of the bebop artist aspired to, or so it seemed then. And in the world of pop, Billy Eckstine and Nat 'King' Cole had smooth, modulated styles. Young black audiences did not want to see Armstrong clowning around with Bing Crosby in *High Society*: an image that had seemed so optimistic to one era now alienated another.

During these years, Armstrong's television appearances, while musically fine, also suffered for the same reason: his image. He made his way into American homes with a fixed regularity on a host of programs: "The Ed Sullivan Show," "The Eddie Condon Floor Show," "The Perry Como Show," "The Hollywood Palace," "The Danny Kaye Show," "The Dean Martin Show," "The Jackie Gleason Show," "The David Frost Show," "The Tonight Show," "The Pearl Bailey Show," and "The Flip Wilson Show" as well as specials.[13]

In these television appearances, Armstrong seemed to be covering old terrain, a giant performing familiar songs. Watching Armstrong grin so broadly as he joked and clowned with Perry Como or smile so passively while Ed Sullivan literally led him by the hand, almost as if Satchmo were a child, was not comfortable for many black viewers. At other times, such as on *Shindig*,[14] Armstrong was supremely effective, recalling the days when his fame was as a jazz musician rather than as a celebrity entertainer.

In his last movie, *Hello Dolly* (United Artists, 1969), Armstrong joins Barbra Streisand for a duet of the title song, which had been a hit for Armstrong long before the film. Frank Driggs Collection.

When Edward R. Murrow and Fred Friendly expanded their "See It Now" profile on Armstrong into a feature film documentary, *Satchmo the Great* (1957), their intelligent and telling portrait presented another identity for Armstrong as a good-will ambassador and a man loved and respected throughout the world. As "an excursion in jazz in which our cameras accompany Satchmo and his trumpet across four continents," narrator Murrow explained, there "are no actors in this film. No scenarios. And the only historian involved is Daniel Louis Armstrong."

In *Satchmo the Great*, Armstrong emerges as a thoughtful, gracious, modest, and warm man who reminisces about his idol King Oliver; discusses jazz, defining the meaning of certain music terms (some of which he is said to have coined) as "gutbucket," "cat," and "barrelhouse"; visits Ghana (then the Gold Coast), partly at the government's invitation (on the eve of the nation's independence) and partly out of personal enthusiasm to see the land he is convinced is his great-grandparents' homeland. At one Armstrong concert, Kwame Nkrumah is in attendance. At another concert in Accra, Armstrong plays to more than 100,000 people. At the airport, crowds give him a rousing reception on his arrival and a tender farewell as he departs.

As he sits on an airplane or train, the great Satchmo looks tired and weary at times. The backbreaking years of touring and one-night stands have taken a toll. But when he picks up his horn, he's a marvel all over again. In his public performance, his emblematic smile is clearly his way, as it always was, of extending himself

PROGRAMS - PEOPLE - WEEK OF SEPT. 16 - 22

1956

Herald New York Tribune **TV** *and Radio Magazine*

SECTION 9

"SATCHMO" LOUIS ARMSTRONG

THE LORD DON'T PLAY FAVORITES! (SEE PAGES 20-21)

Just as he had scored successes in records, radio, and movies, from the 1950s Armstrong triumphed in the new medium of television. In hundreds of broadcasts to millions of homes, Armstrong won new fans who often had little knowledge of his long and illustrious past. Armstrong's appearance in "The Lord Don't Play Favorites" is featured on the cover of *International Herald Tribune TV and Radio Magazine*, September 16-22, 1956. Courtesy Institute of Jazz Studies, Rutgers University.

and his spirit to the audience; a way of acknowledging the shared experience between the audience and artist as he performs.

Satchmo the Great climaxes at New York's Lewisohn Stadium with Armstrong's performance of "The St. Louis Blues" with the New York Philharmonic as Leonard Bernstein conducts. Modest and self-effacing when introduced, Armstrong performs for an audience that includes composer W.C. Handy.

Although it is earnest and reflective, *Satchmo the Great*, never gets to the heart of Louis Armstrong, never fully explains or unlocks his complexity and fierce beauty. But the film provides glimmers of the layers of this remarkable man; it let us hear him speak in his own words on topics of importance to him; and ultimately it preserves a Louis Armstrong that Hollywood never understood.

Satchmo the Great, however, could not reclaim Armstrong for a new generation. Its circulation was limited, unlike the huge audiences that had seen his Hollywood films. Like such other great performers of a previous age as Ethel Waters, Armstrong was viewed as a cultural and political relic; his image in films and television was too conciliatory and accommodating, historically out of step with a movement calling for cultural separatism.

Today it is rather touching to watch Armstrong in such later "jazz films" as *Paris Blues* (1961) and especially *A Man Called Adam* (1966). *Paris Blues* tells the story of two expatriate American musicians (Sidney Poitier and Paul Newman) in Paris. As the legendary jazzman Wild Man Moore, Armstrong turns up for a jam session. "There is no point in Mr. Armstrong's occurrence," *The New York Times* commented,[15] "except to have that jam session with him." Yet obviously once again Armstrong's appearance brings credibility to the film's jazz setting. And fortunately for the audience no dim-witted comic routines were required this time.

His dramatic role in *A Man Called Adam* marks an image change. He plays an old musician called Sweet Daddy, who is treated callously by a restless, self-destructive younger musician Adam (played by Sammy Davis, Jr.), who fears Sweet Daddy's sad exploited fate may one day be his own. Serious, likeable, and a little wistful, Armstrong's Sweet Daddy is frayed at the edges, vulnerable, and even a bit wounded.

His final movie performance was in the 1969 *Hello Dolly*. In a cafe sequence, shortly after star Barbra Streisand descends a red-carpeted stairway to perform the title song with a group of dancing waiters, the camera pans left to reveal the back of an orchestra leader standing in front of his band. When he turns around, we see it is the incomparable Armstrong, dressed in a black tuxedo with a red cummerbund and a red carnation in his lapel. He looks mighty spiffy.

Fashion photographer Genevieve Naylor captures Armstrong on "The Eddie Condon Floor Show" (NBC-TV), an early television showcase of jazz, 1948. Courtesy The Reznikoff Artistic Partnership.

His smile reveals that he even if the production seems moldy and embalmed in old Broadway mists, he, the eternal optimist, is splendidly alive. He joins Streisand for a duet of the title song, which long before the film had been a hit for Armstrong. It's a deliriously pleasurable moment, mildly reminiscent, although different in mood and tone, of his luminous "The Blues Are Brewing" sequence with Billie Holiday in *New Orleans*. Pauline Kael commented that as Armstrong sang to Streisand, 'You're still glowin', you're still crowin', you're still goin' strong,' "one wants them to dump the movie and just keep going."[16] In an otherwise forgettable film, the moment, brief as it is, remains moving and incandescent, a glimpse of a mighty old warrior, who after almost fifty years in films, is still giving his best.

In a discussion of a film's ability to elicit an audience response, Pauline Kael also once wrote, "The greatest moviemakers—men like Griffith and Renoir—were the men who not only wanted to give the audience of their best but had the most to give. This is also, perhaps, the element that, combined with originality of temperament, makes the greatest stars and enables them to last—what links a Louis Armstrong and an Olivier and a Streisand."[17]   She added that when artists were able to give everything they had, then indeed was there "freedom in the arts." "Working one's peak capacity, going beyond one's known self, giving everything one has, makes show business, from time to time, art," Kael wrote.[18] Armstrong always mutually connected to his work, his art, (his pleasure in attaining his highest professional/artistic ideals may be the real reason he smiles so effusively) and to his audience, for whom he was determined to give something. Never could he disregard the patrons who came to see him (indeed, the very idea of performing with his back to them was wholly alien to him). Even when he recorded on sound stages without an audience in sight, the audience was always in his mind. His great gift was that no matter what the setting, role, or concept, he simply gave it his all, went the distance beyond his "known self," and was up-front honest about his desire to entertain.

Today his artistry, coupled with that irreducible part of himself that he held back when acting a role or even singing a song but never when playing his trumpet, enables him to transform and transcend many a rotten movie. It also still gives us, those anonymous figures sitting in the dark, many pleasurable and memorable moments at the movies.

NOTES

1. Robert Benchley, "*Hearts in Dixie* (The First Real Talking Picture)," *Opportunity*, April 1929.

2. Ibid.

3. Mordaunt Hall, "Ex-Flame," *New York Times*, 24 January 1931.

4. Sime, "Ex-Flame," *Variety*, 28 January 1931.

5. Abel, "Artists and Models," *Variety*, 4 August 1937.

6. Land, "Pennies From Heaven," *Variety*, 16 December 1936.

7. Albert Murray, *Stomping the Blues*, (New York: McGraw Hill, 1976), 31.

8. "Satchmo Cancels Tour: 'My People' Mistreated'," *New York Herald Tribune*, 19 September 1957.

9. Jim Miller, "Genius Blended With Ham," *Newsweek*, 10 October 1983, 83.

10. "New Picture: The Glenn Miller Story," *Time*, 1 March 1954.

11. "The Current Cinema: Barry with Ballads," *The New Yorker*, 18 August 1956.

12. Melvin Maddocks, "Crosby, Sinatra, and Grace Kelly in Musical," *The Christian Science Monitor*, 4 August 1956.

13. *The Ed Sullivan Show*, CBS, 1948–1971; *The Eddie Condon Floor Show*, NBC, 1949–1950; *The Perry Como Show*, NBC, 1948–1963; *The Hollywood Palace*, ABC, 1964–1974; *The Danny Kaye Show*, CBS, 1963–1967; *The Dean Martin Show*, NBC, 1965–1974; *The Jackie Gleason Show*, CBS, 1952–1970 *The David Frost Show*, Syndicated, 1969–1972; *The Pearl Bailey Show*, ABC, 1971; *The Flip Wilson Show*, NBC, 1970–1974.

14. *Shindig*, ABC, 4 November 1965, and 11 November 1965.

15. Bosley Crowther, "Paris Blues," *New York Times*, 8 November 1961.

16. Pauline Kael, "Keep Going," *The New Yorker*, 3 January 1970.

17. Pauline Kael, "Numbing the Audience," *The New Yorker*, 3 October 1970.

18. Ibid.

5 Louis Armstrong: A Portrait Record

Marc H. Miller

Today, more than twenty years after his death, Louis Armstrong remains a familiar and alive presence. Armstrong's enduring fame is a tribute to his genius as a musician and entertainer. The vividness of his image, however, is the result of a full, rich legacy of recorded images and sound. While Armstrong's music has been appreciated and analyzed, the extraordinary visual record of his life has never been seriously studied. Spanning seven decades and including tens of thousands of images, the portraits fully chronicle Armstrong's life. They show us "Little Louis," the talented New Orleans youth; "Satchmo," the acclaimed musical innovator and international celebrity; and finally "Pops," the revered founding father of jazz and beloved American original. This pictorial record is an important primary resource for understanding Armstrong's life and career because through his portraits as well as his music, the artist continues to communicate with us.

Although Louis Armstrong would become one of the most frequently depicted personalities of his generation, only a few of these images date from the first twenty-two years of his life. At his birth in 1901, portrait photography was more than fifty years old and practiced throughout America. Quickly done and generally inexpensive, photography was a democratic portrait medium but it was not equally available to all Americans. For the poor Armstrong family living in the "Back o' Town" section of New Orleans, even the most inexpensive photographs were probably prohibitive.

Armstrong was lucky to live in New Orleans with its active

Armstrong as photographed by Annie Leibovitz three weeks before his death in 1971. Courtesy Annie Leibovitz.

He uses words like he strings notes together—artistically and vividly.

Tallulah Bankhead, *Ebony*, 1952

Armstrong's personality came through in his words as well as his music. He was a prolific writer, traveling with a typewriter, working backstage and in hotel rooms on letters, magazine articles, and memoirs. Popsie Randolph shows Armstrong at the typewriter in his dressing room at the Basin Street nightclub in New York, 1955. Frank Driggs Collection.

A 1944 letter from Armstrong to Robert Goffin, written backstage at the Harlem's Apollo on customized "Satchmo" stationery. Courtesy Institute of Jazz Studies, Rutgers University.

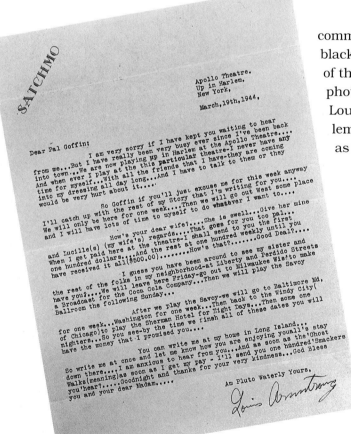

community of over more than seventy thousand blacks and Creoles. In the restrictive racial climate of the South, blacks generally had little access to photography. Had Armstrong grown up in rural Louisiana, he would have encountered the problems jazz musician Bunk Johnson faced as late as 1940:

> ...about my delay in sending you these pictures... The service here is really poor for colored people. We have no colored studios. This is a Cajun town and, in these little country towns, you don't have a chance like the white man, so you just have to stand back and wait until your turn comes.[1]

During the years Armstrong lived in New Orleans (1901–1922), there were at least two African-American photographers with studios in Treme, the city's principal black quarter. The foremost was Arthur P. Bedou (1882–1966), who won a gold medal in photography at Virginia's Jamestown Exposition of 1907 and was Booker T. Washington's personal photographer during his 1911–12 farewell tour (P. 78). In 1917 Villard

Louis Armstrong's popular autobiography was translated into numerous foreign languages including French (above) and Norwegian (below). Louis Armstrong Archives, Queens College, City University of New York.

Actress Grace Kelly reads Armstrong's autobiography, *Satchmo: My Life in New Orleans* (1954), one of the most successful books on jazz. *Satchmo* would help establish Armstrong as a legendary figure in the popular imagination. Courtesy Academy of Motion Picture Arts and Sciences.

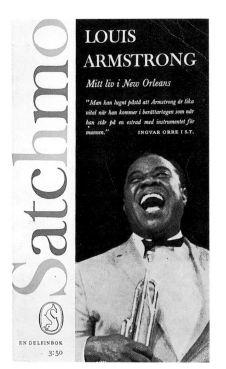

Paddio (c. 1895–1947), a talented student of Bedou, set up a competing studio. Working exclusively for black clients, Bedou and Paddio did portraits, photographs for New Orleans' black publications, and commercial work for the city's many black-owned businesses. Their pictures capture New Orleans' dynamic African-American community and include the first portraits of Louis Armstrong.[2]

Although some portraits of Louis as a young child may have been made, none survive today. The first photo that survives of Armstrong is not the usual family portrait but rather a 1913 photograph showing him at thirteen years old, already a confident musician and central figure in the Colored Waif's Home Brass Band (p. 21). The photograph was probably commissioned by the Waif's Home, a charity operated by the African-American Joseph Jones. Although the photographer has not been conclusively identified, it was likely Bedou, who at this date had a near monopoly on photographing New Orleans' African-American community. The band photograph resembles the publicity pictures used by black and white musical groups in New Orleans and around the country. Compared to photographs of other groups, the youngsters seem disorganized, but the picture shows that the Waif's Home Band was a serious semiprofessional outfit complete with elaborate uniforms.

In the dynamic music scene of New Orleans, Bedou took similar pictures of the many important black bands that participated in the birth of jazz (p. 23). His signature appears on our next portraits of Armstrong: a 1919 picture of the Fate Marable Band

Armstrong's tales of New Orleans and his rags-to-riches story inspired other biographies. Writer Jeanette Eaton collaborated with the African-American illustrator Elton Fax on the children's book, *Trumpeter's Tale: The Story of Young Louis Armstrong* (1955).

Top left: Armstrong's grandmother takes him to the tomb of the Voodoo Queen, Marie Laveau. Drawing by Elton Fax. Twentieth Century Archives, Boston University Libraries.

Top right: In this drawing by Elton Fax, "Little Louis" fires the shot that gets him committed to the Waif's Home. Twentieth Century Archives, Boston University Libraries.

Opposite: Ben Shahn's ink drawings of Armstrong's youth in New Orleans illustrated an interview with Armstrong in the film *Satchmo the Great* (1957). Top to bottom: Little Louis, Coal Cart, Madame John's Legacy. Courtesy Mrs. Ben Shahn.

posed on the riverboat S.S. *Sydney*, and a 1920 picture of the Marable Band on the S.S. *Capitol* (p. 27). Armstrong's two-year tenure working with the accomplished Marable Band on Mississippi pleasure cruises marked an important step in his professional education. The 1919 photo is shot from a distance to show the distinctive ambiance of the indoor dance floor on the *Sydney*, and Captain Streckfus, the owner of the boat, poses with the band. In the 1920 picture, each of the band members strikes a dynamic, but frozen, pose. It is a basic solution to one of the principle issues of jazz portraiture: how to capture the energy of the music at a time when photography still required long exposures.[3]

In 1922 young Louis, like many other Southern blacks, left New Orleans and moved north to Chicago. The separation of the Armstrong family was the occasion for a visit to Villard Paddio's Treme studio to take the only family photograph that still survives (p. 7). Dressed in their best clothes, Louis and his sister Beatrice stand on each side of their mother Mayann, who sits in Paddio's elaborate studio chair. It was a serious occasion befitting the importance attributed to photography at the beginning of the century. A contemporary advertisement in a local black publication states "Nothing affords a more lasting tribute of the donor's thoughtfulness, love and friendship as photographs."[4] Soon after arriving in the north, Armstrong visited one of the many photographers with studios in the thriving black belt of Chicago and posed for a strikingly similar photograph (p. 28). This time it is Joe Oliver, Armstrong's mentor and the man who had brought him north, who

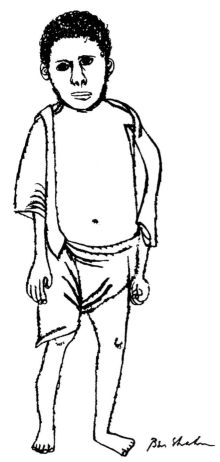

sits in the ornate studio chair. One can easily imagine Louis sending this picture to Mayann to assure her that he had arrived safely and was in good hands.

In these family pictures we can see "Little Louis," as the five-foot six-inch, twenty-one year-old Armstrong was affectionately called by Mayann, Papa Joe, and the others who knew him best. He was a shy, serious young man eager to please his elders. In future years Armstrong would set the style in the African-American community, but in his old-fashioned, box-back suit and natural hairstyle, he must have seemed very rural to the sophisticated blacks on Chicago's South Side. The pianist Lil Hardin, who would soon become Mrs. Armstrong, was certainly not impressed:

> Everything he had on was too small for him. His atrocious tie was dangling down over his protruding stomach and to top it off, he had a hairdo that called for bangs, and I do mean bangs. Bangs that jutted over his forehead like a frayed canopy. All the musicians called him Little Louis and he weighed 226 pounds.[5]

While photography sessions were rare occasions in Armstrong's New Orleans life, they would become familiar in the media-conscious entertainment world of Chicago. Publicity photos were placed outside theaters, reproduced in newspapers, used on sheet music covers, and given out to friends and fans—often with an autograph.[6] Bands kept their photos up to date, so with Armstrong's arrival in 1922 a new photograph was taken of King Oliver's Creole Jazz Band (p. 29). For the rest of his career, Armstrong would be photographed with every group in which he played, leaving an important record of his many professional associations.

In the north, commerce generally spoke louder than race prejudice, and black entertainers could choose any of the city's many theater photographers they could afford. The King Oliver group pictures are by "Daguerre" of Chicago, a European-trained professional who did many portraits of the actors and entertainers working out of the Windy City. By the 1920s publicity photographs followed a well-defined mode. Shot in the studio with a flash, the group is placed against a black curtain to avoid distracting shadows. In some photos the band's instruments were carefully arranged on the floor with the musicians standing behind them; in other pictures the musician hold their instruments and take animated poses to capture the dynamism of jazz music. With the action poses emanating as much from the band as the photographer, Daguerre's pictures capture the energy and confidence of King Oliver's Band as well as the special chemistry developing between Armstrong and his future wife, the pianist Lil Hardin.

In September 1924 Armstrong joined Fletcher Henderson's Band in New York, a one-year association that continued Armstrong's maturation in the profession. In these photographs Armstrong appears comfortable as a member of one of the nation's

185

Armstrong holds his trademark trumpet and handkerchief in a dramatically lit studio shot by photographer Anton Bruehl. The photo, originally published in *Vanity Fair* magazine (November 1935), was one of Armstrong's favorites. Courtesy Vanity Fair. Copyright © 1935 (renewed 1963) by The Condé Nast Publications Inc.

most sophisticated black bands, which regularly performed for black and white audiences in the most prestigious venues (p. 32). At least in terms of his dress, Armstrong had already come a long way from the poverty he grew up with in New Orleans:

> I got me a sharp tuxedo and fell in love with it. $50 for a tuxedo in 1924! You know I had a sharp one. Stiff bosom shirts. Yeah, only tux I had before was a blue coat and I put on a white shirt.[7]

The elegantly composed photographs are by the renowned White Studios, the highly successful firm of Luther S. White (1857–1936) that had a near monopoly on cast photographs of New York's theater world in the years 1910–1929.[8]

In 1925 Armstrong returned to Chicago and began making his legendary Hot Five recordings for OKeh Records. It was the early years of the phonograph record industry, but the use of photographs for marketing was already well established. Kid Ory, the trombone player of the Hot Five, recalled one of OKeh's successful promotional ideas: "for a while the OKeh people gave away a picture of Louis to everyone that bought one of the records. When they did that, the sales went way up, because Louis was so popular."[9]

Daguerre's pictures of the group included a printed inscription announcing that "Armstrong's Hot Five" were "Exclusively OKeh Record Artists" (p. 30). OKeh Records also used Woodard Studios, a successful African-American firm whose portraits of black celebrities appeared regularly in the many publications serving Chicago's black community.[10] Woodard Studios claimed their portrait photographs showed "style & dignity," and these qualities can certainly be seen in a half-length of Armstrong that OKeh Records used for advertisements in the black press (p. 66). OKeh's advertising campaigns regularly alternated dignified formal ads with eye-catching comic imagery.[11] Woodard's portrait of Armstrong was soon being collaged onto drawn cartoon bodies inspired by the songs. For "Basin Street Blues," the drawn body wears the checkered suit, white gloves, and diamond tie clip of the black pimp and dandy. In the more militant social climate of the 1960s, Armstrong would be criticized for seeming to accommodate such racial stereotypes. OKeh's advertisements may bear a similarity to the demeaning cartoon images found on contemporary sheet music intended primarily for whites, but they were intended exclusively for black audiences and must be interpreted within this socia context.[12]

Armstrong's early professional career is well documented in publicity portraits, but these staged photographs give us little insight into his life offstage. Fortunately, Armstrong's crowd was quick to embrace the simplified still cameras and amateur movie cameras that were just coming into vogue in the 1920s (p. 62).[13] The new amateur cameras revolutionized portraiture by facilitating informality and spontaneity. In pictures taken by friends (pp. 28, 31), Louis and Lil mug uninhibitedly for the camera with an upbeat youthful exuberance very different from the mood found in their professional photos. Armstrong is shown at leisure—boating with Earl Hines, and swimming with Tubby Hall—in snapshots that capture his love of outdoor sports and document that his music associates were also his friends offstage.

One set of snapshots captures a pivotal moment in Armstrong's career, when he and the Carrol Dickerson band relocated to New York City in 1929 (p. 36). The long car trip from Chicago included a sightseeing detour to Niagara Falls, and Armstrong sent captioned pictures of the trip to his friends back in the Windy City. In these images Armstrong projects the offstage persona so colorfully described by Rex Stewart:

> What he carried with him was the aroma of red beans and rice, with more than a hint of voodoo and "gris-gris." He conveyed this to the world by the insouciant challenge of his loping walk, the cap on his head tilted at an angle, which back home meant: "Look out! I'm a bad cat—don't mess with me!"[14]

In the early 1930s, cameras accompanied Armstrong's entourage on tour, and snapshots show their life on the road. As Armstrong embarked on one tour he posed with a group that included Alpha, his adopted son Clarence Hatfield, and the white bus driver invariably required when black entertainers toured the South. One picture shows Armstrong with his portly manager from 1930–31, Johnny Collins. Possessively holding a cigar with one hand and Armstrong with the other, Collins looks every bit the disreputable character described by contemporaries.

As Armstrong gained prominence, publications wanted up-to-the-minute photographs shot on location in addition to the stock studio portraits distributed by Armstrong's management. "News" photographs were especially plentiful during Armstrong's three-month triumphal return visit to New Orleans in summer 1931 (pp. 52-54). All the city papers covered Armstrong's visit, but coverage was especially intense in the *Louisiana Weekly*, New Orleans' leading black paper. Both Arthur Bedou and Villard Paddio photographed Armstrong's return to the Colored Waif's Home (renamed the Municipal Boy's Home) where the dapperly dressed, obviously happy (cocky might be a better word) musician posed with his band, the school's administrator Joseph Jones and his wife, Peter Davis (who had given Louis his first formal musical education), and the new boys' band. Paddio became preoccupied with Armstrong's visit, taking pictures of him onstage at the Suburban Gardens, with Armstrong's Secret Nine (a black baseball team named after him), and on-site pictures of his visit to the local black musicians' union. In these early days of photojournalism, Paddio worked with a large camera and slow film. The pictures are posed group portraits rather than candid action shots. Yet they clearly show Paddio's skill and the excitement surrounding Armstrong during an early career high point.

PARTY IN HONOR OF
DUKE ELLINGTON AND LOUIS ARMSTRONG
AT TONY'S TAVERN - 55-W-31ST STREET
FEB-14-1935-CHICAGO-ILL

A party given for Duke Ellington and Armstrong at Tony's Tavern, Chicago, February 14, 1935. Louis Armstrong Archives, Queens College, City University of New York.

By the early 1930s, Armstrong was recognized throughout the country. The official portrait images from this period were two 1931 photographs by Theatrical of Chicago: one showing Armstrong standing (p. 16) and the other a close-up head shot (p. 49). With his processed hair and fashionable clothes, it is clear that rural Little Louis had fully absorbed the high style of Chicago's black entertainment world. Trumpet player Buck Clayton recalled the star quality Armstrong exuded in Los Angeles in the early 1930s:

> He had just come out of the hotel and he looked awfully sharp. His hair looked nice and shiny and he had on a pretty gray suit. He wore a tie that looked like an ascot tie with an extra-big knot in it. Pops was the first one to bring that style of knot to Los Angeles. Soon all the hip cats were wearing big knots in their ties. We called them Louis Armstrong knots. I only saw him for a few minutes, but he sure impressed me just by his appearance.[15]

Clarinet player Mezz Mezzrow recalls Armstrong's impact on the young blacks of Harlem:

> All the raggedy kids, especially those who became vipers [marijuana smokers], were so inspired with self-respect after digging how neat and natty Louis was, they started to dress up real good, and took pride in it too, because if Louis did it it must be right.[16]

Armstrong's glamour and stage charisma is clear in a set of photographs taken by Gibson of Chicago in 1933 (p. 55).[17] A sequence of six dynamic poses captures the animation and liveliness that was a key feature of Armstrong's performances. While Armstrong undoubtedly chose the poses, the effect is enhanced by Gibson's use of a theater spotlight and dramatic cast shadows—a lighting technique that would soon become ubiquitous in photo portraits of jazz musicians. For perhaps the first time in a photograph, Armstrong conspicuously holds a handkerchief, a prop that became a key part of his image:

> Louis always held a handkerchief in his hand because he perspired so much, onstage and off, and he started a real fad—before long all the kids on the Avenue were running up to him with white handkerchiefs in their hands too, to show how much they loved him.[18]

Gibson's photographs also conspicuously feature another Armstrong trademark: the big, broad-faced, clenched-teeth smile. The exaggerated grin, linked to the conventions of minstrel entertainment, was a feature that in later years would be criticized as racial accommodation. Which of Armstrong's ubiquitous smiles were rooted in minstrel stereotypes, based on the conventions of show-business glamour, or rooted in his personality, is difficult to determine. Even when Armstrong was a young boy, people had commented on his large mouth and smile. It was his childhood friends who originally nicknamed him "Dippermouth," "Gatemouth," and "Satchelmouth" (later modified to Satchmo). Like Eskimos who have dozens of words for snow, Armstrong had numerous smiles and each had a different meaning. For those closest to Armstrong, like Rex Stewart, his smile usually had a positive message:

> The youngsters object to his ever-present grin, which they interpret as Tomming. This I feel is a misunderstanding. No matter where Louis had been brought up, his natural ebullience and warmth would have emerged just as creative and strong.[19]

In the early 1930s, following two concert tours of Europe, Armstrong's fame became international. American jazz was already popular in Europe and Armstrong's arrival was an eagerly anticipated event. Seeking to scoop the competition, England's popular music magazine *Rhythm* had a photographer meet Armstrong's boat to get the first pictures of the musician's arrival. In the competitive European press, photojournalism was the norm and the excitement of Armstrong's tour is fully documented in pictures taken in clubs in England, Denmark, Belgium, and France showing him surrounded by local musicians, celebrities, and fans (p. 57).

In late 1933, at the beginning of Armstrong's second visit to Europe, he visited Ava Studios of London for studio portraits to promote his upcoming tour (p. 56). In Jazz Age Europe, the fusion between new music and fashion is clear in Ava's modish photographs. A faddishly dressed Armstrong looks more like a fashion model than a celebrity musician, especially in pictures where he is

Charles Peterson, a jazz musician turned jazz photojournalist, used his flash camera with new abandon to produce spontaneous, candid shots. For this 1937 photo of Armstrong backstage at the Paramount Theatre in New York, he knocked on Armstrong's dressing room door, pushed it open, and snapped. Louis Armstrong Archives, Queens College, City University of New York.

In this photograph, Peterson catches some late night revelry at the Braddock Hotel in Harlem, 1942. Courtesy Don Peterson.

paired with his equally stylish companion Alpha Smith. Soft lighting and careful styling give the photographs an air of sophisticated elegance appropriate for a photographer who called herself "Princess Ava."[20]

In Europe, Armstrong was portrayed in numerous caricatures and portrait drawings, which alternated with photographs in publications and nightclub promotions. Two drawings of Armstrong by a Belgian artist (initialed "M.G.") were distributed by the photographers Delagne et Martin of Brussels for press reproduction and other commercial uses (p. 59). The strongly crosshatched depictions put an emphasis on Armstrong's smile and have the attention-grabbing graphic qualities periodicals require.

The art of caricature, portrait drawing in which a person's features are exaggerated for comic effect, was enjoying new vogue in Europe in the 1920s and 1930s. In a two-page spread covering Armstrong's first European appearance at the London Palladium, *Melody Maker* used eight cartoon drawings showing moments of the performance (p. 58).[21] With their simple exaggerated gestures, the drawings effectively capture the energy and humor of the show at a time when there were no photographs of Armstrong on stage. Some caricatures do not enhance our knowledge of Armstrong but do provide insight into how he was perceived in Europe during his first tour. Advertisements for Armstrong's performances frequently portrayed him with large lips and bulging eyes, racial cliches unconnected to the man himself. Images like these show that racial stereotyping was as common in Europe as in America and convincingly undermine the myth that European audiences uniformly viewed jazz musicians as serious artists.

Some of the most interesting drawings of Armstrong done during his visit to Paris in 1934 are by Charles Delaunay, a talented youth then debating whether to devote his life to music or follow the path of his parents, the esteemed artists Robert and Sonia Delaunay, into the visual arts. Delaunay contrived to meet his musical idol by requesting a sketching session. He produced one set of drawings during a sitting at Armstrong's apartment, but the most successful sketches were executed during a Paris recording session (p. 59). Delaunay later recalled that the emotion of Armstrong's music, "literally carried my crayon on the paper."[22] Delaunay's drawings are rendered in white chalk on a black background, a clever device for sketching black performers that also captures the nighttime mood of jazz. Delaunay became a leading jazz promoter in Europe, and his Armstrong sketches appeared in *Jazz Hot*, the pioneer French jazz magazine he helped found in 1935.

Despite his triumphs in Europe, Armstrong must have felt low when he returned to America in January 1935. He was without management and suffering from an open sore on his lip that had forced him to cancel concerts in Europe. The embouchure wound, formed by pressing his trumpet to his lips, would leave a large and distinctive scar evident in all future portraits. The wound was vividly remembered by Mezz Mezzrow:

Weegee (Arthur Fellig) photographs
Armstrong backstage at Bop City, New
York, c. 1955. Armstrong's open and natural
style was a fitting subject for Weegee, a
pioneer paparazzo who specialized in
unusual, candid images for tabloid
newspapers. Permanent Collection,
International Center of Photography,
Bequest of Wilma Wilcox.

His lip...was so bad, all raw and swole up, that he just sat and looked at it all day in a mirror...To make things worse, he kept picking at the great sore with a needle. I couldn't stand to see it, every prick went all through me, I was so afraid he might infect himself and have to stop playing altogether.[23]

Within months, however, Armstrong had a new manager, Joe Glaser, and his career was again on the upswing. The association between the two men would last for nearly thirty-five years, greatly affecting the direction of Armstrong's career. Before his European tours, Armstrong had been popular with some white audiences, but he clearly enjoyed his greatest popularity among African-Americans. Under Glaser's management his career was increasingly directed toward the broadest possible audience, which was predominantly white. The change would affect both Armstrong's music and look. One aspect of Glaser's successful campaign to expand Armstrong's audience was to present him as an upscale sophisticated performer. Publicity photographs of 1937 by Maurice (Seymour) show a quieter, more elegant Armstrong without the sharp clothing and high energy seen in the early 1930s (p. 107).[24] Maurice's pictures of Armstrong's Orchestra, posed in formal dress before elaborate backdrops and matching music stands, show Glaser's influence. Armstrong's new look fully emerges in a 1941 photograph by James Kriegsmann that would be the official portrait of Armstrong for the next decade. Impeccably dressed in black tie, with blemishes eliminated by careful lighting (not retouching), Armstrong is silhouetted against a clean white background, the new format favored by publications.[25]

In searching for new audiences, Glaser encouraged Armstrong to emphasize his comic abilities and project himself as an entertainer:

I'd say, "Louis, sing and make faces and smile. Smile, goddamn it. Give it to them. Don't be afraid."...An entertainer, singer and musician can make ten times as much money as an ordinary trumpet player.[26]

Armstrong the entertainer emerges most fully in the many Hollywood films he made during the 1930s and 1940s. With Glaser's help, Armstrong was one of a handful of blacks who regularly appeared in American movies, and this led to the remarkable expansion of his career in the late 1930s. The Hollywood films would greatly enhance Armstrong's fame and finances, but because they were made primarily for white audiences and circulated in southern as well as northern states, they accommodated themselves to the basest race politics and prejudices of the day. Black performers who worked in film found themselves limited to the most stereotyped roles. Armstrong appeared as servant, shabbily dressed horse groom, and garbage collector, roles far below his true station as a successful musician. Because the films reached millions of people around the world, and the publicity materials (posters,

An insider's view of jazz is seen in the photos of Milt Hinton, a bass player as well as a photographer. In the early 1950s, Hinton was briefly a member of Armstrong's All Stars. In a Seattle hotel in 1953, Armstrong shows off the case specially designed to carry his tape recorder and phonograph player on the road. © Milton J. Hinton. Courtesy Milton J. Hinton Photographic Collection.

Milt Hinton handed his camera to a bystander to get this picture of himself working with Armstrong backstage during the All Stars' tour of Japan, 1954. The Milton J. Hinton Photographic Collection. © Milton J. Hinton

photographs, caricatures, booklets, and theater displays) reached millions more, the image of Armstrong produced in Hollywood soon challenged and even surpassed his identity as a popular music idol. Hollywood's image of an affable, accommodating Armstrong may have expanded his white audience, but it had an increasingly negative effect on black audiences. Taken at face value, the stereotypes obscure the true character of a musician determined to perform and succeed even under adverse and demeaning circumstances.

Armstrong's growing reputation and his ascension into the mainstream of American culture is signalled by the coverage he received in the trend-setting magazine *Vanity Fair*. The November 1935 issue spotlighted Armstrong's return to America with a full-page portrait by Anton Bruehl (1879–1945), a top commercial photographer whose work was admired and collected in New York's artistic community (p. 186).[27] Dramatically lit and shot from below, Armstrong mops his brow with his trademark handkerchief. Bruehl's portrait may have been Armstrong's favorite of himself. In 1936 it was used as the frontispiece of Armstrong's first autobiography, *Swing That Music*. In 1948 he commissioned Calvin Bailey (1909–1988), a young African-American painter, to make a large oil painting after the image. Bailey added blue and red coloring to the black-and-white portrait, and Armstrong hung the painting prominently in his living room until his death.[28]

In February 1936 Armstrong again appeared in *Vanity Fair*, this time in a regular feature, "Impossible Interviews" by Miguel Covarrubias (1904–1957), which juxtaposed unlikely personalities in a composite caricature (p. 210).[29] Armstrong is paired with Fritz Kreisler, a classical violinist who admired jazz, and the imaginary dialogue humorously alludes to jazz music's new respectability:

> LOUIS: Ah'll give yo' a job playin' fiddle in mah band.
>
> FRITZ: Hot ginger and dynamite! Wait until Heifetz and Zimbalist hear me now.

The theme of jazz music incorporated into the world of classical music nicely parallels Covarrubias's own role as a visual artist. For many cultured observers, the young, Mexican-born illustrator's sophisticated humor and skillful use of abstract line and expressive colors had elevated the popular art of caricature into a fine art. The careers of Armstrong and Covarrubias both reflect the rise of popular culture in the 1920s and 1930s.

In 1939 Armstrong's rise to the top echelons of American popular entertainment took him to Broadway in *Swingin' the Dream*, an elaborate jazz version of Shakespeare's *A Midsummer Night's Dream*. Although the play survived for only sixteen performances, it left an impressive collection of images by some of the most talented artists in the entertainment publicity field (pp. 110–113). The production photographs were by Vandamm Studios, the firm run by Florence Vandamm (1883–1966) and her husband

These pictures of Armstrong performing at a New York nightclub and backstage with singer Velma Middleton were taken by Garry Winogrand for a magazine assignment in 1954. They show the photographer's eye for realist viewpoints and spontaneous moments. © Eileen Adele Hale. Center for Creative Photography, University of Arizona.

George R. Thomas (d. 1944) that in the 1930s had replaced White Studios as Broadway's leading stage photographers.[30] Al Hirschfeld (b. 1903), who became America's preeminent caricaturist, was commissioned to produce the art used to promote *Swingin' the Dream.* For the cover of *Playbill*, Hirschfeld combined portraits of Armstrong, costar Benny Goodman, and a finger-snapping Shakespeare, capturing the play's fashionable blend of high and low culture. In a more ambitious drawing, Hirschfeld exhibits his mastery of expressive line and ability to portray the lively essence of a jazz musical by freely combining caricature portraits of actors dressed in the play's outrageous costumes with dancers, music notes, and abstracted piano keys. The play's elaborate costumes also dominate a photograph of Armstrong and costar Maxine Sullivan taken by the renowned Edward Steichen (1879–1973) that appeared in *Vogue* magazine.[31]

With the end of World War II in 1945, Armstrong's career was again on the ascent. Jazz was increasingly viewed with a new historical perspective, and Armstrong was appreciated not just as a successful musician but as one of the original creators of a unique American music popular around the world. Armstrong's new stature was confirmed on February 21, 1949, when he was portrayed as the "King of Jazz" on the cover of *Time* magazine (p. 14). The portrait illustration by Boris Artzybasheff (1899–1965), one of *Time's* most prolific cover artists, was an original composite image based on photographs. Meticulously rendering such facial features as Armstrong's embouchure scar, Artzybasheff strives to avoid

While recording Armstrong's 1955 visit and performance at Castle Hill, a Massachusetts artists' retreat, for *Life* magazine, photographer Gordon Parks caught the changing audience of jazz. Courtesy Gordon Parks.

caricature and stereotyping. The respectful mood is only slightly offset by the humorous accessory details that were Artzybasheff's trademark. Wearing a crown of tiny gold trumpets, the King is surrounded by a court of brightly colored, anthropomorphized music notes, all smiling except for a crying blue note in the bottom left corner.[32]

The occasion for the *Time* story was Armstrong's coronation as "King Zulu" in New Orleans' annual Mardi Gras celebration. The first African-American group to participate officially in Mardi Gras (in 1909), the Zulus and their raucous parade were a festival highlight. Armstrong's presence at Mardi Gras attracted international attention. Numerous photographers recorded him as King Zulu in the traditional straw skirt and exaggerated blackface makeup with white markings around the eyes (p. 131).[33] In the new postwar racial climate, the pictures proved controversial; the blackface makeup was a stark reminder of the restrictive days of minstrel entertainment. Armstrong's generation of Southern blacks could appreciate the honor of being King Zulu, but the wide distribution of the pictures also reinforced the image of Armstrong propagated by Hollywood as a symbol of racial accommodation.

Armstrong's career was increasingly

Lisette Model took many pictures of jazz musicians in the 1950s and hoped to collaborate with writer Langston Hughes on a book about jazz. Her photograph of Armstrong at the Newport Jazz Festival (1954–56) catches the rhythm of the music. National Portrait Gallery, Smithsonian Institution, Courtesy Lisette Model Foundation.

linked with the renewed interest in the colorful history and music of New Orleans. In 1947 he appeared in the film *New Orleans*, which had a turn-of-the-century setting and numerous allusions to the birth of jazz. Publicity photos for the film show Armstrong with an old-fashioned cornet and as part of small combos like those popular during the early years of jazz (p. 162-163). Soon real life followed the lead of film fiction, for Armstrong broke up his big band and was touring the country with a small combo of veteran New Orleans musicians. At a time when bebop was changing the sound of jazz, Armstrong's All Stars road the crest of the so-called Dixieland Revival.

The publication of Armstrong's autobiography, *Satchmo: My Life in New Orleans* (1954), cemented his association with the city in which both he and jazz were born. Armstrong's colorful telling of his "rags to riches" story and his lively tales about the people, places, and folkways of New Orleans became core legends in the story of jazz. Jeanette Eaton's *Trumpeter's Tale: The Story of Young Louis Armstrong* (1955), a biography intended for young audiences, was one of many books that retold Armstrong's story. Illustrations for the book by the African-American artist Elton Fax (b. 1909) included an invented portrait of young Armstrong, with short pants, a torn shirt, and no shoes (p. 184). This image of Little Louis was soon being repeated by other artists including Ben Shahn (1898–1969) who in 1956 did a series of sketches of Armstrong's childhood for the documentary film *Satchmo the Great* (p. 185).[34] The Little Louis image reflected Armstrong's new stature as a positive role model for children, but in an increasingly sensitive racial climate, the image of a ragged waif—although it conformed to Armstrong's descriptions of himself—was also seen as a reprise of the pickaninny stereotype rooted in turn-of-the-century reality.[35]

The story of Armstrong's emergence as one of the twentieth-century's leading cultural figures and the full contours of his image were realized in the documentary film *Satchmo the Great* (1957) by Edward R. Murrow and Fred Friendly. Armstrong had sporadically been featured in the newsreels in the 1930s and 1940s, but *Satchmo the Great* was the first full-length film documentary of his life. *Satchmo the Great*, an outgrowth of a shorter documentary on Armstrong originally seen on the television series *See It Now*, was, as its title implies, typical of the powerful advocacy journalism of Murrow and Friendly.[36] Mixing commentary and interviews with footage of Armstrong traveling and performing, the film establishes Armstrong's importance as one of the originators of jazz. Footage of Armstrong performing with Leonard Bernstein and the New York Philharmonic Orchestra suggests that jazz has become an honored part of musical tradition. The film also highlights Armstrong's postwar identity as "Ambassador Satch." Scenes of Armstrong in Berlin, the city whose partition symbolized the cold war, and during his first tour of Africa present him as America's goodwill ambassador and the man responsible for spreading jazz around the world.[37]

In the last two decades of his life Armstrong joined that small elite of the most photographed people on earth. Most of the pictures were generated by the publicity apparatus that supported Armstrong's nonstop, international schedule of concerts, recording sessions, and film and television appearances. Always at ease with people, Armstrong was one celebrity who made himself accessible to both professional and amateur photographers. The resulting collection of images reflects the full creative range of photo portraiture and includes work by some of this century's most respected photographers.[38]

By the late 1930s innovations in photography, including faster film and portable flash units, changed our image of Armstrong. Pictures were increasingly shot on location, and cameras that could catch figures in action allowed for unposed shots unlike anything done earlier. Charles Peterson (1900–1976), a former jazz musician who became a photojournalist and who specialized in the world of jazz, was one of the first to use the flash camera effectively.[39] As a trusted friend of the musicians he photographed, Peterson used his 4 x 5" camera with a new abandon (p. 190). For an unusually candid image of Armstrong backstage at

The photographic decision, like the jazz decision, must be instantaneous.

Dennis Stock, *Jazz Street*, 1960

Photographing Armstrong over a number of weeks, photojournalist Dennis Stock created an extended portrait with a range of moods and details. These pictures were taken at the Latin Casino, Philadelphia, about 1960. Courtesy Dennis Stock/Magnum Photos.

the Paramount Theatre in 1937, Peterson knocked on the dressing room door, pushed it open and quickly snapped. Following a performance in 1942, Peterson joined Armstrong and friends at the Braddock Hotel in Harlem, catching lively pictures of the late-night revelry that was a common but usually undocumented part of Armstrong's life.

In the 1950s Armstrong was frequently photographed by the tabloid photojournalist Weegee [Arthur Fellig] (1899–1968). The pioneer paparazzo often made late-night rounds of New York nightclubs searching for celebrities and newsworthy events, and he specialized in unusual action photos with a sensational bent (p. 192). The open, extroverted Armstrong was a conducive subject, and at Bop City, Weegee caught the uninhibited side of Armstrong, surrounded by friends and fans as he relaxed in his dressing room, half naked at one of his weightier moments (his weight fluctuated by as much as ninety-five pounds).

An insider's view of Armstrong's world can be seen in the photographs of Milt Hinton (b. 1910), a professional bass player who seriously developed his photography skills in the 1930s by setting up a darkroom in hotel rooms as he toured with the Cab Calloway Band (p. 194).[40] Hinton's intimate knowledge of the jazz world allows him to catch subtleties overlooked by others. In 1953 Hinton, then a member of Armstrong's All Stars, photographed Armstrong relaxing in a Seattle hotel room with the special travel crate he had constructed to take his tape recorder and record player on the road.

A dynamic new kind of candid photography can be seen in

Garry Winogrand's pictures of Armstrong performing at an unnamed New York nightclub and during a recording session (p.196). Probably taken around 1954 for a magazine story, the pictures show Winogrand's remarkable eye for candid moments and unique camera viewpoints. Shooting quickly in rapid succession and moving the camera with the action, Winogrand captures a world in flux. Armstrong's high energy and spirits effectively come across, especially in pictures showing him onstage and off with Velma Middleton, the female vocalist who worked with Armstrong for well over a decade.[41]

Photo coverage of Armstrong was often unrelenting, with serious photojournalists diligently taking numerous pictures over extended periods of time and striving to accurately show the performer's life. The documentary photo projects commissioned by the Farm Security Administration during the Depression and the picture stories featured in *Life* helped popularize and develop the art of the photo in the U.S. Gordon Parks (b.1912) was a veteran of both these enterprises. As an African-American and an accomplished musician and composer, Parks often covered the world of jazz. In 1955 *Life* sent him to cover Armstrong's visit to Castle Hill, an upscale New England artist community. (p. 197).The event showed jazz's stature in the U.S. and Parks's photographs of

Armstrong, taken throughout the day, show both the affluent environment and the mix of artists, students, and society dowagers in attendance.[42]

Dennis Stock (b. 1928), who in the late 1950s was just beginning his successful career as a photojournalist, followed Armstrong for days, capturing him onstage, offstage, on the road, and back home, compiling one of the most complete photo stories about Armstrong (pp. 200–201, 220–221). While Parks aimed to capture definitive moments, Stock is more diverse in his approach, open to all sorts of moments in his quest to present a full portrait. Focusing on both the man and his environment, Stock mixed close-ups and distant shots, unconventional cropping, evocative layout, and captions featuring Armstrong's own words, to capture the range of the musician's life and moods. In his written introduction to *Jazz Street* (1960), Stock compared his approach to photography to the way jazz musicians approach music: "Improvisation, the essence of their art, dictated the form of this book. It often happened quickly, the photographic decision like the jazz decision must be instantaneous."[43]

Many effective portraits of Armstrong are not important examples of art photography. Some of the most telling images are by the nightclub photographers who by 1940 were a staple in jazz clubs, replacing the sketch artists popular in the 1920s and 1930s. Much of Armstrong's socializing took place at clubs between sets, and over the years he amassed a large collection of souvenir pictures. When Armstrong returned to the popular Club De Lisa in the

Using a special darkroom technique in which negative and positive images are superimposed slightly off register, Robert Parent transforms his photo of Armstrong into animated lines that evoke both mood and sound, 1956. Courtesy Don Parent.

heart of Chicago's Black Belt in the early 1940s, tables were reserved for reunions with his adopted son Clarence, ex-wife Lil, and other old friends (p.126). Surprisingly the majority of the club pictures in Armstrong's personal collection show him with the many anonymous fans who had their picture taken with him between sets (pp. 212-213). The photographs capture his openness to people and willingness to engage in the public relations side of show business. That Armstrong saved so many of these pictures with fans, however, may reveal something deeper. Like many performers, Armstrong needed the approval of audiences and thrived on attention.[44]

Many of the best-known portraits of Armstrong done in the postwar period were taken in a studio setting against simplified backdrops under controlled lighting. Done for major magazines by leading portrait and fashion photographers, the pictures strive primarily for an easy-to-read, emblematic image, but many also reveal much about Armstrong's appearance and character. In 1948 Irving Penn (b. 1917) photographed Armstrong for a *Vogue* article entitled "Inside N.Y.C.," which featured celebrities squeezed into a tight-fitting corner space with a minimum of props (p. 202).[45] By first isolating his subjects and then allowing them to pose themselves, Penn's photos succeed in both revealing specific individuals and projecting an expressive mood that one writer has called "existential."[46] While Penn's portraits can seem quite severe, his picture of a well-dressed Armstrong, clutching his trumpet, with one foot propped on a cloth-covered chair, projects ease and geniality.

In 1957 Bert Stern (b. 1929) did a portrait of Armstrong for

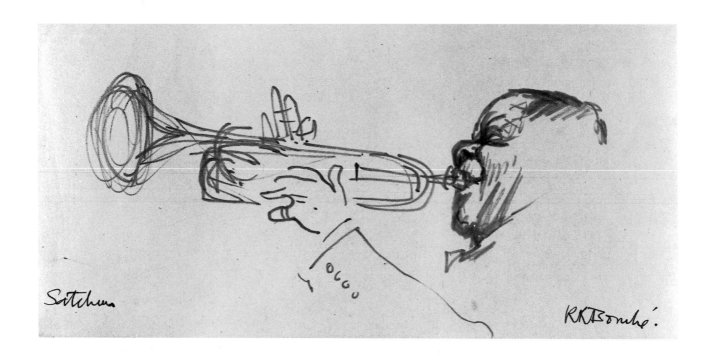

The society portraitist and *Vogue* magazine fashion illustrator René Bouché sketched Armstrong's performance at the Newport Jazz Festival in 1954. Queens Museum of Art, New York, Gift of Mrs. Rene Bouché.

Polaroid Corporation using their new film (p. 203). The picture of Armstrong was used in a Polaroid advertising campaign, reflecting the musician's growing popularity with corporate sponsors, which at that time also included Chesterfield cigarettes and Pepsi Cola. Using a 4 x 5" view camera and a massive bank of fluorescent lights, Stern achieved remarkable sharpness and detail.[47] Because every line and blemish of Armstrong's face and hands is clearly visible, the photo is a unique document of his visual appearance. Despite its intense scrutiny, the close-up view of Armstrong with his clenched-teeth smile resting on his horn is surprisingly natural.

In 1966 Armstrong was featured on the cover of *Life* in a striking color photograph taken by the acclaimed portrait photographer Philippe Halsman (1906–1979). Halsman, who specialized in unique images designed to catch the attention of magazine readers, certainly succeeded with his cover photo of Armstrong, shot with a wide-angle lens from above (p. 11). The unusual picture inventively captures a vertical standing figure within a horizontal format, and the effect was spotlighted by *Life's* specially designed pullout cover. At their best, Halsman's innovative techniques increased the emotional impact of his pictures. In another photo of Armstrong, done at the same session, Halsman experiments with radically cropping the head to intensify the focus on those facial features that most strongly convey expression (p. 1).[48] It is unfortunate that Halsman's pictures show Armstrong once again popping his eyes. The wide circulation of the *Life* cover would expand Armstrong's fame but also reinforce his image as a symbol of racial accommodation.

JAZZ
SKETCHBOOK

By Rene Bouché

The 1955 Newport Jazz Festival program featured Bouché's *Jazz Sketchbook*, a distinctive group of freely executed drawings inspired more by the music than the subject's physical appearance. Courtesy Institute of Jazz Studies, Rutgers University.

In the 1950s and 1960s many fine art photographers, painters, filmmakers, and graphic artists found inspiration in the world of jazz. Sponsored by Louis and Elaine Lorillard, yearly jazz festivals held in the rarified atmosphere of the affluent estates of Newport, Rhode Island,[49] attracted a fashionable audience. The first Newport Festival in 1954 was attended by Lisette Model (1906–1983), an influential photographer and teacher who specialized in expressive shots of people in action. Armstrong was the star of the festival, and Model's pictures of him on stage reveal her sharp aesthetic sense (p.198). The closely cropped prints show Armstrong holding his trumpet and surrounded by fragments of arms and instruments that create a lively composition with an abstract rhythm expressive of the music. In a deceptively simple way, Model achieves the basic goal of jazz portraiture, a static visual that evokes both the person and his animated music.[50]

The blending of art and jazz at Newport can be seen in the souvenir catalogues, which included portfolios by photographers and graphic artists. The 1955 catalogue featured "Jazz Portraits" by Richard Avedon, photographs of Armstrong, Ellington, and other musicians starkly silhouetted against a white background. The 1956 catalogue included a portfolio by Bob Parent (1923–1987), called "Solarized Jazz."[51] Parent was inspired by Man Ray's famous solarized photographs of the 1920s, but his images are distinctly different (p. 205). Utilizing a special darkroom technique in which negative and positive images are combined slightly off register, the pictures transform Armstrong and other performers into animated lines evocative of both mood and sound. Parent's work can be compared to the abstracted photo portraits that Weegee experimented with in the 1950s and 1960s (p. 204). At their best Weegee's distorted images are clever caricatures. His picture of Armstrong popping his eyes, however, is not one of his better efforts and apparently was never published (p.208).

The Newport Jazz Festivals were also a magnet for graphic artists and painters. At the 1954 festival, the society portraitist and *Vogue* magazine fashion illustrator René Bouché (1905–1963) did stylish sketches of Armstrong in performance (p. 206). The 1955 Newport program featured Bouche's "Jazz Sketchbook," a distinctive group of freely executed drawings with an abstract rhythm of line inspired more by the live music than the portrait subject's appearance (p. 207). Radically departing from Bouche's fashion illustration style, these drawings reflect his close association with abstract expressionist painters in the 1940s.

The fusion of portraiture with abstraction rooted in the sound of jazz music is perhaps best seen in the work of the illustrator and painter LeRoy Neiman (b. 1927). Neiman's illustrations, originally featured in his "Man at His Leisure" column in *Playboy* magazine, set the tone for an art career consistently dedicated to expressing the extracurricular interests of the modern urban male. Jazz was a part of this world and Neiman regularly sketched performers at clubs and festivals. Beginning in Chicago in 1956 he sketched Armstrong numerous times sometimes using sketches as the basis for paintings (pp. 214–215). In both his paintings and drawings, rendered in a fauve-expressionist tradition, Neiman used line and color to capture feelings and moods as well as the appearances of his portrait subjects, as he explained:

> The work is the result of being there...I'm not just drawing a musician, I'm not just copying them, sketching them, painting them. What the musician is doing is the thing that counts the most. The vibrations I get. The sounds of the music.[52]

The African-American painter and collage artist Romare Bearden (1912–1988) developed a very different way to combine portraiture with the feeling of jazz (pp. 218-219). As a child Bearden lived across from the Lafayette Theatre in Harlem, and later as an artist he frequently used jazz themes in paintings and collages expressing his black heritage. In 1961 Bearden accepted an offer from a friend, the photojournalist Sam Shaw (b. 1912) to design "Paris Blues Suite," a book project inspired by the popular movie *Paris Blues*. Shaw, who produced the film drama that featured Armstrong in a supporting role and a sound track by Duke Ellington, supplied photographs for Bearden's collages celebrating not the movie, but rather Armstrong, Ellington, and the history of jazz. The book was never completed, and most of Bearden's designs were executed only as sketches. But one large collage that was finished features photographs of Armstrong and Ellington combined with an African mask, a symbol of the cultural roots out of which their music emerged.[53] Carefully manipulating the abstract components of his art as well as his images, Bearden's choice of colors and placement of objects capture the spirit of jazz:

> At [Stuart] Davis's suggestion, I listened for hours to recordings of Earl Hines at the piano. Finally, I was able to block out the melody and concentrate on the silences between the notes. I found that this was very helpful to me in the transmutation of sound into colors and in the placement of objects in my paintings and collages.[54]

Bearden's collages for "Paris Blues Suite" anticipated his increasing preoccupation with jazz themes in the 1970s and 1980s. A seminal series of collages done in 1975 and entitled "Of the Blues" celebrates key moments in the history of jazz. Many of the works, *New Orleans Farewell* and *Connie's Inn*, seem rooted in Armstrong's career and one image, *Showtime*, actually features Armstrong with his trumpet and trademark handkerchief (p. 15).[55] In the 1980s Bearden collaborated with Shaw again on another unrealized book project about the history of jazz. He made four collages with Shaw's photographs, each pairing Armstrong with different members of his All Stars. The collage of Armstrong with Trummy Young is especially effective, catching the mood of the music as well as Armstrong's relationship with his best friend in the All Stars.

Bearden's success in creating collages that express the spirit of jazz is rooted in part in similarities between the mediums of collage and jazz, art forms that fragment and rearrange pictures and written tunes, respectively. Parallels between collage and jazz have long been acknowledged, and it is perhaps not surprising that when Armstrong sought to express himself pictorially in the 1950s and 1960s, he did so in collage. While Bearden reflects a sophisticated tradition of fine arts collage, Armstrong's collages may be rooted as much in the folk art of assembling scrapbooks and in the commercial use of collage in jazz graphics.

Although Armstrong made collages for more than fifteen years and nearly five hundred survive, his works were made primarily for his own satisfaction (pp. 82-83,131, 220-223). His collages, tenuously held together by cellophane tape, were probably not viewed by Armstrong as significant works of art. Band member Marty Napoleon thought Armstrong made them primarily as memory aids:

> (Louis was always) carrying a pair of scissors around with him and constantly cutting up newspapers, *Jet* and *Life* magazines and anything that he wanted to remember. He would cut out pictures, words, headlines, etc. and paste them all together in little notebooks that he carried around. It was a hobby of his. We'd see him in between sets—cutting and pasting these bits together.[56]

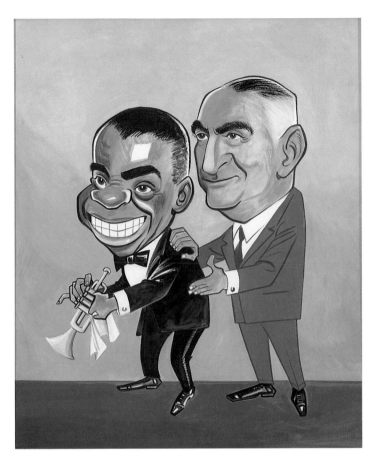

Top left: An anonymous watercolor caricature of Armstrong with his manager Joe Glaser, c. 1950. Louis Armstrong Archives, Queens College, City University of New York.

Top right: Jeanette Eaton's *Trumpeter's Tale: The Story of Young Louis Armstrong* featured illustrations by Elton Fax. Courtesy Institute of Jazz Studies, Rutgers University.

Right: Louis Armstrong's autobiography, *Satchmo: My Life in New Orleans*, was published by Prentice-Hall in 1954. Louis Armstrong Archives, Queens College, City University of New York.

Opposite: Miguel Covarrubias's caricature of Armstrong with Fritz Kreisler, a classical musician who admired jazz, was published in *Vanity* Fair, February 1936. In the 1920s and 1930s, the popular arts were widely embraced by intellectuals, advancing the careers of both the jazzman Armstrong and the illustrator Covarrubias. Courtesy Institute of Jazz Studies, Rutgers University.

Armstrong also referred to his collage making as a hobby, but in a letter that accompanied a collage sent to a friend, he also alluded to creative goals:

> I guess you've wondered why all the regalia (the photo) that I sent to you...huh? Well, you know my hobbie (one of them anyway) is using a lot of scotch tape....My hobbie is to pick out the different things during what I read and piece them together and making a little story of my own.[57]

Created out of photographs, personal letters, and bits of paper linked to his daily life, Armstrong's collages are like an extended diary rich in personal history. They show Armstrong's active role in perpetuating his own story and parallel his prolific writings during this same period. A large and elegant 1952 scrapbook contains some of Armstrong's most finished collages. On the first page, a photo of Armstrong is combined with the heads of jazz players that he admired; a tiny photo of his mentor King Oliver is tellingly placed in the center of his forehead. Most of the surviving collages decorate the cardboard boxes that contain Armstrong's reel-to-reel audiotape collection. They show the people close to Armstrong: his wife Lucille, manager Joe Glaser, and the manufacturer of the laxative that Armstrong endorsed ("This is the lady that makes Swiss Kriss"). In the best of his collages, Armstrong's spontaneous style catches his moods and feelings. *That Happy Feeling* combines those words with an upbeat photograph of Armstrong. A similar exuberant mood can be seen in another collage where a photo of

To Louis from Hiram

Love that "Pops"

Armstrong is encircled by four identical floating Armstrong heads.

In 1968 Armstrong's health started to deteriorate, beginning the slow slide to his death in 1971. With the end clearly in sight, "Pops," as the aged Armstrong was now affectionately called, was increasingly lionized and photographed. Pictures taken during a 1968 summer tour of England show the once-hefty Armstrong as thin and frail; shortly thereafter, coronary problems forced a half-year layoff. During these last years Jack Bradley (b. 1934), a jazz fan and photographer whom Armstrong befriended in the 1950s, spent long periods with him creating a full photo record of his life and moods. Bradley's pictures of Armstrong at the special 70th Birthday Salute at the 1970 Newport Jazz Festival show him thin but energetic, and this impression is confirmed in the documentary film produced for the occasion by jazz promoter George Wein (b. 1925).

In March 1971 Armstrong was hospitalized, but he was back home and planning to go on the road again on June 16 when he was photographed by Annie Leibovitz (b. 1950), a young photographer on her first travel assignment for *Rolling Stone* magazine (pp. 180, 217). Leibovitz hoped to do unposed photo reportage on Armstrong and was disappointed to find that the show business veteran had his own ideas about picture taking. Without any encouragement from Leibowitz, he went through his complete repertoire of poses: taking out his handkerchief, pretending to blow his trumpet, and giving her his famous smile. After a few hours, Leibowitz left, feeling that the session was largely a failure. It was only later that she saw the true poignancy of the photos, which

In the oil painting *Satchmo Head* (1967), LeRoy Neiman fuses portraiture with abstraction rooted in the sound of jazz, using line and color to capture feeling and mood as well as appearance. Collection of Alvin and Joan Wolf. © LeRoy Neiman, 1967.

Sketches by LeRoy Neiman show Armstrong backstage at the Olympia Theatre, Paris, April 24, 1962. Neiman began sketching Armstrong in Chicago in 1956, returned to the subject often, and sometimes used the drawings as the basis for paintings. © LeRoy Neiman, 1962.

The work is the result of being there. . . . I'm not just drawing a musician, I'm not just copying them, sketching them, painting them. What the musician is doing is the thing that counts the most, The vibrations I get. The sounds of the music.

LeRoy Neiman, 1992

were among the last taken of Armstrong. In looking at the photos now, she says:

> You know something is not 100 percent right. You admire the professionalism. You admire that the show must go on. You admire that even in this sort of tired and exhausted state, he's going to give you his best. Those are all very fascinating and admirable moments.[58]

Three weeks later, on July 6, Armstrong was dead. All over the country, the passing of the jazz giant was front-page news, many papers featured photos and special illustrations, including Paul Conrad's cartoon in the *Los Angeles Times* showing Armstrong in heaven out-trumpeting the angel Gabriel (p. 225). Even in death Armstrong was photographed. On July 8, as his body lay in state at a National Guard armory in Manhattan, Fred McDarrah (b. 1926) of the *Village Voice* photographed him resting peacefully in an open coffin as thousands of fans filed by to pay their last respects (p. 224). Although in these photos Armstrong's legendary energy had now given way to a serene calm, even in death, he is surrounded by friends and fans.

The story of Armstrong portraiture does not end with his death. In the years that followed, interest in the jazz giant remained strong and a host of new record albums, publications, souvenirs, and art tributes reused old Armstrong portraits and developed new ones. The most conspicuous of these posthumous images are the statuettes, coffee mugs, dress up dolls, liquor decanters, ceramic hash pipes, and other Armstrong souvenirs that reflect his broad popularity. These items show the codification of Armstrong's image, invariably depicting him in a tuxedo, holding a handkerchief and trumpet, and flashing his ubiquitous smile.

Some posthumous portraits more thoughtfully show Armstrong's place in American culture. David Stone Martin (1913–1992), a talented artist/illustrator who created a host of memorable jazz album covers starting in the early 1940s, rarely portrayed Armstrong while he was alive,[59] but his 1973 drawing successfully captures Armstrong's transformation from living entertainer into jazz legend. Folk artist Malcah Zeldis did a number of painted tributes to Armstrong, including a "Peaceable Kingdom" in which Armstrong joins Abraham Lincoln, the Reverend Martin Luther King, Jr., and others as a symbol of racial harmony (p. 226).[60] In the 1980s the expressionist painter Jean-Michel Basquiat (1960–1988) frequently incorporated references to Armstrong in energetic works full of allusions to American pop culture and his own African-American heritage.[61]

Certainly the most significant of the posthumous Armstrong portraits is the ten-foot-high bronze statue by Elizabeth Catlett (b. 1919) that now stands at the center of Louis Armstrong Park in New Orleans (p. 227).[62] Begun in 1970 and financed by Bing Crosby and other Hollywood entertainers, the statue's history touches on

What I remember the most about this shoot was that he was trying so hard to give me what he thought I, as a photographer, wanted....He had lost a lot of weight and wasn't very well. That effort of having to be 'on' all the time, it was so exhausting.

Annie Leibovitz, 1992

Opposite: Annie Leibovitz photographed Armstrong for *Rolling Stone* magazine on June 16, 1971, just three weeks before his death. Courtesy Annie Leibovitz.

In 1961 Bearden and Shaw collaborated on "Paris Blues Suite," a never-realized book project inspired by the movie *Paris Blues*. In this collaging of Shaw's photos, Bearden shows Armstrong with Duke Ellington. The success of the work reflects similarities between jazz and collage—two improvisational art forms that take elements of a composition, shake them up, and put them back together into something entirely new. Sam Shaw Collection.

Artist Romare Bearden often found inspiration in jazz. These collages from the 1980s show Armstrong with the group's singer, Velma Middleton, and with the All Stars' trombonist, Trummy Young. Done in collaboration with photojournalist Sam Shaw, the collages were intended for a book on the history of jazz. Sam Shaw Collection.

Beginning in the early 1950s, Armstrong made hundreds of collages out of personal papers, photographs, and clippings from newspapers and magazines. The collages survive today in scrapbooks and on the cardboard boxes that contain Armstrong's reel-to-reel audiotape collection. As shown in these 1960 photographs by Dennis Stock, at one time Armstrong's passion for collage filled the walls and even the ceiling of his Corona, New York, house. Courtesy Dennis Stock/Magnum Photos.

many of the artistic and social issues that have surrounded Armstrong and his portraits. Initial debates centered around the appropriate style for the statue. While some people favored a modern abstract statue reflecting jazz music's importance as a modern art form, the committee ultimately opted for the safer approach articulated by Ward Kimball, an artist at Walt Disney Studios:

> This is no time for new horizons in sculpture. The monument just has to be classical and in bronze, and preferably by a *black* artist. Old hat? Yes, but just try to imagine the alternatives: ...A Picasso Louis with two heads? A Calder Louis mobile hanging by multiple nooses?...A 1-inch by 25-ft. Giacometti Louis?...Can you imagine what the black population would say if they looked

Armstrong's collages form an extended self-portrait or diary, incorporating the people and events of life and the world around him.

Opposite

Top: This collage, assembled on a cardboard reel-to-reel tape container, shows Armstrong with his manager, Joe Glaser. Louis Armstrong Archives, Queens College, City University of New York.

Bottom: Armstrong and his wife Lucille are featured on this collage. Louis Armstrong Archives, Queens College, City University of New York.

Above: The words "That Happy Feeling" are a conspicuous element in this collage on a cardboard reel-to-reel tape container. Louis Armstrong Archives, Queens College, City University of New York.

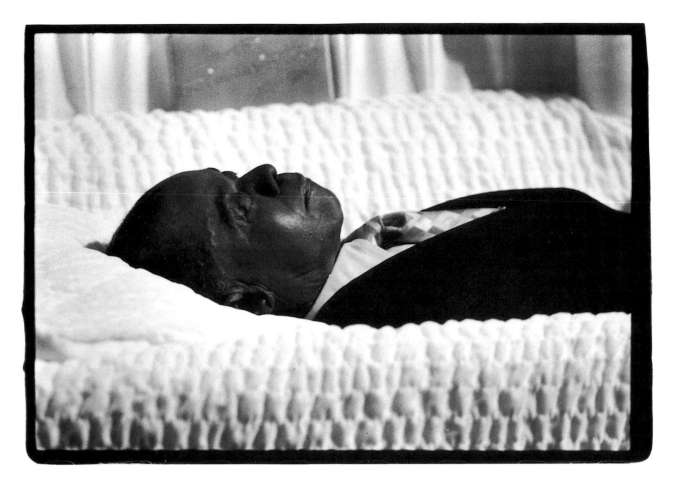

When Armstrong died of heart failure on July 6, 1971, his passing was mourned throughout the world. More than 25,000 people filed past his open coffin as he lay in state at a New York National Guard Armory. Photograph by and courtesy of Fred W. McDarrah.

up to see a George Segal lily-white plaster effigy of Louis Armstrong?[63]

When the successful African-American sculptor Richmond Barthé (1901–1989) turned down the commission because of poor health, the monument committee selected Elizabeth Catlett, a relatively unknown artist eager to succeed with her first major public work. Catlett would have preferred producing a semiabstract statue expressing the "rhythm, movement, joy, and strength" of Armstrong, but she accepted the committee's preference for a realistic, standing figure. In the charged racial environment that followed the civil rights movement of the 1960s and the assassination of Martin Luther King, Jr., however, controversy could not be avoided. For many African-Americans, Armstrong's upbeat persona, molded in the repressed racial climate of the 1920s, was out of tune with the times, which raised serious questions about the mode of his representation. When the statue backers requested a smiling Armstrong, Catlett felt compelled to refuse: "As a black person living at that time, I understand the reasons behind Louie's clowning, but I don't want to perpetuate it and it shouldn't be part of a monument."[64]

Ultimately the Armstrong statue would be physically scarred as it was forced to conform to the new racial climate. At the suggestion of the monument committee, Catlett had depicted Armstrong waving to his fans, but she was shocked when Louisiana locals

Paul Conrad's editorial cartoon of Armstrong in heaven out-trumpeting the Archangel Gabriel (*The Los Angeles Times*, July 7, 1971) was one of many newspaper tributes to Armstrong following his death. Paul Conrad. Copyright 1971 *The Los Angeles Times*. Reprinted with permission.

compared the pose to that of "The Happy Darky," a statue in nearby Baton Rouge. After much soul searching and debate, right before the unveiling of the statue, Catlett modified the position of Armstrong's already cast arm despite clear aesthetic harm.

Catlett's statue has retained a vitality reflecting the true importance of Armstrong's cultural contribution and his power as a symbol of success and goodwill. On July 4, 1976, the U.S. Bicentennial and the date Armstrong chose to celebrate his birthday, the statue was officially unveiled before a large and enthusiastic multiracial audience. Armstrong certainly would have approved the confluence of events that effectively projected his rise from poverty to world acclaim into a testimonial to the American dream. In 1980 the statue became the centerpiece of Louis Armstrong Park, an ambitious thirty-one-acre site that reflects New Orleans' recognition of the importance of jazz and the emergence of Armstrong as the popular personification of the music. Incorporating the historic site of Congo Square, an adjacent concert hall, and plans for a jazz museum, the park pays tribute to both the roots of jazz and its living vitality.[65] Bigger than life, Catlett's statue of Armstrong looms over the park named after him. The struggle had left its mark, but he stands with dignity and pride. In the city where both he and jazz were born, Louis Armstrong was king.

Love baby love. That's the secret. Yeahh.

   Louis Armstrong, 1970

Soon after Armstrong's death, folk artist Malcah Zeldis painted the first of many versions of the *Peaceable Kingdom* that included Armstrong. In this composition of 1990, Armstrong is joined by Abraham Lincoln, Martin Luther King, Jr., Gandhi, John F. Kennedy, Beethoven, Mother Theresa, Albert Einstein, and others. Collection of Cori and Rick Chertof.

Dedicated on July 4, 1976, Elizabeth Catlett's statue of Armstrong stands in New Orleans' Louis Armstrong Park, less than a mile from Armstrong's birthplace. © Jan White Brantley.

NOTES:

1. Letter from Bunk Johnson to Frederic Ramsey, Jr.1940, quoted in Nat Shapiro and Nat Hentoff, eds., *Hear Me Talkin' To Ya; The Story of Jazz as Told by the Men Who Made It* (New York: Dover Publications Inc, 1986) 68.

2. Girard P. Mouton III and Alma D. Williams, "The Eyes of Jazz," *The Jazz Archivist* (A newsletter of the William Hogan Jazz Archive, Tulane University), 8–11. Also see Paddio obituary, *Louisiana Weekly*, 26 May 1947, 1.

3. The posed action photos are rooted in a long tradition of theater photography. See Mary Henderson, *Broadway Ballyhoo; the American Theatre in Posters, Photographis, Magazines, Caricatures, and Programs* (New York, Harry N. Abrams, 1989).

4. Advertisement for Arthur P. Bedou Studio in Allen T. Woods, W*oods Directory; Being a Colored Business, Professional and Trades Directory of New Orleans, Louisiana* (New Orleans, 1914).

5. Lil Hardin Armstrong in Chris Albertson, *Giants of Jazz: Louis Armstrong* (Alexandria, Virginia: Time-Life Books, 1978), 13.

6. Lil Hardin Armstrong recalled that Joe Oliver sent Armstrong a picture of his band to encouraged him to come to Chicago. Louis wrote back, "tell Miss Lil I like her." Lil Armstrong quoted in Shapiro & Hentoff, op. cit., 101

7. Richard Meryman (interview with Louis Armstrong), *Louis Armstrong - A Self Portrait* (New York: Eakins Press, 1971), p. 32.

8. Luther White obituary, *New York Times*, 25 August 1936; Henderson, op. cit., 72–80.

9. Kid Ory, Quoted in Shapiro & Hentoff, op. cit., 109.

10. The signature "Woodard Studio, Chg." or "Woodard Studio N.Y." is frequently found on photographs of black celebrities of the 1920s and 1930s. Unfortunately little is known about the firm. Even Woodard's full name has yet to be identified. An advertisement for the firm appears in Irvin C. Miller, *The Official Theatrical World of Colored Artists the World Over, 1928 Edition*, 66; See also "What of the Receptionist?," *The Light* (Chicago), 14 January 1928.

11. OKeh's advertising philosophy was "based on the idea that the thing people like best is entertainment and that folks love to laugh." See "OKeh Window Display Service," *Talking Machine World*, January 1922 quoted in Ronald Clifford Foreman, Jr., "*Jazz and Race Records; Their Origins and Their Significance For the Record Industry and Society*, Ph.D. dissertation, University of Illinois, 1968.

12. See Bogle essay, in this volume, pp.157-159.

13. George Eastman began developing cameras for amateurs in the 1890s but it was a number of years before the cameras became widely affordable. The key feature was removable film that could be sent to professional processors. See Beaumont Newhall, *The History of Photography* (New York: Museum of Modern Art, 1964).

14. Rex Stewart, "Boy Meets King," *Downbeat*, 15 July 1965. p. 23. The Armstrong in these snapshots contrasts markedly with the professional image of Armstrong recorded shortly after his arrival in New York by the theatrical photographer Apeda (P. 37).

15. Buck Clayton, *Buck Clayton's Jazz World* (New York: Oxford University Press, 1987), 36.

16. Mezz Mezzrow and Bernard Wolfe, *Really The Blues* (New York: Random House, 1946), 183.

17. Because the pictures included the inscription "Johnny Collins presents....," they would receive little distribution when Armstrong relationship with Collins ended a few months after the photo session.

18. Mezzrow and Wolfe, op. cit., 183.

19. Rex Stewart, op. cit., 24.

20. Frank Driggs & Harris Lewine, *Black Beauty, White Heat; A Pictorial History of Classic Jazz* (New York: William Morrow, 1982), 215. Armstrong's sartorial splendor was much discussed amongst English musicians. Dan Ingham recalled that "he had 75 suits." Nat Gonella remembered, "Louis was always a sharp dresser, smart and a bit loud." See Max Jones & John Chilton, *Louis; The Louis Armstrong Story* (Boston and Toronto: Little Brown and Company, 1971), 149-150

21. Dan S. Ingman, "England's Welcome to Louis Armstrong," *Melody Maker*, August 1932.

22. Charles Delaunay, *Delaunay's Dilemma: de la Peinture au Jazz*, (Macon: Editions W., 1985), 83-88; Charles Delaunay, *Noirs Au Blanc: Images de Jazzmen*, (Paris: Editions Porte du Sud, 1986).

23. Mezzrow and Wolfe, op. cit., 222.

24. Armstrong's extroverted, energetic style of the eary 1930s, is still evident in the portrait photos taken by Apeda soon after his return to America in 1935. The pictures were taken to promote Selmer Trumpet, a European musical instrument company with which Armstrong first became associated with in Europe.

25. Kriegsmann first photographed Armstrong for the Cotton Club in 1939 (P. 94). His dynamic double exposures lit by a theater spotlight were designed to match similar shots of Cab Calloway and Bill Robinson used in the club's souvenir picture book. By the 1940's, Kriegsmann was the music industry's leading photographer. Author interview with James Kriegsmann, 14 January 1992. See also: Pat Hackett, "James J. Kriegsmann," *Interview Magazine*, May 1986, 108–13.

26. Richard Meryman (interviewer), "Manager Joe Glaser on Louis," *Life*, 15 April 1966, 114.

27. Joe Deal, "Anton Bruehl," *Image* (Rochester, NY), June 1976.

28. Calvin Bailey primarily did pencil and pastel caricatures for the movie industry and in the nightclubs of Los Angeles. He probably met Armstrong while sketching the cast of "Cabin in the Sky." Letter from Bailey to Claude Barnett, 3 July 1949, Barnett Papers, Manuscripts Division, Chicago Historical Society; Letter from Armstrong to Bailey, 14 June 1949, Collection of Marcella Bailey, Los Angeles.

29. Beverly J. Cox and Denna Jones Anderson, *Miguel Covarrubias Caricatures*, exhibition catalogue (National Portrait Gallery, Washington, D.C.: Smithsonian Institution Press, 1985).

30. John K. Hutchens, "50,000 photos by Vandamm," *New York Times*; for information on Vandamm Studios see: Henderson, op. cit., pp. 81-90. ; "Swingin' the Dream" was also photographed by Lucien Aigner. See: *Aigner's New York*, exhibition catalogue, (Museum of the City of New York, 1992).

31. "Swingin' the Dream" had already closed when Steichen's photograph appeared in the February 1940 issue of *Vogue*. The picture shows Armstrong and Sullivan in the "Swingin' the Dream" costumes, but the text promotes them in a new show at the Cotton Club, the famed Harlem night spot that had recently moved to Broadway in midtown Manhattan.

32. Boris Artzybasheff obituary, *New York Times*, 18 July 1965. A 1931 handbill includes a cartoon drawing of Armstrong wearing a crown and labeled "King of the Trumpet."

33. Among those who photographed Armstrong as King Zulu were Leonard Feather, William Russell and Don Perry.

34. Ben Shahn, "Satch," *Nugget*, December 1957, 49–53.

35. "(*The Trumpeter's Tale*) is loaded with pen sketches by one Elton C. Fax that, if anything, are more insultingly stereotyped than the text." Ron Anger, "Swing that Music: A Survey of Louis Armstrong Literature," *Coda* (Canada) Aug. 1973, 34.

36. Erik Barnouw, *Documentary; A History of the Non-Fiction Film* (New York: Oxford University Press, 1974), 222–228.

37. A frequently reproduced studio portrait from this period, which shows Armstrong in a tuxedo and carrying a suitcase, captures the "Ambassador Satch" image. The photographer has not been identified (P. 88).

38. Among the many notable photographers who portrayed Armstrong and who are not specifically covered by this essay are Otto Hess (p. 109), Bill Gottlieb, Richard Merrill (p. 120), Phil Stern (p. 163), Bob Willoughby, Irving Haberman, Bill Mark (p. 106), Ron Gaella, John-Pierre Leloir, and Sam Shaw (p. 171).

39. Peterson was a guitar player in Rudy Vallee's band who later studied at the Clarence White School of Photography. J. Lee Anderson, "Jazz Images by Charles Peterson," *The Mississippi Rag*, May 1989, 1–6; J. Lee Anderson, "Jazz Images by Charles Peterson, Part II," *The Mississippi Rag*, June 1989, 1–5.

40. Milt Hinton and David G. Berger, *Bass Line: The Stories and Photographs of Milt Hinton* (Philadelphia: Temple University Press, 1988); Milt Hinton, David G.Berger, and Holly Maxson, *OverTime: The Jazz Photographs of Milt Hinton*, (Petaluma, CA: Pomegranate Art Books, 1991).

41. John Szarkowski, *Winogrand: Figments from the Real World (New York: Museum of Modern Art, 1988)*. For more information on Winogrand's ealry work as a photo journalist, see Gerald Marzorati, "El Morocco's Night Watch: A Glimpse of Garry Winogrand's Underexposed Work for the Fifties;" *Vanity Fair*, April 1986, 198–109.

42. Author interview with Gordon Parks, October 14, 1992.

43. Dennis Stock, *Jazz Street* (New York: Doubleday & Company, Inc., 1960), 9.

44. James Lincoln Collier's controversial biography of Armstrong, harshly overstates this aspect of his personality. "There was that everpresent emotional disability: his inability to accept himself and his endless need for approving audiences that followed from it." James Lincoln Collier, *Louis Armstong, An American Genius* (New York: Oxford University Press, 1983) 300.

45. Irving Penn "Inside New York," *Vogue*, July 1948, 61–66. Other celebritites include Truman Capote, Igor Stravinsky, and Georgia O'Keeffe.

46. Alexander Liberman quoted in Vicki Goldberg, "Irving Penn is Difficult. Can't You Tell?," *New York Times*, 24 November 1974.

47. John Cornfield, *Bert Stern: The Photo Illustration* (New York: Alskog Book with Thomas Y. Crowell Company, Inc., 1974).

48. Yvonne Halsman, *Philippe Halsman at Work* (New York: Harry N. Abrams, 1989)

49. Notable photographers who focused on jazz in the 1950s included Eugene Smith, Gjon Mili, and Roy DeCarava. The Newport Jazz Festivals were photographed by Bert Goldblatt, Ken Heyman, Bruce Davidson and Jay Maisel. In 1958 Bert Stern produced *Jazz on a Summer Day*, an innovative feature–length film documentary on the Newport Jazz Festival, which includes footage of Armstrong.

50. Model hoped to collaborate with writer Langston Hughes on a book about jazz. Ann Thomas, *Lisette Model* (Ottawa: National Gallery of Canada, 1970), 136–138.

51. J. Lee Anderson, "Bob Parent," *Mississippi Rag*, February 1991.

52. Author interview with Neiman, March 2, 1991. Also: LeRoy Neiman, *LeRoy Neiman: Art & Life Style* (New York: Felicie, 1974), 248–249. Armstrong attended the opening of Neiman's 1962 exhibition at Hammer Gallery, New York, and purchased a portrait of jazz musician Gerry Mulligan.

53. Shaw recalls that the finished collage of Armstrong and Ellington dates from the early 1960s but one Bearden specialist has questioned this on stylistic grounds. In the 1980s, the image was used as a poster for the Jazzmobile and may date from that time.

54. Bearden quoted in *Riffs and Takes: Music in the Art of Romare Bearden*, Raleigh: North Carolina Museum of Art, 1988).

55. Myron Schwartzman, *Romare Bearden, His Life and Art* (New York: Harry N. Abrams, 1990) 230–239.

56. Quoted in Bert Goldblatt, *Gallery of Jazz*, 126.

57. Letter from Armstrong to Mrs. Marili Mardon c/o Jazz Man Record Shop, 27 September 1953. Louis Armstrong Archives, Queens College, City University of New York

58. Author interview with Annie Leibovitz, 17 March 1992; The photographs illustrated Ralph J. Gleason, "God Bless Louis Armstrong," *Rolling Stone*, 5 August 1971.

59. Manek Daver, *David Stone Martin: Jazz Graphics* (Tokyo: Graphic-sha Publishing Co., 1991).

60. Letter from Malcah Zeldis to Marc Miller, 4 May 1990.

61. Klaus Kertess, "Brushes with Beatitude," in Richard Marshall, *Jean-Michel Basquiat* (New York: Whitney Museum of American Art, 1992), 50–55.

62. Author interview with Elizabeth Catlett, 1 July 1992; author interview with Floyd Levin (director, Louis Armstrong Statue Fund), 22 January 1992. The artist selection committee included Walter Hopps (Corcoran Gallery of Art) James Byrnes (Delgado Museum of Art), Ward Kimball (Walt Disney Productions), Gerard Nordland (San Francisco Museum of Art), and David Stuart (David Stuart Gallery).

63. Letter from Ward Kimball to David Stuart, 19 October 1970, Records of the Louis Armstrong Statue Fund, possession of Floyd Levin, Los Angeles, California.

64. Elizabeth Catlett to Floyd Levin, 30 September 1975, Catlett manuscript collection, Amistad Research Center, Tulane Univsersity, New Orleans.

65. In addition to Congo Square, the site where African-Americans congregated to sing and dance in nineteenth-century New Orleans, Louis Armstrong park also includes three historical buildings associated with Creole life in Treme.

Selected Bibliography

ARMSTRONG MANUSCRIPT COLLECTIONS

Louis Armstrong Archives, Queens College, Flushing, NY. Collection contains 17 original Armstrong manuscripts including: "Louis Armstrong & the Jewish Family in New Orleans," begun March 31, 1969, 76 leaves; "New Orleans a Letter from Larry Amadee" (copied and expanded on by Armstrong), c. 1968, 42 leaves; "Open Letter to Fans," March 15, 1970, 22 leaves; "Our Neighborhood," c. 1969, six leaves. Collection of 15 letters written by Armstrong includes: Armstrong to Bing Crosby, n.d.; Armstrong to his sister Beatrice Armstrong, n.d.

Institute of Jazz Studies, Rutgers University, Newark, NJ. Collection contains two Armstrong manuscripts: An autobiography written at the request of Robert Goffin, c. 1944, 128 leaves on 5 writing tablets; Carbon typescript of unedited text for *Satchmo: My Life in New Orleans* (New York: Prentice-Hall, 1954), c. 1954, 149 leaves. Collection of letters includes: Armstrong to jazz critic Leonard Feather, 6 letters, 1941–1969; Armstrong to jazz writer Robert Goffin, 5 letters, 1944.

Music Division, Library of Congress, Washington D.C. Collection of 22 letters, telegrams, and memoes sent by Armstrong to his manager Joe Glaser, 1955–1960.

BOOKS, ARTICLES, INTERVIEWS BY ARMSTRONG (by date)

Armstrong, Louis (with music section edited by Horace Gerlach), *Swing That Music*. London: Longmans, 1936. Reprint: New York: Da Capo Press, 1993.

_____. "Special Jive." *Harlem Tatler*, July 1940.

_____. "I'll Still Be Swinging When I'm Sixty." *The Baton*, October 1941.

_____. "Chicago, Chicago, That Toddlin' Town: How King and Ol' Satch Dug It in the Twenties." *Esquire's 1947 Jazz Book*, 1946.

_____. "Storyville— Where the Blues were Born," *True*, November 1947.

_____. "Europe - With Kicks." *Holiday* 7, June 1950.

_____. "Jazz on a High Note." *Esquire*, December, 1951.

_____. "Why I Like Dark Women." *Ebony* 9, August, 1954.

_____. *Satchmo: My Life in New Orleans*. New York: Prentice-Hall, 1954. Reprints: New York: Signet, 1955; New York: Da Capo, 1986.

—— (interviewed). "They Cross Iron Curtain To Hear American Jazz." *U.S. News & World Report* 39, December 2, 1955.

_____. "Its Tough to Top A Million." *Our World*, August 1956.

_____ (as told to David Dachs). "Daddy, How The Country Has Changed!" *Ebony* 61, May 1961.

—— (interview with Richard Meryman). "An Interview with Louis Armstrong." *Life* 60, April 15, 1966. Reprint: Meryman, Richard. *Louis Armstrong: A Self-Portrait*. New York: Eakins Press, 1971.

_____. "Scanning the History of Jazz," *Esquire* 26, December 1971.

ARMSTRONG BIOGRAPHIES

Albertson, Chris. *Giants of Jazz: Louis Armstrong*. Alexandria, VA: Time-Life Books Inc., 1978.

Collier, James Lincoln. *Louis Armstrong, An American Genius*. New York: Oxford University Press, 1983.

Eaton, Jeanette. *Trumpeter's Tale: The Story of Young Louis Armstrong*. New York: William Morrow & Company, 1955.

Giddins, Gary. *Satchmo*. New York: Doubleday, 1988.

Goffin, Robert. *Horn of Plenty: The Story of Louis Armstrong*. New York: Allen, Towne & Heath, 1947.

Jones, Max, and John Chilton. *Louis: The Louis Armstrong Story*. Boston and Toronto: Little, Brown, and Company, 1971.

McCarthy, Albert J. *Louis Armstrong*. London: Cassell, 1960.

Panassie, Hugues. *Louis Armstrong*. New York: Charles Scribner's Sons, 1971.

Pinfold, Mike. *Louis Armstrong*. New York: Universe Books, 1987.

Richards, Kenneth G. *People of Destiny: Louis Armstrong*. Chicago: Childrens Press, 1967.

Sanders, Ruby Wilson. *Jazz Ambassador: Louis Armstrong*. Chicago: Childrens Press, 1973.

Tanenhaus, Sam. *Louis Armstrong: Musician*. New York: Chelsea House, 1989.

Westerberg, Hans. *Boy From New Orleans: A Discography of Louis "Satchmo" Armstrong*. Copenhagen: Jazzmedia, 1981.

GENERAL REFERENCE

Barker, Danny. *A Life in Jazz*. London: Macmillan, 1986.

Bechet, Sidney. *Treat It Gentle*. New York: Hill and Wang, 1960.

Bigard, Barney, with Barry Martyn. *With Louis and the Duke*. New York: Oxford University Press, 1986.

Bogle, Donald. *Blacks in American Films and Television: An Illustrated Encyclopedia*. New York: Fireside, 1989.

_____. *Toms, Coons, Mulattos, Mammies, & Bucks: An Interpretive History of Blacks in American Films*. New York: Continuum, 1989.

Clayton, Buck, with Nancy Miller Elliott. *Buck Clayton's Jazz World*. New York: Oxford University Press, 1987.

Dance, Stanley. *The World of Earl Hines*, New York: Charles Scribner's Sons, 1977.

Daver, Manek. *Jazz Graphics - David Stone Martin*. Tokyo, Japan: Graphic-sha Publishing Co., Ltd., 1991.

Driggs, Frank, and Harris Lewine. *Black Beauty, White Heat; A Pictorial History of Classic Jazz*. New York: William Morrow and Company, Inc, 1982.

Ellington, Edward Kennedy (Duke). *Music is My Mistress*. Garden City, NY: Doubleday, 1973.

Foster, George "Pops" with Tom Stoddard. *The Autobiography of George "Pops" Foster*. Berkeley and Los Angeles: University of California Press, 1971.

Hadler, Mona. "Jazz and the Visual Arts," *Arts Magazine* 57, June 1983.

Hammond, John, with Irving Townsend. *John Hammond on Record*. New York: Summit, 1977.

Henderson, Mary. *Broadway Ballyhoo; the American Theatre in Posters, Photographs, Magazines, Caricatures, and Programs*. New York: Harry N. Abrams, 1989.

Hughes, Langston and Milton Meltzer. *Black Magic: A Pictorial History of the Negro in Entertainment*. Englewood Cliff, NJ: Prentice-Hall, 1967.

Kellner, Bruce, editor. *The Harlem Renaissance: A Historical Dictionary for the Era*. New York: Methuen, 1984.

Kenny, William Howland. *Chicago Jazz: A Cultural History 1904–1930*. New York: Oxford University Press, 1993.

Kisch, John, and Edward Mapp. *A Separate Cinema: Fifty Years of Black Cast Posters*. New York: Farrar, Straus and Giroux, 1992.

Lewis, David Levering. *When Harlem Was in Vogue*. New York: Knopf, 1981.

Locke, Alain, editor. "Harlem: Mecca of the New Negro." *Survey Graphics*, March 1925.

_____. *The New Negro: An Interpretation*. New York: Boni, 1925. Reprint: New York: Atheneum, 1968.

Lomax, Alan. *Mr. Jelly Roll: The Fortunes of Jelly Roll Morton, New Orleans Creole and "Inventor" of Jazz*. New York: Duell, Sloane, and Pearce, 1950.

Long, Richard. *African Americans: A Portrait*: New York: Crescent Books, 1993.

MacDonald, J. Fred. *Blacks and White TV: Afro-Americans in Television since 1948*. Chicago: Nelson-Hall Publishers, 1983.

Marquis, Donald. *The Search for Buddy Bolden*. Baton Rouge: Louisiana State University Press, 1978.

McElroy, Guy C. *Facing History The Black Image in American Art, 1710–1940*. San Francisco: Bedford Arts and Washington, D.C.: The Corcoran Gallery of Art, 1990.

Meeker, David. *Jazz in the Movies: A Guide to Jazz Musicians, 1917–1977*. New Rochelle, NY: Arlington House, 1977.

Mezzrow, Mezz, and Bernard Wolfe. *Really The Blues*. New York: Random House, 1946.

North Carolina Museum of Art. *Riffs and Takes: Music in the Art of Romare Bearden*. Raleigh: North Carolina Museum of Art, 1988.

Powell, Richard J. *The Blues Aesthetic: Black Culture and Modernism*. Washington, D.C.: Washington Project for the Arts, 1989.

Ramsey Jr., Frederick, and Charles Edward Smith, editors. *Jazzmen: The Story of Hot Jazz Told in the Lives of the Men Who Created It*. New York: Harcourt, Brace, 1939.

Rose, Al and Edmond Souchon. *New Orleans Jazz; A Family Album*, Baton Rouge: Louisiana State University Press, 1967.

Schuller, Gunther. *Early Jazz: Its Roots and Musical Development*. New York: Oxford University Press, 1968.

Shapiro, Nat, and Nat Hentoff, editors. *Hear Me Talkin' To Ya: The Story of Jazz as Told by the Men Who Made It*. New York: Rhinehart, 1955. Reprinted: New York: Dover, 1986.

Wolbert, Klaus. *That's Jazz: Der Sound des 20. Jahrhunderts*, exh. cat. Darmstadt, Germany: Ausstellunghallen Mathildenhohe, 1989.

Wright, John S., and Tracy E. Smith. *A Stronger Soul Within A Finer Frame: Portraying African-Americans in the Black Renaissance*. Minneapolis: University Art Museum, University of Minnesota, 1990.

Louis Armstrong: A Cultural Legacy

Organized by the Queens Museum of Art and the Smithsonian Institution Traveling Exhibition Service (SITES).

Exhibition Curator: Marc H. Miller

SITES Project Director: Marquette Folley

Designed and edited by Office of Exhibits Central, Smithsonian Institution

Object list for the complete show at the Queens Museum of Art. An abridged version of this exhibition will travel to other venues.

Dimensions are given in inches, unless otherwise stated.

SECTION I. NEW ORLEANS

A. THE NEW ORLEANS OF ARMSTRONG'S YOUTH, 1901-1922

Jules Pascin
The Balconies, New Orleans, 1916
Oil on canvas, 29¼ x 25½
Collection of Melba and Moise Steeg, New Orleans

William Woodward
St. Louis Cathedral Viewed from Orleans Street, 1901
Oil crayon on board, 22½ x 28½
New Orleans Museum of Art; Gift of the Edgar Stern Family, New Orleans

William Woodward
Second Ursulines Convent and Priest's House, 1912
Oil crayon on board, 22 x 28
New Orleans Museum of Art; Gift of the Edgar Stern Family, New Orleans

Arnold Genthe
Off Pirate's Alley, c. 1925
Platinum print, 13⅜ x 10¼
New Orleans Museum of Art, Museum Purchase: City of New Orleans Capital Fund

Arnold Genthe
Street Vendor, c. 1925
Platinum print, 12³/₁₆ x 9¾
New Orleans Museum of Art, Museum Purchase: City of New Orleans Capital Fund

Arnold Genthe
Batten Shutters and Stucco Walls, c. 1925
Platinum print, 13 x 9³/₁₆
New Orleans Museum of Art, Museum Purchase: City of New Orleans Capital Fund

Arnold Genthe
A Quadroon Belle, c. 1925

Platinum print, 13³/₁₆ x 10⅜
New Orleans Museum of Art, Museum Purchase: City of New Orleans Capital Fund

B. BIRTH OF A LEGEND

Villard Paddio
Louis Armstrong with His Mother, Mayann, and His Sister, Beatrice, c. 1922, reprinted c. 1940
Hand-tinted photograph, 18 x 12½ (oval)
Louis Armstrong Archives, Queens College, City University of New York

Unidentified (photographer)
Will Armstrong, Father of Louis Armstrong, c. 1920, reprinted c. 1940
Hand-tinted photograph, 18 x 12½ (oval)
Louis Armstrong Archives, Queens College, City University of New York

Sanborn Map Co.
Insurance Maps of New Orleans, La., Map 291 (neighborhood of Armstrong's birth), 1908
Printed map, 26⅜ x 19⅝
Louisiana Division, New Orleans Public Library

Unidentified (photographer)
The Karnofsky Family, c. 1917
Black-and-white photograph (copy), 8 x 10
Courtesy the Karnofsky Family

Louis Armstrong
"When I would be on the junk wagon with Alex Karnofsky . . . ," 1969
Manuscript page, ink on paper, 10 x 8 (approx.)
Louis Armstrong Archives, Queens College, City University of New York

Arthur P. Bedou (attributed)
Colored Waifs Home Brass Band with Louis Armstrong, c. 1913
Black-and-white photograph (copy), 8 x 10
Frank Driggs Collection

Villard Paddio
The Jones Home for Colored Waifs, c. 1931
Printed postcard, 6 x 4¾
Louis Armstrong Archives, Queens College, City University of New York

"Section J" Sign from the Home for Colored Waifs
Wooden sign, 6 x 5½
New Orleans Jazz Club Collections, Louisiana State Museum

C. MUSIC ALL AROUND

"A Charity Pic-nic for the Benefit of the Charity Hospital Annex for Colored

Female Patients, Lincoln Park...Music by Magnolia Orchestra," 1911
Printed broadside, 14½ x 18
William Ransom Hogan Jazz Archive, Howard-Tilton Memorial Library, Tulane University

"A Grand Soiree Dansante to be given by the Lilac Social and Pleasure Club, Economy Hall," 1909
Printed broadside, 14½ x 18
William Ransom Hogan Jazz Archive, Howard-Tilton Memorial Library, Tulane University

Sidewalk Tiles and Piano Keys from Economy Hall, n.d.
Floor tiles (2) and piano keys (4) with hammers
Historic New Orleans Collection, William Russell Collection

Arthur P. Bedou
The John Robichaux Orchestra, c. 1910
Black-and-white photograph, 5 x 7
William Ransom Hogan Jazz Archive, Howard-Tilton Memorial Library, Tulane University

Arthur P. Bedou
The Arnold Metoyer Band at Tom Anderson's Cafe, 1923
Black-and-white photograph, 7½ x 13⅞
William Ransom Hogan Jazz Archive, Howard-Tilton Memorial Library, Tulane University

Arthur P. Bedou
The Manuel Perez Orchestra at the Pythian Temple, c. 1924
Black-and-white photograph, 8 x 10
William Ransom Hogan Jazz Archive, Howard-Tilton Memorial Library, Tulane University

Arthur P. Bedou
Piron-Williams Band in Uniform, 1914
Black-and-white photograph, 5¼ x 9½
William Ransom Hogan Jazz Archive, Howard-Tilton Memorial Library, Tulane University

Arthur P. Bedou
Piron-Williams Band Dressed for Vaudeville Appearance, 1914.
Black-and-white photograph, 4⅝ x 6⅝
William Ransom Hogan Jazz Archive, Howard-Tilton Memorial Library, Tulane University

Williams & Piron Music Publishing Co., New Orleans
Mama's Baby Boy, A Jazz Song, 1917
Sheet music, 13¾ x 10⅝

William Ransom Hogan Jazz Archive,
Howard-Tilton Memorial Library,
Tulane University

Clarence Williams Music Publishing
Co., New York
*I Wish I Could Shimmy Like My Sister
Kate*, 1922
Sheet music, 12¼ x 9¼
William Ransom Hogan Jazz Archive,
Howard-Tilton Memorial Library,
Tulane University

Apeda, New York City
Original Dixieland Jazz Band, c. 1917
Black-and-white photograph, 9¼ x 13⅞
William Ransom Hogan Jazz Archive,
Howard-Tilton Memorial Library,
Tulane University

D. STORYVILLE

Romare Bearden
Storyville, 1974
Collage with acrylic and lacquer on
board, 15¼ x 20
Barbara and Ronald Balser

E.J. Bellocq
Women of Storyville, c. 1911–1913
Black-and-white photographs (2),
10 x 8 each
Fraenkel Gallery, San Francisco

William Fitzner (architect)
*Elevation for Brothel, Basin Street, and
Iberville*, 1900
Ink on tracing paper, 19½ x 18½
Notarial Archives, New Orleans

William Fitzner (architect)
*Floor Plan for Brothel, Basin Street,
and Iberville*, 1900
Ink on tracing paper, 16½ x 24¼
Notarial Archives, New Orleans

William Fitzner (architect)
*Tom Anderson's Saloon, Basin Street,
and Iberville*, 1900
Ink on tracing paper, 17¼ x 23¾
Notarial Archives, New Orleans

E. RIVERBOATS

Arthur P. Bedou
*The Fate Marable Band on the
Riverboat S.S. Capitol*, c. 1918
Black-and-white photograph (copy),
8 x 10
Frank Driggs Collection

Charles Franck
*New Orleans Wharf with Streckfus
Steamboats*, 1920s
Black-and-white photograph reprinted
from original negative, 11 x 14
Historic New Orleans Collection

Unidentified (photographer)
Ballroom on S.S. Capitol, 1920s
Black-and-white photograph, 4½ x 6½
Special Collections, Tulane University
Library

*Dance Excursions on the S.S. Capitol
(Advertisement)*, 1920s
Newspaper clipping mounted on
scrapbook page, 10 x 7⅞
Special Collections, Tulane University
Library

William Aiken Walker
*Comin' From the Market Near Baton
Rouge*, c. 1885
Oil on canvas, 14 x 20
The David Warner Foundation,
Tuscaloosa, Alabama

SECTION II. CHICAGO

A. MOVING NORTH

Aaron Douglas and Langston Hughes
Bound No'th Blues (from *Weary Blues*),
c. 1926
Offset lithograph, 16 x 11
Art & Artifacts Division, Schomburg
Center for Research in Black
Culture, The New York Public
Library, Astor, Lenox and Tilden
Foundations

Stokely Webster
Chicago Rail Yard, 1933
Oil on canvas, 10½ x 13⅞
Illinois State Museum

Archibald Motley, Jr.
Black Belt, 1934
Oil on canvas, 31¾ x 39⅜
Hampton University Museum, Hampton, Virginia

Archibald Motley, Jr.
Saturday Night, 1935
Oil on canvas, 32 x 40
Howard University Gallery of Art,
Washington, D.C.

Archibald Motley, Jr.
Barbecue, 1935
Oil on canvas, 36¼ x 40⅛
Howard University Gallery of Art,
Washington, D.C.

B. ARMSTRONG AND JAZZ IN CHICAGO, 1922–1929

Daguerre of Chicago
King Oliver's Creole Jazz Band, c.
1922–1924
Black-and-white photograph, 11 x 14
Floyd Levin

Blanding Sloan
Jazz—The New Possession, c. 1925
Woodcut, 12 x 9
National Museum of American Art,
Smithsonian Institution, Museum
Purchase made possible by Emily
Tuckerman and Charles Albert

Louis Armstrong
Cornet Chop Suey (A Jazz Fox Trot),
1924
Handwritten music score, 13 x 9½
Music Division, Library of Congress

Louis Armstrong
Gully Low Blues, 1927
Handwritten music score, 13 x 9½
Music Division, Library of Congress

Harry P. Jay of Chicago (manufacturer)
*"Columbia" Trumpet in B Flat (once
owned by Louis Armstrong)*, c. 1920
Brass trumpet
J.I. Kislak Mortgage Corporation

Consolidated Music
*Heebie Jeebies (with portrait of
Armstrong's Hot Five on cover)*, 1926
Printed sheet music, 12½ x 9⅜
New Orleans Jazz Club Collections,
Louisiana State Museum

Melrose Bros. Music Company,
Chicago
*Sugar Foot Stomp (with portrait of King
Oliver's Creole Jazz Band on cover)*,
1927
Printed sheet music, 12 x 9 (approx.)
William Ransom Hogan Jazz Archive,
Howard-Tilton Memorial Library,
Tulane University

Melrose Bros. Music Company,
Chicago
*Louis Armstrong's 125 Jazz Breaks for
Cornet*, 1927
Book of sheet music, 10⅛ x 7
Historic New Orleans Collection,
William Russell Collection

*Clippings Showing Armstrong Career in
Chicago (in scrapbook assembled by
Alpha Smith)*, c. 1929
Newspaper clippings mounted on
scrapbook pages (2), 7¼ x 10 each
Louis Armstrong Archives, Queens
College, City University of New York

Adolf Dehn
Jazz Babies, 1927
Ink on paper, 13½ x 19
Mrs. Adolf Dehn

Romare Bearden
Jazz (Chicago) Grand Terrace—1930,
1964
Photograph projection, 66 x 50
Howard University Gallery of Art,
Washington, D.C.

C. LIL HARDIN ARMSTRONG AND ALPHA SMITH ARMSTRONG

Maurice of Chicago
Lil Hardin Armstrong, c. 1935
Black-and-white photograph, 10 x 8
Frank Driggs Collection

Louis Armstrong
"My Romance with Lil Armstrong,"
c. 1944
Handwritten pages (2), 10¼ x 6¼ each
Institute of Jazz Studies, Rutgers
University

Unidentified (artist)
Silhouettes of Louis Armstrong and Alpha Smith, c. 1929
Cut paper silhouettes mounted on scrapbook page, 7¼ x 10
Louis Armstrong Archives, Queens College, City University of New York

D. ARMSTRONG'S EARLY PHONOGRAPH RECORDINGS

Woodard Studios
Louis Armstrong, c. 1928
Black-and-white photograph, 8⅞ x 7
Historic New Orleans Collection, William Russell Collection

Daguerre of Chicago
Louis Armstrong's Hot Five, c. 1925
Black-and-white photograph, 7 x 9½
Historic New Orleans Collection, William Russell Collection

Victor Talking Machine Company
Victrola Electrola, 1928
Wood and mixed media, 63 x 25¼ x 23¾
Smithsonian Institution

Okeh Truetone
"Heebie Jeebies," 1926
78 rpm phonograph record, 10 (diameter)
Institute of Jazz Studies, Rutgers University

Okeh Electric
"West End Blues," 1928
78 rpm phonograph record, 10 (diameter)
Institute of Jazz Studies, Rutgers University

Okeh Electric
"Ain't Misbehavin'," 1929
78 rpm phonograph record, 10 (diameter)
Institute of Jazz Studies, Rutgers University

Jan Matulka
Still life Arrangement with Phonograph and African Sculpture, 1929
Oil on canvas, 30 x 40
National Museum of American Art, Smithsonian Institution

SECTION III. NEW YORK

A. FIRST VISIT TO NEW YORK, 1924–1925

Winold Reiss
Dawn in Harlem, c. 1925
Ink and ink wash on paper, 19 x 14
James DeWoody, New York

Winold Reiss
Interpretation of Harlem Jazz, c. 1925
Ink and watercolor on paper, 20 x 15
Mr. and Mrs. W. Tjark Reiss

John Held, Jr.
Teaching Old "Dogs" New Tricks

(original art for *Life* magazine cover), 1926
Gouache and ink on paper, 16 x 13
Courtesy of James Graham & Sons, New York

Charles Demuth
Negro Jazz Band, 1916
Watercolor on paper, 13 x 8
Dr. Irwin Goldstein

Stuart Davis
Dancer in Newark, c. 1916
Charcoal on paper
Earl Davis

Miguel Covarrubias
Blues (Woman Singing), (original illustration for W.C. Handy, *Blues: An Anthology*), 1926
Ink on illustration board, 15 x 10
Library of Congress, Prints and Photographs Division

White Studios, New York
Fletcher Henderson Orchestra (inscribed by Armstrong to Fate Marable), Fall 1924
Black-and-white photograph with ink inscription, 11 x 14
Frank Driggs Collection

Perry Bradford Music Publishing Company
Crazy Blues (with portrait of Mamie Smith and Her Jazz Hounds on cover), c. 1920
Printed sheet music, 12⅛ x 9
Historic New Orleans Collection, William Russell Collection

Clarence Williams Music Publishing Co.
New Orleans Hop Scop Blues (with portrait of Clarence Williams on cover), 1920s
Printed sheet music, 12⅛ x 9¼
Historic New Orleans Collection, William Russell Collection

Clarence Williams Music Publishing Co.
Oh Daddy Blues (with portrait of Bessie Smith on cover), 1923
Printed sheet music, 12 x 9 (approx.)
Frank Driggs Collection

W.C. Handy (composer)
Beale Street Blues (with portrait of W.C. Handy on cover), 1917
Printed sheet music, 12 x 9 (approx.)
Moorland-Spingarn Research Center, Howard University

B. SECOND VISIT TO NEW YORK, 1929

Unidentified (photographer)
On the Road from Chicago to New York: "Having lots of fun in Niagra Fall"; "On Our Way to New York"; "In New York"; "2 Real Buddies in N.Y.", (inscribed by Louis Armstrong), 1929
Black-and-white snapshots (5) mounted on scrapbook pages (2), 7¼ x 10, each page
Louis Armstrong Archives, Queens College, City University of New York

Apeda, New York City
Armstrong with Carroll Dickerson's Orchestra, 1929
Sepia-toned photograph (copy), 10⅞ x 13⅞
New Orleans Jazz Club Collections, Louisiana State Museum

Otis C. Butler
Interior, Connie's Inn, c. 1930
Black-and-white photograph, 9 x 11
Photographs & Prints Division, Schomburg Center for Research in Black Culture, The New York Public Library, Astor, Lenox and Tilden Foundations

Mills Music Inc. (publisher), Leff (illustrator)
"Ain't Misbehavin'" from Connie's Hot Chocolates
Printed sheet music, 9¼ x 12½
Estate of Estelle Newmark

Rex Studio, Columbus, Ohio
Andy Razaf (inscribed "Yours Truely Andy Razaf"), 1920s
Black-and-white photograph with ink inscription, 8 x 10 (approx.)
Photographs & Prints Division, Schomburg Center for Research in Black Culture, The New York Public Library, Astor, Lenox and Tilden Foundations

Campbell Studios, New York City
Fats Waller, 1924
Black-and-white photograph (copy), 10 x 8
Institute of Jazz Studies, Rutgers University

Winold Reiss
Hot Chocolates, 1929
Crayon and pastel on paper, 22 x 28½
Shepherd Gallery, New York

C. JAZZ AGE HARLEM

E. Simms Campbell
A Night-Club Map of Harlem, 1932
Photocopy of ink drawing, 26 x 36
Elizabeth Campbell Rollins

Reginald Marsh
Tuesday Night at the Savoy Ballroom, 1930
Tempera on composition board, 36 x 48½
Rose Art Museum, Brandeis University, Waltham, Massachusetts; Gift of the Honorable William Benton

Jules Pascin
Dance in Harlem, c. 1925
Pen and charcoal on paper, 20 x 21 (framed)
E. William Judson

Stephen Longstreet
Scenes from Jazz-Age New York: "Flapper," "Reefer Man," "Late Night," c. 1927

Ink drawings (3), 8½ x 11 each
Stephen Longstreet Collection, Special
Collections, Boston University

Jacob Lawrence
Rooftops No. 1 (This is Harlem), 1942–
1943
Gouache and pencil on paper, 15⅜ x
22 11/16
Hirshhorn Museum and Sculpture
Garden, Smithsonian Institution

SECTION IV. THE WORLD'S GREATEST TRUMPETER

A. SPREADING HIS WINGS

Gibson, Chicago
Louis Armstrong, 1933
Black-and-white photographs (6), 10 x
8 each
Louis Armstrong Archives, Queens
College, City University of New York

Theatrical of Chicago
Louis Armstrong (inscribed "To my
cousin Isaac Miles, 8/9/31"), 1931
Black-and-white photograph, 14⅛ x 11
William Ransom Hogan Jazz Archive,
Howard-Tilton Memorial Library,
Tulane University

Unidentified (photographer)
*Armstrong with His Manager Johnny
Collins*, 1930–1932
Black-and-white snapshot, 2½ x 3½
(approx.)
Louis Armstrong Archives, Queens
College, City University of New York

Unidentified (photographer)
Band Waiting for the Bus, 1930–1932
Black-and-white snapshot, 2½ x 3½
(approx.)
Louis Armstrong Archives, Queens
College, City University of New York

Unidentified (photographer)
Bus, 1930–1932
Black-and-white snapshot, 2½ x 3½
(approx.)
Louis Armstrong Archives, Queens
College, City University of New York

Unidentified (photographer)
*Louis Armstrong, Alpha Smith, Bus
Driver, and Others*, 1930–32
Black-and-white snapshot, 2½ x 3½
(approx.)
Louis Armstrong Archives, Queens
College, City University of New York

Unidentified (photographer)
Looking at a Buck and Bubbles Poster,
1930–32
Black-and-white snapshot, 2½ x 3½
(approx.)
Louis Armstrong Archives, Queens
College, City University of New York

*TO NIGHT—Louis Armstrong King of
the Trumpet...for White Patrons*,
Palace (Cleveland), 1931

Broadside, 6 x 4½
Louis Armstrong Archives, Queens
College, City University of New York
*Johnnie Collins Presents the World's
Greatest Trumpet Player...Royal
Theatre, Baltimore*, 1931
Handbill, 9 x 6
Louis Armstrong Archives, Queens
College, City University of New York

Adolf Dehn
That's Jazz, 1929
Ink on paper, 15 x 22
Collection of Virginia Dehn, Courtesy
of Harmon-Meek Gallery, Naples,
Florida

Franz Kline
Drummer and *Trombonist*, 1933
Oil on wood panels (2), 40 x 40
(approx.) each
From the "Jazz Mural" Collection of
Larry and Charlene Graver

B. BACK IN NEW ORLEANS, 1931

Villard Paddio
*On Stage at Suburban Gardens, New
Orleans*, 1931
Sepia-toned photographs (2), 8 x 10
(approx.) each
Historic New Orleans Collection,
William Russell Collection

Villard Paddio
*Banquet Honoring Louis Armstrong,
Astoria Hotel, New Orleans*, 1931
Black-and-white photograph, 8 x 10
(approx.)
Frank Driggs Collection

Villard Paddio
*Banquet Honoring Louis Armstrong,
Crowd Outside the Astoria Hotel,
New Orleans*, 1931
Black-and-white photograph, 8 x 10
(approx.)
Frank Driggs Collection

*Louis Armstrong Cigar Label and
Advertising Broadside* ("Smoke Louis
Armstrong"), 1931
Label and broadside mounted on
scrapbook page, 15½ x 11³/₁₆
Louis Armstrong Archives, Queens
College, City University of New York

*Letter from the Municipal Boys Home
Thanking Armstrong for Dedicating a
Radio Broadcast to Them*, 1931
Typewritten letter mounted on
scrapbook page, 15½ x 11³/₁₆
Louis Armstrong Archives, Queens
College, City University of New York

Villard Paddio
*Louis Armstrong, Lil Armstrong,
Captain Joseph Jones, and Peter
Davis at the Municipal Boys Home*,
1931
Black-and-white photograph, 7⅛ x 9¼
(approx.)
Historic New Orleans Collection

Arthur P. Bedou
*The Louis Armstrong Band at the
Municipal Boys Home*, 1931
Black-and-white photograph, 4½ x 6⅜
William Ransom Hogan Jazz Archive,
Howard-Tilton Memorial Library,
Tulane University

Villard Paddio
*Armstrong's Secret Nine Baseball
Team*, 1931
Black-and-white photograph, 8 x 10⅛
Historic New Orleans Collection,
William Russell Collection

Louis Armstrong Day! Base-ball, 1931
Printed broadside, 9 x 6
Louis Armstrong Archives, Queens
College, City University of New York

C. FIRST VISITS TO EUROPE, 1932–1935

*"England's Welcome to Louis
Armstrong," Melody Maker* (London),
August 1932
Magazine, 8½ x 5½
Institute of Jazz Studies, Rutgers
University

*"Armstrong Arrive!" Music: Le Maga-
zine du Jazz* (Brussels), November
1934
Printed newspaper, 11½ x 8½
Institute of Jazz Studies, Rutgers
University

Ava Studio, London
Louis Armstrong, 1933
Black-and-white photograph, 9 x 7
Frank Driggs Collection

Delacre et Martin, Brussels (after "M.G.")
Louis Armstrong, 1934
Black-and-white photographs of ink
sketches (2), 8⅞ x 6½ each
Louis Armstrong Archives, Queens
College, City University of New York

Rhythm Studio, London
*With Jack Hylton and Band in Louis's
Dressing Room, Palladium, London*,
1932
Black-and-white photograph, 7½ x 9½
Louis Armstrong Archives, Queens
College, City University of New York

Unidentified (photographer)
*Entering the Ace of Spades' Road
House, England*, 1934
Black-and-white photograph, 8 x 10
(approx.)
Louis Armstrong Archives, Queens
College, City University of New York

Peddy-Foto (B.A. "Peddy" Moberg)
Louis Armstrong in Stockholm, 1933
Black-and-white photographs (2),
7 x 9¼ each
Louis Armstrong Archives, Queens
College, City University of New York

U.S. Department of State
Passport Issued to Louis Armstrong,
July 6, 1932

Passport, 3½ x 5
Louis Armstrong Archives, Queens
 College, City University of New York

Unidentified (photographer)
*Louis Armstrong, Alpha Smith and
 John Hammond on Ship*, 1932
Black-and-white snapshot, 3 x 2
 (approx.)
Louis Armstrong Archives, Queens
 College, City University of New York

Unidentified (photographer)
*Louis Armstrong and Alpha Smith in
 Paris*, 1934
Black-and-white snapshot, 2½ x 4
 (approx.)
Louis Armstrong Archives, Queens
 College, City University of New York

Delacre et Martin, Brussels
Louis Armstrong and Robert Goffin, 1934
Black-and-white photograph, 7 x 5
 (approx.)
Louis Armstrong Archives, Queens
 College, City University of New York

Unidentified (photographer)
*Armstrong with Entourage and Band,
 Wolverhampton, England*, May 1934
Black-and-white snapshot, 2 x 3
 (approx.)
Louis Armstrong Archives, Queens
 College, City University of New York

D. Jazz Age Europe

Paul Colin
*Jazz Band (from portfolio Le Tumulte
 Noir)*, 1927
Lithograph, 18 x 25
Art & Artifacts Division, Schomburg
 Center for Research in Black
 Culture, The New York Public
 Library, Astor, Lenox & Tilden
 Foundations

Paul Colin
*Cubist Dancer (from portfolio Le
 Tumulte Noir)*, 1927
Lithograph, 18 x 12½
Art & Artifacts Division, Schomburg
 Center for Research in Black
 Culture, The New York Public
 Library, Astor, Lenox & Tilden
 Foundations

Paul Colin
*Dancer on Piano (from portfolio Le
 Tumulte Noir)*, 1927
Lithograph, 18 x 12½
Art & Artifacts Division, Schomburg
 Center for Research in Black
 Culture, The New York Public
 Library, Astor, Lenox & Tilden
 Foundations

Paul Colin
*Topic of the Day (Josephine Baker),
 (from portfolio Le Tumulte Noir)*, 1927
Lithograph, 18 x 12½
Art & Artifacts Division, Schomburg
 Center for Research in Black

Culture, The New York Public
 Library, Astor, Lenox & Tilden
 Foundations

Paul Colin
*Untitled (Josephine Baker) (from
 portfolio Le Tumulte Noir)*, 1927
Lithograph, 18¾ x 12½
Art & Artifacts Division, Schomburg
 Center for Research in Black
 Culture, The New York Public
 Library, Astor, Lenox & Tilden
 Foundations

SECTION V. SWING THAT MUSIC

A. Armstrong: The Swing Era, 1935–1943

James J. Kriegsmann
Louis Armstrong, 1941
Sepia-toned photograph, 27¼ x 23¼
Louis Armstrong Archives, Queens
 College, City University of New York

*"Joe Glaser Presents the King of the
 Trumpet,"* early 1940s
Autographed poster, 16 x 13
New Orleans Jazz Club Collections,
 Louisiana State Museum

Maurice (Seymour), Chicago
Louis Armstrong, c. 1937
Black-and-white photograph, 8 x 10
 (approx.)
Institute of Jazz Studies, Rutgers
 University

Arsene Studio
*Loew's State Theater Marquee: On
 Stage—Louis Armstrong & Orchestra,
 Times Square, New York City*, early
 1940s
Black-and-white photograph, 8 x 10
Louis Armstrong Archives, Queens
 College, City University of New York

Richard Merrill
Armstrong in Performance, c. 1940
Black-and-white photographs (3),
 11 x 8½ each
Louis Armstrong Archives, Queens
 College, City University of New York

Consco Candid Camera, Indianapolis
Armstrong in Performance, early 1940s
Black-and-white photographs (3),
 10 x 8 each
Louis Armstrong Archives, Queens
 College, City University of New York

Harry Rossner, Brooklyn
Armstrong in Performance, early 1940s
Black-and-white photographs (3),
 10 x 8 each
Louis Armstrong Archives, Queens
 College, City University of New York

Charles Peterson
*Backstage at the Paramount Theatre,
 New York City*, 1937
Sepia-toned photograph, 10 x 8

Louis Armstrong Archives, Queens
 College, City University of New York

Charles Peterson
*With Friends at the Braddock Hotel,
 New York City*, 1942
Black-and-white photograph, 8 x 10
Louis Armstrong Archives, Queens
 College, City University of New York

Charles Peterson
*Ordering Room Service at the Braddock
 Hotel, New York City*, 1942
Black-and-white photograph, 10 x 8
Louis Armstrong Archives, Queens
 College, City University of New York

Otto Hess
*Recording with Pee Wee Hunt, New
 York City*, February 20, 1939
Black-and-white photograph, 7 x 9
Louis Armstrong Archives, Queens
 College, City University of New York

Unidentified (photographer)
*Party in Honor of Duke Ellington and
 Louis Armstrong, Tony's Tavern,
 Chicago*, February 14, 1935
Sepia-toned photograph, 8 x 10
 (approx.)
Louis Armstrong Archives, Queens
 College, City University of New York

Unidentified (photographer)
*Club DeLisa, Chicago: Louis
 Armstrong, Lucille Armstrong,
 Clarence Armstrong, and Two
 Unidentified Women*, c. 1943
Black-and-white photograph in
 printed mat, 7 x 9
Louis Armstrong Archives, Queens
 College, City University of New York

B. Jazz and Art

William H. Johnson
Jitterbug V, c. 1941–1942
Tempera, pen and ink on paper,
 18 1/16 x 11 15/16
National Museum of American Art,
 Smithsonian Institution; Gift of The
 Harmon Foundation

Claude Clark
Downbeat, 1944–1946
Oil on canvas, 16 x 20
Claude Clark

Miguel Covarrubias
The Lindy Hop, 1936
Lithograph, 14 x 10
Howard University Gallery of Art,
 Washington, D.C.

Misha Reznikoff
Cornet Chop Suey, 1938
Oil on canvas, 38 x 36 (approx.)
Misha Reznikoff/Genevieve Naylor/
 Reznikoff Artistic Partnership

C. Joe Glaser

Unidentified (photographer)
Joe Glaser, n.d.

Hand-tinted photograph, 8 x 10
Louis Armstrong Archives, Queens
    College, City University of New York

Unidentified (photographer)
*Joe Glaser and Louis Armstrong Sign
    Contract for "Fleischmann's Yeast
    Hour" Radio Program*, 1937
Black-and-white photograph, 7 x 5
Louis Armstrong Archives, Queens
    College, City University of New York

Bill Mark
Louis Armstrong and Joe Glaser, 1949
Black-and-white photograph, 9 x 8
Louis Armstrong Archives, Queens
    College, City University of New York

Louis Armstrong
Telegram to Joe Glaser, August 6,
    1955
Western Union telegram, 5 x 7
    (approx.)
Music Division, Library of Congress

Louis Armstrong
*"Just between you and me and the
    gatepost.." (letter to Joe Glaser)*,
    1950s
Typewritten letter
Music Division, Library of Congress

Louis Armstrong
*"To My Manager and Pal Mr. Joe Glaser
    . . . ,"* 1969
Handwritten manuscript page, 10 x 8
Louis Armstrong Archives, Queens
    College, City University of New York

D. LUCILLE WILSON ARMSTRONG
Woodard Studio
*Chorus Dancers (with Lucille Wilson,
    far left, second row)*, 1930s
Black-and-white photograph, 8 x 10
    (approx.)
Louis Armstrong Archives, Queens
    College, City University of New York

Unidentified (photographer)
*Wedding of Lucille Wilson and Louis
    Armstrong (with inscriptions identify-
    ing guests)*, 1942
Black-and-white photograph with ink
    inscriptions, 8 x 10
Louis Armstrong Archives, Queens
    College, City University of New York

Unidentified (photographer)
*Louis and Lucille Armstrong Backstage
    at Howard Theatre, Washington,
    D.C.*, 1942–1943
Black-and-white photograph, 10 x 8
Louis Armstrong Archives, Queens
    College, City University of New York

E. THE ENTERTAINER
Unidentified (artist)
*Armstrong and His Manager Joe
    Glaser*, n.d.
Watercolor on illustration board, 32 x 28
Louis Armstrong Archives, Queens
    College, City University of New York

Vandamm Studios
*Louis Armstrong in "Swingin' the
    Dream,"* 1939
Black-and-white photograph, 14 x 10
Museum of the City of New York

Al Hirschfeld
*Louis Armstrong and Benny Goodman
    in "Swingin' the Dream,"* 1939
Pen and ink on paper, 18⅞ x 20¼
The Margo Feiden Galleries Ltd.,
    exclusive representative of Al
    Hirschfeld

Frances Feist
*Louis Armstrong, Cotton Club (Costume
    Design)*, 1939
Watercolor on paper, 19¼ x 14
Museum of the City of New York

Frances Feist
*Set Design for "Tall, Tan, and Terrific"
    (with Cab Calloway and Louis
    Armstrong), The Cotton Club*, 1939
Watercolor on paper, 15 x 20
Museum of the City of New York

Jacob Lawrence
Playing Records, 1949
India ink on paper, 27 x 22½
John H. and Vivian D. Hewitt

Ralph Van Lehmden
Saturday Night Swing, c. 1945
Oil on canvas, 21 x 28
Michael Rosenfeld Gallery

Polydor Records; Dan Shapiro (illus-
    trator)
Louis Armstrong—Paris 1934, 1947
Record album cover, 10½ x 12½
Institute of Jazz Studies, Rutgers
    University

Columbia Records; Flora (illustrator)
Louis Armstrong's Hot Five, Vol. 2, c. 1941
Record album cover, 10½ x 12½
Institute of Jazz Studies, Rutgers
    University

Columbia Records; Steinweiss
    (illustrator)
Hot Jazz Classics—King Louis, c. 1940
Record album cover, 10½ x 12½
Institute of Jazz Studies, Rutgers
    University

Columbia Records
Hot Jazz Classics—Louis and Earl,
    1943
Record album cover, 10½ x 12½
Institute of Jazz Studies, Rutgers
    University

Philco
Radio Model 37-34 (Cathedral Model),
    1937
Wood and mixed media, 17 x 13½ x 9
Smithsonian Institution

Raymond Steth
Evolution of Swing, c. 1943

Lithograph, 13 x 16¼
National Museum of American Art,
    Smithsonian Institution

SECTION VI. ARMSTRONG ON FILM

A. THE EARLY FILMS, 1932–1944
Rhapsody in Black and Blue (Para-
    mount Pictures; director, Aubrey
    Scotto), 1932
Black-and-white photograph (copy),
    11 x 14
Frank Driggs Collection

*Armstrong with Bing Crosby in Pennies
    from Heaven*, (Columbia Pictures;
    director, Norman Z. McLeod), 1936
Black-and-white photograph (copy),
    11 x 14
Frank Driggs Collection

*Armstrong performing "Skeleton in the
    Closet" in Pennies from Heaven*,
    (Columbia Pictures; director,
    Norman Z. McLeod), 1936
Black-and-white photograph, 8 x 10
Louis Armstrong Archives, Queens
    College, City University of New York

Unidentified (artist)
*Storyboard for Haunted House Cafe
    sequence from Pennies from Heaven*,
    (Columbia Pictures; director,
    Norman Z. McLeod), 1936
Ink on illustration board, 11¼ x 8⅝
Norman Z. McLeod Collection,
    Margaret Herrick Library, Academy
    of Motion Picture Arts and Sciences

Every Day's a Holiday (Paramount
    Pictures; director, A. Edward
    Sutherland), 1937
Black-and-white photograph (copy),
    11 x 14
Frank Driggs Collection

*Swing Wedding/Minnie the Moocher's
    Wedding Day*, (MGM Harmonies
    cartoon), 1937
Black-and-white photograph (copy),
    11 x 14
Academy of Motion Picture Arts and
    Sciences Library

Martha Raye in Artists and Models,
    (Paramount Pictures; director, Raoul
    Walsh), 1937
Black-and-white photograph (copy),
    10 x 8
Photofest, New York

Louis Armstrong in Artists and Models,
    (Paramount Pictures; director, Raoul
    Walsh), 1937
Black-and-white photograph (copy),
    10 x 8
Frank Driggs Collection

*Armstrong performing "Jeepers
    Creepers" in Going Places*, (Warner
    Brothers; director, Ray Enright), 1938

Black-and-white photographs (3 copies), 10 x 8 each
Warner Brothers Archives, University of Southern California

Armstrong with Maxine Sullivan and the Dandridge Sisters in Going Places, (Warner Brothers; director, Ray Enright), 1938
Lobby card, 11 x 14
John Kisch Separate Cinema Collection

Louis Armstrong and Maxine Sullivan in Going Places, (Warner Brothers; director, Ray Enright), 1938
Black-and-white photograph (copy), 11 x 14
Frank Driggs Collection

"When It's Sleepy Time Down South", (Soundies Distributing Co. of America), 1942
Black-and-white photograph (copy), 11 x 14
Institute of Jazz Studies, Rutgers University

Armstrong with Mantan Moreland, Willie Best, Eddie Anderson, and Rex Ingram in Cabin in the Sky, (MGM Pictures; director, Vincente Minnelli), 1943
Black-and-white photograph (copy), 11 x 14
Institute of Jazz Studies, Rutgers University

Cabin in the Sky (MGM Pictures; director, Vincente Minnelli), 1943
Poster, 41 x 27
John Kisch Separate Cinema Collection

"Hytten i Himlen," Danish Poster for Cabin in the Sky (MGM Pictures; director, Vincente Minnelli), 1943
Poster, 41 x 27
John Kisch Separate Cinema Collection

"Svart Extas," Swedish poster for Cabin in the Sky (MGM Pictures; director, Vincente Minnelli), 1943
Poster, 40 x 27 (approx.)
John Kisch Separate Cinema Collection

Jam Session (Columbia Pictures; director, Charles Barton), 1944
Lobby card, 11 x 14
John Kisch Separate Cinema Collection

B. The Later Films, 1947–1969
New Orleans (United Artists; director, Arthur Lubin), 1947
Black-and-white photograph (copy), 11 x 14
Frank Driggs Collection

Phil Stern
Armstrong with Billie Holiday in New Orleans, (United Artists; director, Arthur Lubin), 1947
Black-and-white photograph, 16 x 20
Phil Stern

Glory Alley (MGM Pictures; director, Raoul Walsh), 1952
Lobby card, 11 x14
John Kisch Separate Cinema Collection

The Glenn Miller Story (Universal; director, Anthony Mann), 1954
Black-and-white photograph (copy), 11 x 14
Frank Driggs Collection

High Society (MGM Pictures; director, Charles Walters), 1956
Lobby card, 11 x 14
John Kisch Separate Cinema Collection

Jazz on a Summer's Day (director, Bert Stern), 1958
Lobby cards (2), each 11 x 14
John Kisch Separate Cinema Collection

The Five Pennies (Paramount Pictures; director, Melville Shavelson), 1959
Poster, 41 x 27
John Kisch Separate Cinema Collection

Sam Shaw
Armstrong with Paul Newman in Paris Blues, (United Artists; director, Martin Ritt), 1961
Black-and-white photograph, 11 x 14
Louis Armstrong Archives, Queens College, City University of New York

Sam Shaw
Louis Armstrong et Ses Musiciens à Paris pour "Paris Blues" (United Artists; director, Martin Ritt), 1961
Black-and-white photograph, 11 x 14
Louis Armstrong Archives, Queens College, City University of New York

When the Boys Meet the Girls (director, Alvin Ganzer), 1965
Lobby card, 11 x 14
John Kisch Separate Cinema Collection

A Man Called Adam (Embassy Films; director, Leo Penn), 1966
Lobby card, 11 x 14
John Kisch Separate Cinema Collection

With Barbra Streisand in Hello, Dolly!, (United Artists; director, Gene Kelly), 1969
Black-and-white photograph (copy), 11 x 14
Frank Driggs Collection

***Armstrong on Film* video program includes:**
"I'll Be Glad When You're Dead You Rascal, You" from *Rhapsody in Black and Blue* (Paramount Pictures), 1932. Courtesy of Douris Corporation.

Hotel Hades scene from *Cabin in the Sky* (MGM Pictures), 1943. Courtesy Turner Entertainment Co.

"I'll Be Glad When You're Dead, You Rascal, You" from *Betty Boop* (Paramount Pictures/Max Fleischer),

1932. Courtesy of Republic Pictures.

"Skeleton in the Closet" from *Pennies from Heaven*, 1936. Courtesy of Columbia Pictures.

"Mahogany Hall Stomp" from *New Orleans* (United Artists Jules Levey Production), 1947. Courtesy of Video-Cinema Films, Inc.

"Jeepers Creepers" from *Going Places* (Warner Brothers), 1938. Courtesy of Turner Entertainment Co.

Armstrong and Danny Kaye perform "When The Saints Go Marching In," from *The Five Pennies*, 1959. Courtesy of Paramount Pictures.

Armstrong and Barbra Streisand perform "Hello Dolly" from *Hello Dolly!*, 1969. Courtesy of Twentieth Century Fox Corporation.

Armstrong and Bing Crosby perform "High Society Calypso" and "Now You Has Jazz" from *High Society* (MGM), 1956. Courtesy of Turner Entertainment Co.

"Battle Royal" from *Paris Blues* (United Artists), 1961. Courtesy of Metro-Goldwyn-Mayer, Inc.

SECTION VII. DO YOU KNOW WHAT IT MEANS TO MISS NEW ORLEANS?

A. King Zulu, New Orleans Mardi Gras, 1949
Louis Armstrong
Hail King Zulu, c. 1952
Mixed media collage, 9 x 12
Louis Armstrong Archives, Queens College, City University of New York

Zulu Coconut, 1973
Painted coconut on wood pedestal with Mardi Gras coins, 8⅜ x 10¼ x 7½
Louis Armstrong Archives, Queens College, City University of New York

Don Perry
Louis Armstrong—King of the Zulus, New Orleans Mardi Gras, 1949
Black-and-white photographs (6), 5 x 7¼ each
Historic New Orleans Collection, William Russell Collection

Boris Artzybasheff (illustrator)
Time Magazine with Louis Armstrong on Cover, February 21, 1949
Printed magazine, 8¼ x 11
Louis Armstrong Archives, Queens College, City University of New York

B. Armstrong the Writer
Unidentified (photographer)
Armstrong Typing Backstage at the Band Box, Chicago, 1940s

Black-and-white photograph, 5 x 7 (approx.)
Louis Armstrong Archives, Queens College, City University of New York

Louis Armstrong
Letter to Robert Goffin, March 19, 1944
Typewritten on "Satchmo" letterhead, 10 x 8
Institute of Jazz Studies, Rutgers University

Louis Armstrong
"Scanning the History of Jazz," 1956
Handwritten manuscript on grey "Satchmo" letterhead (11 pages), 10½ x 7¼ each
J.I. Kislak Mortgage Corporation

Louis Armstrong
Swing That Music (London: Longmans), 1936
Book with dust jacket
Phoebe Jacobs

Louis Armstrong
Satchmo: My Life in New Orleans (New York: Prentice Hall), 1954
Book with dust jacket
Louis Armstrong Archives, Queens College, City University of New York

Louis Armstrong
Ma Vie Ma Nouvelle Orleans (Paris: Julliard Publishers), 1950s
Book
Louis Armstrong Archives, Queens College, City University of New York

Louis Armstrong
Mitt Liv I New Orleans (Norway: H. Aschehoug & Co.), n.d.
Book with dust jacket
Louis Armstrong Archives, Queens College, City University of New York

Louis Armstrong
Mein Leben in New Orleans (Berlin: Henschelverlag), 1967
Book
Louis Armstrong Archives, Queens College, City University of New York

C. The New Orleans of Armstrong's Youth Revisited, 1940s and 1950s

Jeanette Eaton; Elton Fax (illustrator)
Trumpeter's Tale: The Story of Young Louis Armstrong (New York: William Morrow & Company), 1955
Book with dust jacket, 8¼ x 5½
Louis Armstrong Archives, Queens College, City University of New York

Elton Fax
Young Louis Armstrong with Grandmother (illustration for Trumpeter's Tale: The Story of Young Louis Armstrong), 1955
Pen and ink on paper, 10 x 7
Elton Fax Collection, Special Collections, Boston University

Elton Fax
Young Louis Armstrong Shooting Gun (illustration for Trumpeter's Tale: The Story of Young Louis Armstrong), 1955
Pen and ink on paper, 12 x 14½
Elton Fax Collection, Special Collections, Boston University

Elton Fax
Mississippi Riverboat (illustration for Trumpeter's Tale: The Story of Young Louis Armstrong), 1955
Pen and ink on paper, 14½ x 20
Elton Fax Collection, Special Collections, Boston University

Elton Fax
Louis Armstrong, 1955
Pen and ink on paper, 15 x 11
Elton Fax Collection, Special Collections, Boston University

Ben Shahn
Louis Armstrong as a Child, 1957
Photostat of pen and ink drawing, 15 x 8
Mrs. Bernarda Shahn

Ben Shahn
Images of New Orleans: Coal Cart, Lady of Guadeloupe, Madame John's Legacy, and Unidentified Building, 1957
Photostats of pen and ink drawings (4), 7½ x 9½ each
Mrs. Bernarda Shahn

Ben Shahn
Louis Armstrong, 1957
Pen and ink, 18 x 15¼
Drs. John and Nicole Dintenfass

Ralston Crawford
Colored Waifs Home, 1956
Black-and-white photographs (2), 15 x 20 each
William Ransom Hogan Jazz Archive, Howard-Tilton Memorial Library, Tulane University

Ralston Crawford
Jazz Funeral (Eureka Brass Band and Second Line), 1958
Black-and-white photographs (5), 15 x 20 each
William Ransom Hogan Jazz Archive, Howard-Tilton Memorial Library, Tulane University

Lee Friedlander
Johnny St. Cyr and "Fess" Manetta, 1957
Black-and-white photograph, 9⅜ x 6⅜
Fraenkel Gallery, San Francisco

Lee Friedlander
Isidore Barbarin, 1957
Black-and-white photograph, 7½ x 11¼
Fraenkel Gallery, San Francisco

Lee Friedlander
Edmond Hall, 1957
Black-and-white photograph, 9½ x 6¼
Fraenkel Gallery, San Francisco

Lee Friedlander
"Punch" Miller, 1957
Black-and-white photograph, 6¼ x 9⅝
Fraenkel Gallery, San Francisco

David Stone Martin
New Orleans Street Scene, early 1950s
Ink on paper, 16¾ x 19¾
Phoebe Jacobs

David Stone Martin
New Orleans Marching Band, early 1950s
Ink on paper, 16¾ x 19¾
Phoebe Jacobs

Gene Johnson
Design for Frontierland, Rivers of America, 1963
Mixed media with Magic Marker and grease pencil, 21¼ x 34¾
Walt Disney Imagineering

Unidentified (photographer)
Bunk Johnson, c. 1940
Black-and-white photograph, 7 x 5
Louis Armstrong Archives, Queens College, City University of New York

Bunk Johnson
Letter to Louis Armstrong, March 1, 1939
Handwritten letter (3 pages), 11 x 8½ each
Historic New Orleans Collection, William Russell Collection

A Night in New Orleans, Bunk Johnson's New Orleans Jazz Band...Town Hall, New York, January 1, 1946
Printed handbill
Moorland-Spingarn Research Center, Howard University

D. The New World of Jazz

Stuart Davis
Hot Still Scape for Six Colors—Seventh Avenue Style, late 1950s
Silkscreen print, 20 x 20 (approx.)
Earl Davis

George Wettling
Jazz Is In, c. 1949
Oil on canvas, 22 x 30¼
Collection of Hank O'Neal and Shelley M. Shier

George Wettling
Condon's, c. 1949
Oil on canvas, 22 x 30¼
Collection of Hank O'Neal

William P. Gottlieb
52nd Street, c. 1948
Color photograph, 14½ x 19
Collection of Hank O'Neal

Souvenir Nightclub Photo Covers: The Band Box (Chicago), The Blue Note (Chicago), Famous Door (New York), Small's Paradise (New York), Club

Harlem (Atlantic City, N.J.), late
1940s-1950s
Printed cardboard mats (5), 7 x 9
(approx.) each
Louis Armstrong Archives, Queens
College, City University of New York

Unidentified (photographer)
*Armstrong with Nightclub Photographer
Gerrie Reagan*, 1955
Black-and-white photograph, 10 x 8
(approx.)
Louis Armstrong Archives, Queens
College, City University of New York

Unidentified (photographer)
*Armstrong, Dizzy Gillespie, and Others
at the Beige Room, Chicago*, late
1940s-1950s
Black-and-white photograph, 7¼ x 9¼
Louis Armstrong Archives, Queens
College, City University of New York

Harry Edelman
*With "Hiram," a Fan, at the Blue Note,
Chicago*, 1950s
Black-and-white photograph, 7¼ x 9¼
Louis Armstrong Archives, Queens
College, City University of New York

Unidentified (photographer)
*With Family of Fans, Blue Note,
Chicago*, 1950s
Black-and-white photograph, 7¼ x 9¼
Louis Armstrong Archives, Queens
College, City University of New York

Herman Leonard
Dizzy Gillespie, 1948
Black-and-white photograph, 11 x 14
National Museum of American
History, Smithsonian Institution

Herman Leonard
Charlie Parker, 1949
Black-and-white photograph, 11 x 14
National Museum of American
History, Smithsonian Institution

Herman Leonard
Miles Davis, n.d.
Black-and-white photograph, 11 x 14
National Museum of American
History, Smithsonian Institution

E. TELEVISION

Sam Shaw
*Armstrong and Jack Teagarden,
Rehearsing for "The Timex All-Star
Jazz Show" Television Special (CBS-
TV)*, 1957
Black-and-white photograph, 16 x 20
Louis Armstrong Archives, Queens
College, City University of New York

Genevieve Naylor
*Armstrong on "The Eddie Condon Floor
Show" (NBC-TV)*, 1948
Black-and-white photograph, 11 x 14
Misha Reznikoff/Genevieve Naylor/
Reznikoff Artistic Partnership

Genevieve Naylor
*Misha Reznikoff on "The Eddie Condon
Floor Show" (NBC-TV)*, 1948
Black-and-white photograph, 11 x 14
Misha Reznikoff/Genevieve Naylor/
Reznikoff Artistic Partnership

Misha Reznikoff
Struttin' With Some Barbecue, 1948
Pastel on paper, 30 x 24
Misha Reznikoff/Genevieve Naylor/
Reznikoff Artistic Partnership

*"Hollywood Palace: 50th Show Biz
Anniversary of Our Host Louis
Armstrong" (ABC-TV)*, May 1, 1965
Printed poster, 17 x 6
Floyd Levin

Sylvania
Television, 1958-1959
Mixed media, 40 x 19½ x 25
Smithsonian Institution

Armstrong on Television video program includes:

Armstrong and Frank Sinatra perform
"Birth of the Blues" on *The Edsel
Show* (CBS-TV), 1957. Courtesy of
Gonzaga University.

Armstrong and Jack Teagarden
perform "Rockin' Chair" on the
Timex All Star Jazz Show (CBS-TV),
1957. Courtesy of Tommy Productions.

Armstrong and Dizzy Gillespie
perform "The Umbrella Man" on the
Timex All Star Jazz Show (CBS-TV),
1959. Courtesy of Tommy Productions.

Armstrong and Velma Middleton
perform "That's My Desire" on
Cavalcade of Bands (DuMont
Network), 1950. Courtesy of Chertok
Associates.

Armstrong and Perry Como perform
"Ko Ko Mo, I Love You So" on *The
Perry Como Show* (CBS-TV), 1955.
Courtesy of Liggett Group.

SECTION VIII.
AMBASSADOR SATCH

A. AMERICA'S AMBASSADOR OF GOODWILL

Voice of America Microphone, n.d.
Mixed media
Division of Electricity, National
Museum of American History,
Smithsonian Institution

United States Information Agency
Louis Armstrong with Willis Connover,
mid-1950s
Black-and-white photograph, 8 x 10
(approx.)
Institute of Jazz Studies, Rutgers
University

Mischa Richter
*"This is a Diplomatic Mission of
Outmost Delicacy. The Question is,
Who's the best man for it—John
Foster Dulles or Satchmo?"* (cartoon
for *The New Yorker*), 1958
Ink on paper
Prints and Photographs Division,
Library of Congress

B. AROUND THE WORLD

*"Jazz Kongen, New Orleans, Louis
Armstrong, og Hans Band" (Concert
Poster from Denmark)*, 1958–1959
Printed poster mounted on board,
33 x 24
Institute of Jazz Studies, Rutgers
University

*Louis Armstrong Concert Poster
(Japan)*, 1954
Printed paper poster, 34½ x 24
Louis Armstrong Archives, Queens
College, City University of New York

Walker Hill Photo Shop, Korea
Armstrong in Korea, 1953
Black-and-white photographs in
printed mats (4), 8½ x 6½ each
Louis Armstrong Archives, Queens
College, City University of New York

Casey's Photo Service, Tokyo
*Reception for Louis Armstrong and
Princess Suka in Japan*, 1954
Black-and-white photographs (3),
4½ x 6 each
Louis Armstrong Archives, Queens
College, City University of New York

Unidentified (photographer)
*Armstrong in Egypt (United Arab
Republic)*, 1961
Black-and-white photographs (3),
6¹³/₁₆ x 8½ each
Louis Armstrong Archives, Queens
College, City University of New York

Unidentified (artist)
*Hot Club, Berlin ("To Louis Armstrong
for the Golden 50th")*, 1950
Watercolor on paper, 10 x 14⁷/₁₆
Louis Armstrong Archives, Queens
College, City University of New York

U.S. Department of State
*Stamped Passport Issued to Louis
Armstrong*, December 14, 1957
Green cover with accordion extension
pages, 6 x 27 (open)
Louis Armstrong Archives, Queens
College, City University of New York

*Selection of Louis Armstrong Postage
Stamps from Rwanda, Senegal, Mali,
Gabon, Chad, Upper Volta, Tanzania,
Dominica, and Guyana*, 1960s–1980s
Postage stamps (12)
Dr. William Hill

Frank Travel Service
Itinerary for Armstrong's Tour of Africa,
1960

Photocopy on paper, 10 x 8
Floyd Levin

The Ambassador of Jazz: Louis Armstrong and His Concert Group, late 1950s–1960s
Concert program, 11 x 8½
Louis Armstrong Archives, Queens College, City University of New York

C. AFRICA

Unidentified (photographer)
Armstrong Carried in Triumph, Leopoldville, Congo (now Kinshasa, Zaire), 1960
Black-and-white photograph, 23 x 19 (framed)
Louis Armstrong Archives, Queens College, City University of New York

Unidentified (Nigerian artist)
African Musicians, n.d.
Wood relief, 22 x 34 x 2½
Louis Armstrong Archives, Queens College, City University of New York

Drum Presented to Louis Armstrong by De Black Evening Follies of Salisbury, Southern Rhodesia (now Harare, Zimbabwe), 1960
Wood, animal skin, bronze plaque, 36 (height) x 12½ (diameter)
Louis Armstrong Archives, Queens College, City University of New York

"Armstrong Akwaba!" Welcome Sign, Gold Coast (Ghana), 1956
Ink on paper, 6 x 8¼
Louis Armstrong Archives, Queens College, City University of New York

Unidentified (photographer)
Armstrong Dining with Kwame Nkrumah, Gold Coast (Ghana), 1956
Black-and-white photograph, 6 x 8¼
Louis Armstrong Archives, Queens College, City University of New York

Lobby Cards from the film "Satchmo the Great" showing Armstrong's Visit to the Gold Coast (Ghana): Armstrong with African Dancers; On Stage in Africa; Lucille Armstrong with African Chief; Farewell at Airport, 1957
Lobby cards (4), 11 x 14 each
John Kisch Separate Cinema Collection

Unidentified (photographer)
Louis Armstrong Tour of Ghana and Nigeria Sponsored by Pepsi-Cola, 1960
Black-and-white photographs (4), 8 x 10 each
Louis Armstrong Archives, Queens College, City University of New York

D. ARMSTRONG AND CIVIL RIGHTS

Norman Rockwell
"The Problem We All Live With" (preliminary study for *Look* magazine), c. 1963

Tempera on board, 11 x 19⅞
Norman Rockwell Museum at Stockbridge, Norman Rockwell Art Collection Trust

Elton Fax
Orville Faubus, c. 1957
Ink on paper, 11½ x 8½ (approx.)
Elton Fax Collection, Special Collections, Boston University

Elton Fax
Dwight Eisenhower, c. 1957
Ink on paper, 11½ x 8½ (approx.)
Elton Fax Collection, Special Collections, Boston University

Louis Armstrong
"Negroes Who Work on Broadway," 1950s
Mixed media collage, 9 x 12
Louis Armstrong Archives, Queens College, City University of New York

Louis Armstrong
Jackie Robinson, 1950s
Mixed media collage, 9⅝ x 12
Louis Armstrong Archives, Queens College, City University of New York

SECTION IX. PORTRAITS OF ARMSTRONG

A. ARMSTRONG IN FOCUS

Weegee (Arthur Fellig)
Louis Armstrong Backstage, Bop City, New York, c. 1955
Black-and white photographs reprinted from original negatives (2), 11 x 14 each
International Center of Photography, The Weegee Archive; Bequest of Wilma Wilcox

Milt Hinton
Louis Armstrong in Seattle Hotel, 1953
Black-and-white photograph, 11 x 14 (approx.)
Louis Armstrong Archives, Queens College, City University of New York

Garry Winogrand
Louis Armstrong on Stage with Nightclub Patrons in Foreground, 1954
Black-and-white photograph, 11 x 14
The Center for Creative Photography, University of Arizona, Tucson

Garry Winogrand
Louis Armstrong and Velma Middleton on Stage, 1954
Black-and-white photograph, 11 x 14
The Center for Creative Photography, University of Arizona, Tucson

Garry Winogrand
Louis Armstrong and Velma Middleton off Stage, 1954
Black-and-white photograph, 11 x 14
The Center for Creative Photography, University of Arizona, Tucson

Dennis Stock
Backstage, Latin Casino, Philadelphia, c. 1960
Black-and-white photograph, 14 x 11
Dennis Stock/Magnum Photos

Dennis Stock
Trumpet Case, c. 1960
Black-and-white photograph, 11 x 14
Dennis Stock/Magnum Photos

Gordon Parks
Louis Armstrong at Castle Hill, Massachusetts, 1955
Black-and-white photographs (3), 11 x 14 each
Gordon Parks

Lisette Model
Louis Armstrong at the Newport Jazz Festival, c. 1954-1956
Black-and-white photograph, 10½ x 13¾
Estate of Lisette Model, courtesy Sander Gallery, Inc.

B. STUDIO PORTRAITS

Irving Penn
Louis Armstrong, 1948
Black-and-white photograph, 8 x 10
Fondation Suisse pour la Photographie, Zurich

Bert Stern
Louis Armstrong, 1957
Black-and-white photograph from Polaroid negative, 24 x 20
Bert Stern

Philippe Halsman
Louis Armstrong (Close-Up), 1966
Black-and-white photograph reprinted from original negative, 14 x 11
Philippe Halsman—Halsman Family Collection

Philippe Halsman
Louis Armstrong (Full-Length), 1966
Color photograph reprinted from original negative, 16 x 20
Philippe Halsman—Halsman Family Collection

C. DARKROOM EXPERIMENTS

Weegee (Arthur Fellig)
Louis Armstrong (Abstracted), late 1950s
Black-and-white photograph reprinted from original negative, 11 x 14 (approx.)
International Center of Photography, The Weegee Archive; Bequest of Wilma Wilcox

Robert Parent
Louis Armstrong (from the portfolio Solarized Jazz), 1956
Black-and-white photograph reprinted from original negative, 14 x 11
Don Parent

D. Paintings, Drawings, and Collages

E. Richard Freniere
Newport Doodling, 1958
Collage of pen and ink drawings,
  17⅝ x 22½
New Orleans Jazz Club Collections,
  Louisiana State Museum

René Bouché
Satchmo, 1954
Marker on paper, 8 x 16½ (image)
Queens Museum of Art, New York; Gift
  of Mrs. René Bouché

René Bouché
Satchmo (With Trumpet), 1954
Marker on paper, 8 x 16½ (image)
Queens Museum of Art, New York; Gift
  of Mrs. René Bouché

LeRoy Neiman
Satchmo Head, 1967
Oil on canvas, 20¾ x 20¾
Alvin and Joan Wolf, Miami, Florida

LeRoy Neiman
Satchmo, Paris, Olympia #1 and #2,
  April 24, 1962
Ink and watercolor on paper (2),
  9 x 11½ each
LeRoy Neiman

LeRoy Neiman
*Louis Armstrong and Duke Ellington,
  Madison Square Garden, 2/23/70*,
  1970
Felt-tipped pen and ink on paper,
  12¼ x 15¾
LeRoy Neiman

Romare Bearden and Sam Shaw
Paris Blues (Armstrong and Ellington),
  1961
Mixed media collage, 28 x 20
Sam Shaw

Romare Bearden
Paris Blues (Armstrong and Ellington),
  n.d.
Silkscreened poster, 28 x 20
Institute of Jazz Studies, Rutgers
  University

Romare Bearden
*Louis Armstrong (Layout Page for Paris
  Blues Suite)*, 1961
Ink and tempera on tracing paper,
  18 x 24
Sam Shaw

Romare Bearden
*Showtime (with Louis Armstrong)
  (from "Of the Blues" series)*, 1974
Collage with acrylic and lacquer on
  board, 50 x 40
Stanley and Dolores Feldman

Romare Bearden and Sam Shaw
Louis Armstrong and Trummy Young,
  1980s
Mixed media collage, 14 x 22
Sam Shaw

E. Collages by Louis Armstrong

Dennis Stock
*Armstrong Pasting Photographs on
  Ceiling of Home*, c. 1960
Black-and-white photograph, 11 x 14
Dennis Stock/Magnum Photos

Dennis Stock
Collage on Wall of Armstrong's Home,
  c. 1960
Black and white photograph, 14 x 11
Dennis Stock/Magnum Photos

Louis Armstrong
*Louis Armstrong, King Oliver, Duke
  Ellington, Bunny Berigan, and
  Florence Mills*, early 1950s
Mixed media collage, 9⅝ x 12⅝
Louis Armstrong Archives, Queens
  College, City University of New York

Louis Armstrong
That Happy Feeling, 1950s–1960s
Mixed media collage on cardboard
  reel-to-reel tape container,
  7⅜ x 7⅜
Louis Armstrong Archives, Queens
  College, City University of New York

Louis Armstrong
Trumpet, 1950s–1960s
Mixed media collage on cardboard
  reel-to-reel tape container,
  7⅜ x 7⅜
Louis Armstrong Archives, Queens
  College, City University of New York

Louis Armstrong
Joe Glaser and Louis Armstrong,
  1950s-1960s
Mixed media collage on cardboard
  reel-to-reel tape container,
  7⅜ x 7⅜
Louis Armstrong Archives, Queens
  College, City University of New York

Louis Armstrong
Louis and Lucille Armstrong, 1950s–
  1960s
Mixed media collage on cardboard
  reel-to-reel tape container,
  7⅜ x 7⅜
Louis Armstrong Archives, Queens
  College, City University of New York

Louis Armstrong
The Lady Who Makes Swiss Kriss,
  1950s–1960s
Mixed media collage on cardboard
  reel-to-reel tape container,
  7⅜ x 7⅜
Louis Armstrong Archives, Queens
  College, City University of New York

Louis Armstrong
*Reel 163 (Armstrong with Multiple
  Heads)*, 1950s-1960s
mixed media collage on cardboard
  reel-to-reel tape container,
  7⅜ x 7⅜
Louis Armstrong Archives, Queens
  College, City University of New York

SECTION X. THE MUSIC GOES ON

A. Death and Legacy

Annie Leibovitz
Louis Armstrong, June 16, 1971
Black-and-white photographs (2),
  20 x 16 each
Annie Leibovitz

Louis Armstrong
Satchmo Talking, 1959
Mixed media collage on cardboard
  reel-to-reel tape container (top and
  bottom), 7⅜ x 7⅜ each
Louis Armstrong Archives, Queens
  College, City University of New York

Fred W. McDarrah
Armstrong in Coffin, 1971
Black-and-white photograph, 11 x 14
Fred W. McDarrah

Paul Conrad
Armstrong in Heaven with Gabriel
  (cartoon from *The Los Angeles
  Times*), July 7, 1971
Photostat of lithograph, 14 x 10
Courtesy Queens Museum of Art, New
  York

Malcah Zeldis
Peaceable Kingdom, 1994
Oil on board, 24 x 36
Malcah Zeldis

James Leonard
*Wind Machine with Gabriel, Eleanor
  Roosevelt, and Louis Armstrong*,
  1984
Copper with liver-of-sulphate mark-
  ings on wood base, 28 x 18½ x 10
National Museum of American Art,
  Smithsonian Institution

Elizabeth Catlett
*Trumpet (model for Louis Armstrong
  statue, New Orleans)*, 1975
Wood, 38 (length) (approx.)
Elizabeth Catlett

Index

Italic numbers refer to pages where illustrations appear.